Thomas De Witt Talmage

Every-Day Religion

Sermons Delivered in the Brooklyn Tabernacle

Thomas De Witt Talmage

Every-Day Religion
Sermons Delivered in the Brooklyn Tabernacle

ISBN/EAN: 9783337826871

Printed in Europe, USA, Canada, Australia, Japan

Cover: Foto ©Lupo / pixelio.de

More available books at **www.hansebooks.com**

EVERY-DAY RELIGION:

SERMONS DELIVERED IN THE BROOKLYN TABERNACLE,

BY

T. DE WITT TALMAGE,

AUTHOR OF

"FIRST SERIES OF SERMONS," "SECOND SERIES OF SERMONS," "ABOMINATIONS OF MODERN SOCIETY," "CRUMBS SWEPT UP," "OLD WELLS DUG OUT," "AROUND THE TEA-TABLE," "SPORTS THAT KILL," ETC.

REVISED FROM PHONOGRAPHIC REPORTS.

NEW YORK:
HARPER & BROTHERS, PUBLISHERS,
FRANKLIN SQUARE.
1875.

PREFACE.

THESE discourses attempt to bring the Gospel to the hearts and homes of the people, as a present comfort, warning, and necessity. Hence the title of the book.

I thank the public for their kind reception of former volumes, and also the Christian newspapers which each week put my sermons before one million three hundred and eighty thousand readers in Great Britain and the United States; thus giving me the opportunity of preaching Christ to multitudes whom I can not hope to meet till on that day when we must answer for words spoken or heard. My Christian greeting to all!

T. DE WITT TALMAGE.

BROOKLYN, *September,* 1875.

CONTENTS.

	PAGE
EVERY-DAY RELIGION	7
LIFE AT HOME	21
THE OLD CORN OF CANAAN	33
ZIKLAG IN ASHES	46
THE RELIGION OF GHOSTS	59
SNOW-WATER AND ALKALI INSUFFICIENT	75
STRIPPING THE SLAIN	89
A SUM IN GOSPEL ARITHMETIC	101
SWIMMING FOR LIFE	114
THE CHRISTIAN AT THE BALLOT-BOX	126
THE OVERFLOWING CUP	136
THE WRECK OF THE "SCHILLER"	149
EXASPERATING COMFORTERS	160
A GOOD WOMAN PROMOTED	174
THE CRIMSON COAT	189
THE SYRACUSE CALAMITY	198
THINGS WE NEVER GET OVER	208
THE BROKEN-UP FUNERAL	220
BARTERING FOR ETERNITY	231
A BASKET OF SUMMER FRUIT	243
THE LAST ACT OF THE TRAGEDY	254
DROWNED IN THE LAKE	266
THE RED CORD IN THE WINDOW	276

	PAGE
THE LAMP	288
THE DYING NEED OF THE CHURCH	300
VIEW FROM THE PALACE WINDOW	313
PAUL'S VALEDICTORY	325
HONEY FROM A STRANGE HIVE	337
THE KNELL OF NINEVEH	350
PILLOWS UNDER THE ARMS	362
WHAT KILLS MINISTERS	380
THE SUPERHUMAN JESUS	395
WRECKED FOR TWO WORLDS	409

EVERY-DAY RELIGION.

EVERY-DAY RELIGION.

"Whether therefore ye eat or drink, or whatsoever ye do, do all to the glory of God."—1 *Corinthians* x., 31.

WHEN the apostle, in this text, sets forth the idea that so common an action as the taking of food and drink is to be conducted to the glory of God, he proclaims the importance of religion in the ordinary affairs of our life. In all ages of the world there has been a tendency to set apart certain days, places, and occasions for worship, and to think those were the chief realms in which religion was to act. Now, holy days and holy places have their importance. They give opportunity for especial performance of Christian duty, and for regaling of the religious appetite; but they can not take the place of continuous exercise of faith and prayer. In other words, a man can not be so much of a Christian on Sunday that he can afford to be a worldling all the rest of the week. If a steamer put out for Southampton, and go one day in that direction, and the other six days go in other directions, how long before the steamer will get to Southampton? It will never get there. And though a man may seem to be voyaging heavenward during the holy Sabbath-day, if, during the following six days of the week, he is going toward the world, and toward the flesh, and toward the devil, he will never ride up into the peaceful harbor of heaven. You can not eat so much at the Sabbath banquet that you can afford religious abstinence the other six days. Heroism and princely behavior on great occasions are no apology for lack of right demeanor in circumstances insignificant and inconspicuous. The genuine Christian life is not spasmodic; does not go by fits and starts. It toils on through heat and cold, up steep mountains and along dangerous declivities, its eye on the everlasting hills crowned with the castles of the blessed.

I propose, this morning, to make a plea in behalf of what I shall call "every-day religion."

In the first place, we want to bring the religion of Christ into our *every-day conversation*. When a dam breaks, and two or three villages in Massachusetts are overwhelmed, or an earthquake in South America swallows a whole city, then people begin to talk about the uncertainty of life, and they imagine that they are engaged in positively religious conversation. No. You may talk about these things, and have no grace of God at all in your heart. We ought every day to be talking religion. If there is any thing glad about it, any thing beautiful about it, any thing important about it, we ought to be continuously discussing it. I have noticed that men, just in proportion as their Christian experience is shallow, talk about funerals, and grave-yards, and tombstones, and death-beds. The real, genuine Christian man talks chiefly about this life, and the great eternity beyond, and not so much about the insignificant pass between these two residences. And yet how few circles there are where the religion of Jesus

Christ is welcome. Go into a circle, even of Christian people, where they are full of joy and hilarity, and talk about Christ or heaven, and every thing is immediately silenced. As on a summer day, when the forests are full of life, chatter, and chirrup, and carol—a mighty chorus of bird-harmony, every tree-branch an orchestra—if a hawk appear in the sky, every voice stops, and the forests are still; just so I have seen a lively religious circle silenced on the appearance of any thing like religious conversation. No one had any thing to say, save, perhaps, some old patriarch in the corner of the room, who really thinks that something ought to be said, under the circumstances; so he puts one foot over the other, and heaves a long sigh, and says, "Oh yes; that's so, that's so!"

My friends, the religion of Jesus Christ is something to talk about with a glad heart. It is brighter than the waters; it is more cheerful than the sunshine. Do not go around groaning about your religion, when you ought to be singing it or talking it in cheerful tones of voice. How often it is that we find men whose lives are utterly inconsistent, who attempt to talk religion, and always make a failure of it! My friends, we must *live* religion, or we can not talk it. If a man is cranky, and cross, and uncongenial, and hard in his dealings, and then begins to talk about Christ and heaven, every body is repelled by it. Yet I have sometimes heard such men say, in whining tones, "We are miserable sinners;" "The Lord bless you;" "The Lord have mercy on you;" their conversation interlarded with such expressions, which mean nothing but canting; and canting is the worst form of hypocrisy. If we have really felt the religion of Christ in our hearts, let us talk it, and talk it with an illuminated countenance, re-

1*

membering that when two Christian people talk, God gives especial attention, and writes down what they say. Malachi iii., 16: "Then they that feared the Lord spake often one to another; and the Lord hearkened and heard it, and a book of remembrance was written."

Again I remark: we must bring the religion of Christ into our *every-day employments*. "Oh," you say, "that is very well if a man handle large sums of money, or if he have an extensive traffic; it is very well for this importer of silks, for the bankers and shippers, for the Rothschilds and the Barings; but in my thread-and-needle store, in my trimming establishment, in the humble work in life that I am called to, the sphere is too small for the action of such grand heavenly principles." Who told you so? Do you not know that God watches the faded leaf on the brook's surface as certainly as he does the path of a blazing sun? And the moss that creeps up the side of the rock makes as much impression upon God's mind as the waving tops of Oregon pine and Lebanon cedar; and the alder, crackling under the cow's hoof, sounds as loud in God's ear as the snap of a world's conflagration. When you have any thing to do in life, however humble it may seem to be, God is always there to help you to do it. If your work is that of a fisherman, then God will help you, as he helped Simon when he dragged Gennesaret. If your work is drawing water, then he will help you, as when he talked at the well-curb to the Samaritan woman. If you are engaged in the custom-house, he will lead you, as he led Matthew sitting at the receipt of customs. A religion that is not good in *one* place is not worth any thing in another place. The man who has only a day's wages in his pocket as certainly needs the guidance of religion, as he who rattles the keys of a bank, and could abscond with a hundred thousand hard dollars.

There are those prominent in the churches who seem to be, on public occasions, very devout, who do not put the principles of Christ's religion into practice. They are the most inexorable of creditors. They are the most grasping of dealers. They are known as sharpers on the street. They fleece every sheep they can catch. A country merchant comes in to buy spring or fall goods, and he gets into the store of one of these professed Christian men who have really no grace in their hearts, and he is completely swindled. He is so overcome that he can not get out of town during the week. He stays in town over Sunday, goes into some church to get Christian consolation, when, what is his amazement to find that the very man who hands him the poor-box in the church is the one who relieved him of his money! But never mind; the deacon has his black coat on now. He looks solemn, and goes home talking about "the blessed sermon." If the wheat in the churches should be put into a hopper, the first turn of the crank would make the chaff fly, I tell you. Some of these men are great sticklers for Gospel preaching. They say, "You stand there in bands and surplice and gown, and preach—preach like an angel, and we will stand out here and attend to business. Don't mix things. Don't get business and religion in the same bucket. You attend to your matters, and we will attend to ours." They do not know that God sees every cheat they have practiced in the last six years; that he can look through the iron wall of their fire-proof safe; that he has counted every dishonest greenback they have in their pocket, and that a day of judgment will come. These inconsistent Christian men will sit on the Sabbath night in the house of God, singing, at the close of the service, "Rock of Ages cleft for Me," and then, when the benediction is pronounced, shut the pew-door, and say, as they go out, "Good-bye, Religion. I'll be back next Sunday."

I think that the Church of God and the Sabbath are only an armory where we are to get weapons. When war comes, if a man wants to fight for his country he does not go to Troy or Springfield to do battling, but he goes there for swords and muskets. I look upon the Church of Christ and the Sabbath-day as only the place and time where and when we are to get armed for Christian conflict; but the battle-field is on Monday, Tuesday, Wednesday, Thursday, Friday, and Saturday. "St. Martin's," and "Lenox," and "Old Hundred" do not amount to any thing unless they sing all the week. A sermon is useless unless we can take it with us behind the plow and the counter. The Sabbath-day is worthless if it last only twenty-four hours.

There are many Christians who say, "We are willing to serve God, but we do not want to do it in these spheres about which we are talking; it seems so insipid and monotonous. If we had some great occasion, if we had lived in the time of Luther, if we had been Paul's traveling companion, if we could serve God on a great scale, we would do it; but we can't in this every-day life." I admit that a great deal of the romance and knight-errantry of life has disappeared before the advance of this practical age. The ancient temples of Rouen have been changed into store-houses and smithies. The residences of poets and princes have been turned into brokers' shops. The classic mansion of Ashland has been cut up into walking-sticks. The groves where the poets said the gods dwelt have been carted out for fire-wood. The muses that we used to read about have disappeared before the emigrant's axe and the trapper's gun, and a Vermonter can go over the Alleghany and Rocky Mountains, and never see an oread or a sylph; and that man who is waiting for a life bewitched of wonders will never find it. There is, however, a field for endurance and great achievement, but it is in every-day life. There are Alps to scale, there are Hellesponts to swim, there are fires to brave; but they are all around us now. This is the hardest kind of martyrdom to bear. It took grace to lead Latimer and Ridley through the fire triumphantly when their armed enemies and their friends were looking on; but it requires more grace now to bring men through persecution, when nobody is looking on. I could show you in this city a woman who has had rheumatism for twenty years, who has endured more suffering and exhausted more grace than would have made twenty martyrs pass triumphantly through the fire. If you are not faithful in an insignificant position in life, you would not be faithful in a grand mission. If you can not stand the bite of a midge, how could you endure the breath of a basilisk?

Do not think that any work God gives you to do in the world is on too small a scale for you to do. The whole universe is not ashamed to take care of one little daisy. I say, "What are you doing down here in the grass, you poor little daisy? Are you not afraid nights? You will be neglected, you will die of thirst, you will not be fed. Poor little daisy!" "No," says a star, "I'll watch over it to-night." "No," says a cloud, "I'll give it drink." "No," says the sun, "I'll warm it in my bosom." Then I see the pulleys going, and the clouds are drawing water, and I say, "What are you doing there, O clouds?" And they reply, "We are giving drink to that daisy." Then the wind rises, and comes bending down the wheat, and sounding its psalm through the forest, and I cry, "Whither away on such swift wing, O wind?" And it replies, "We are going to cool the cheek of that daisy." And then I bow down and say, "Will God take care of the grass of the field?" And a flower at my foot responds, "Yes; he clothes the lilies of the field, and never yet has forgotten me, a poor little daisy." Oh! when I see the great heavens bending themselves to what seems insignificant ministration, when I find out that God does not forget any blossom of the spring or any snow-flake of the winter, I come to the conclusion that we can afford to attend to the minute things in life, and that what we do we ought to do well, since there is as much perfection in the construction of a spider's eye as in the conformation of flaming galaxies. Plato had a fable which I have now nearly forgotten, but it ran something like this: He said spirits of the other world came back to this world to find a body and find a sphere of work. One spirit came and took the body of a king, and did his work. Another spirit came and took the body of a poet, and did his work. After a while Ulysses came, and he said, "Why, all the fine bodies are taken, and all the grand work is taken. There is nothing left for me." And some one replied, "Ah! the best one has been left for you." Ulysses said, "What's that?" And the reply was, "The body of a common man, doing a common work, and for a common reward." A good fable for the world, and just as good a fable for the Church. Whether we eat or drink, or whatsoever we do, let us do it to the glory of God.

Again, we need to bring the religion of Christ into our *every-day trials*. For severe losses, for bereavement, for trouble that shocks like an earthquake and that blasts like a storm, we prescribe religious consolation; but, business man, for the small annoyances of last week, how much of the grace of God did you apply? "Oh!" you say, "these trials are too small for such application." My brother, they are shaping your character, they are souring your temper, they are wearing out your patience, and they are making you less and less of a man. I go into a sculptor's studio, and see him shaping a statue. He has a chisel in one hand and a mallet in the other, and he gives a very gentle stroke—click, click, click! I say, "Why don't you strike harder?" "Oh!" he replies, "that would shatter the statue. I can't do it that way; I must do it this way." So he works on, and after a while the features come out, and every body that enters the studio is charmed and fascinated. Well, God has your soul under process of development, and it is the little annoyances and vexations of life that are chiseling out your immortal nature. It is click, click, click! I wonder why some great providence does not come, and with one stroke prepare you for heaven. Ah, no. God says that is not the way. And so he keeps on by strokes of little annoyances, little sorrows, little vexations, until at last you shall be a glad spectacle for angels and for men. You know that a large fortune may be spent in small change, and a vast amount of moral character may go away in small depletion. It is the little troubles of life that are having more effect upon you than great ones. A swarm of locusts will kill a grain-field sooner than the incursion of three or four cattle. You say, "Since I lost my child, since I lost my property, I have been a different man." But you do not recognize the architecture of little annoyances that are hewing, digging, cutting, shaping, splitting, and interjoining your moral qualities. Rats may sink a ship. One lucifer-match may send destruction through a block of store-houses. Catherine de Medicis got her death from smelling a poisonous rose. Columbus, by stopping and asking for a piece of bread and a drink of water at a Franciscan convent, was led to the discovery of a new world. And there is an intimate connection between trifles and immensities, between nothings and everythings.

Now, be careful to let none of those annoyances go through your soul unarraigned. Compel them to administer to your spiritual wealth. The scratch of a sixpenny nail sometimes produces locked-jaw, and the clip of a most infinitesimal annoyance may damage you forever. Do not let any annoyance or perplexity come across your soul without its making you better.

Our National Government does not think it belittling to put a tax on pins, and a tax on buckles, and a tax on shoes. The individual taxes do not amount to much, but in the aggregate to millions and millions of dollars. And I would have you, O Christian man, put a high tariff on every annoyance and vexation that comes through your soul. This might not amount to much, in single cases, but in the aggregate it would be a great revenue of spiritual strength and satisfaction. A bee can suck honey even out of a nettle; and if you have the grace of God in your heart, you can get sweetness out of that which would otherwise irritate and annoy. A returned missionary told me that a company of adventurers rowing up the Ganges were stung to death by flies that infest that region at certain seasons. I have seen the earth strewed with the carcasses of men slain by insect annoyances. The only way to get prepared for the great troubles of life is to conquer these small troubles. What would you say of a soldier who refused to load his gun, or to go into the conflict because it was only a skirmish, saying, "I am not going to expend my ammunition on a skirmish; wait until there comes a general engagement, and then you will see how courageous I am, and what battling I will do." The general would say to such a man, "If you are not faithful in a skirmish, you would be nothing in a general engagement." And I have to tell you, O Christian men, if you can not apply the principles of Christ's religion on a small scale, you will never be able to apply them on a large scale. If you can not successfully contend against these small sorrows that come down single-handed, what will you do when the greater disasters of life come down with thundering artillery, rolling over your soul?

Again, we must bring the religion of Christ into our *every-day blessings*. When the autumn comes, and the harvests are in, and the governors make proclamation, we assemble in churches, and we are very thankful. But every day ought to be a thanksgiving-day. We do not recognize the common mercies of life. We have to see a blind man led by his dog before we begin to bethink ourselves of what a grand thing it is to have eye-sight. We have to see some one afflicted with St. Vitus's dance before we are ready to thank God for the control of our physical energies. We have to see some wounded man hobbling on his crutch, or with his empty coat-sleeve pinned up, before we learn to think what a grand thing God did for us when he gave us healthy use of our limbs. We are so stupid that nothing but the misfortunes of others can rouse us up to our blessings. As the ox grazes in the pasture up to its eyes in clover, yet never thinking who makes the clover, and as the bird picks up the worm from the furrow, not knowing that it is God who makes every thing, from the *animalcula* in the sod to the seraph on the throne, so we go on eating, drinking, and enjoying, but never thanking, or seldom thanking; or, if thanking at all, with only half a heart.

I compared our indifference to the brute; but perhaps I wronged the brute. I do not know but that, among its other instincts, it may have an instinct by which it recognizes the Divine hand that feeds it. I do not know but that God is, through it, holding communication with what we call "irrational creation." The cow that stands at this hour under the willow by the water-course, chewing its cud, *looks* very thankful; and who can tell how much a bird means by its song? The aroma of the flowers smells like incense, and the mist arising from the river looks like the smoke of a morning sacrifice. Oh that we were as responsive! Yet who thanks God for the water that gushes up in the well, and that foams in the cascade, and that laughs over the rocks, and that patters in the showers, and that claps its hands in the sea? Who thanks God for the air, the fountain of life, the bridge of sunbeams, the path of sound, the great fan on a hot summer's day? Who thanks God for this wonderful physical organism — this sweep of the vision — this chime of harmony struck into the ear — this soft tread of a myriad delights over the nervous tissue — this rolling of the crimson tide through artery and vein — this drumming of the heart on our march to immortality? We take all these things as a matter of course.

But suppose God should withdraw these common blessings! Your body would become an Inquisition of torture, the cloud would refuse rain, every green thing would crumple up, and the earth would crack open under your feet. The air would cease its healthful circulation, pestilence would swoop, and every house would become a place of skulls. Streams would first swim with vermin, and then dry up; and thirst, and hunger, and anguish, and despair would lift their sceptres. Oh, compare such a life as that with the life you live this morning with your families about you! Is it not time that, with every word of our lips and with every action of our life, we began to acknowledge these every-day mercies? "Whether ye eat or drink, or whatsoever ye do, do all to the glory of God." Do I address a man or a woman this morning who has not rendered to God one single offering of thanks?

I was preaching one Thanksgiving-day, and announced my text: "Oh, give thanks unto the Lord; for he is good; for his mercy endureth forever." I do not know whether there was any blessing on the sermon or not; but the text went straight to a young man's heart who sits in this assembly to-day. He said to himself, as I read the text, "'Oh, give thanks unto the Lord; for he is good—' Why, I have never rendered him any thanks. Oh, what an ingrate I have been!" Can it be, my brother, that you have been fed by the good hand of God all these days—that you have had clothing and shelter and all beneficent surroundings, and yet have never offered your heart to God? Oh, let a sense of the Divine goodness shown you in the every-day blessings melt your heart; and if you have never before uttered one earnest note of thanksgiving, let this be the day which shall hear your song. What I say to one,

I say to all of this audience. Take this practical religion I have recommended into your every-day life. Make every day a Sabbath, and every meal a sacrament, and every room you enter a Holy of Holies. We all have work to do; let us be willing to do it. We all have sorrows to bear; let us cheerfully bear them. We all have battles to fight; let us courageously fight them. If you want to die right, you must live right. Negligence and indolence will win the hiss of everlasting scorn, while faithfulness will gather its garlands, and wave its sceptre, and sit upon its throne, long after this earth has put on ashes, and eternal ages have begun their march. You go home to-day, and attend to your little sphere of duties. I will go home, and attend to my little sphere of duties. Every one in his own place. So our every step in life shall be a triumphal march, and the humblest footstool on which we are called to sit will be a conqueror's throne.

LIFE AT HOME.

"Let them learn first to show piety at home."—1 *Timothy* v., 4.

A CHURCH within a church, a republic within a republic, a world within a world, is spelled by four letters—Home! If things go right there, they go right everywhere; if things go wrong there, they go wrong everywhere. The door-sill of the dwelling-house is the foundation of Church and State. A man never gets higher than his own garret or lower than his own cellar. In other words, domestic life overarches and undergirds all other life. The highest house of Congress is the domestic circle; the rocking-chair in the nursery is higher than a throne. George Washington commanded the forces of the United States, but Mary Washington commanded George. Chrysostom's mother made his pen for him. If a man should start out and run seventy years in a straight line, he could not get out from under the shadow of his own mantel-piece. I therefore talk to you this morning about a matter of infinite and eternal moment when I speak of your home.

As individuals we are fragments. God makes the race in parts, and then he gradually puts us together. What I lack, you make up; what you lack, I make up; our deficits and surpluses of character being the cog-wheels in the great social mechanism. One person has the patience, another has the courage, another has the placidity, another has the enthusiasm: that which is lacking in one is made up by another, or made up by all. Buffaloes in herds, grouse in broods, quails in flocks, the human race in circles. God has most beautifully arranged this. It is in this way that he balances society; this conservative and that radical keeping things even. Every ship must have its mast, cutwater, taffrail, ballast. Thank God, then, for Princeton and Andover, for the opposites. I have no more right to blame a man for being different from me than a drivingwheel has a right to blame the iron shaft that holds it to the centre. John Wesley balances Calvin's Institutes. A cold thinker gives to Scotland the strong bones of theology: Dr. Guthrie clothes them with a throbbing heart and warm flesh. The difficulty is that we are not satisfied with just the work that God has given us to do. The water-wheel wants to come inside the mill and grind the grist, and the hopper wants to go out and dabble in the water. Our usefulness and the welfare of society depend upon our staying in just the place that God has put us, or intended we should occupy.

For more compactness, and that we may be more useful, we are gathered in still smaller circles in the home group. And there you have the same varieties again: brothers, sisters, husband, and wife; all different in temperaments and tastes. It is fortunate that it should be so. If the husband be all impulse, the wife must be all prudence. If one sister be sanguine in her temperament, the other must be lymphatic. Mary and Martha are necessities. There will be no dinner for Christ if there be no Martha; there will be no audience for Jesus if there be no Mary. The home organization is most beautifully constructed. Eden has gone; the bowers are all broken down; the animals that Adam stroked with his hand that morning when they came up to get their names have since shot forth tusk and sting, and growled panther at panther; and, mid-air, iron beaks plunge till with clotted wing and eyeless sockets the twain come whirling down from under the sun in blood and fire. Eden has gone, but there is just one little fragment left. It floated down on the river Hiddekel out of Paradise. It is the marriage institution. It does not, as at the beginning, take away from man a rib. Now it is an addition of ribs.

This institution of marriage has been defamed in our day. Socialism, and polygamy, and Mormonism, and the most damnable of all things, free-lovism, have been trying to turn this earth into a Turkish harem or a great Salt Lake City. While the pulpits have been comparatively silent, novels—their cheapness only equaled by their nastiness—are trying to educate, have taken upon themselves to educate, this nation in regard to holy marriage, which makes or breaks for time and eternity. Oh, this is not a mere question of residence or wardrobe! It is a question charged with gigantic joy or sorrow, with heaven or hell. Alas for this new dispensation of George Sands! Alas for this mingling of the nightshade with the marriage garlands! Alas for the venom of adders spit into the tankards! Alas for the white frosts of eternal death that kill the orange-blossoms! The Gospel of Jesus Christ is to assert what is right and to assert what is wrong. Attempt has been made to take the marriage institution, which was intended for the happiness and elevation of the race, and make it a mere commercial enterprise; an exchange of houses and lands and equipage; a business partnership of two stuffed up with the stories of romance and knight-errantry, and unfaithfulness and feminine angelhood. The two after a while have roused up to find that, instead of the paradise they dreamed of, they have got nothing but a Van Amburgh's menagerie, filled with tigers and wild cats. Eighty thousand divorces in Paris in one year preceded the worst revolution that France ever saw. It was only the first course in that banquet of hell; and I tell you what you know as well as I do, that wrong notions on the subject of Christian marriage are the cause at this day of more moral outrage before God and man than any other cause.

There are some things that I want to bring before you. I know there are those of you who have had homes set up for a great many years; and, then, there are those here who have just established their home. They have only been in it a few months or a few years. Then, there are those who will, after a while, set up for themselves a home, and it is right that I should speak out upon these themes.

My first counsel to you is, *have Jesus in your new home*, if it be a new home; and let him who was a guest at Bethany be in your household: let the divine blessing drop upon your every hope and plan and expectation. Those young people who begin with God end with heaven. Have on your right hand the engagement ring of the Divine affection. If one of you be a Christian, let that one take the Bible and read a few verses in the evening-time, and then kneel down and commend yourselves to him who setteth the solitary in families. I want to tell you that the destroying angel passes by without touching or entering the door-post sprinkled with blood of the everlasting covenant. Why is it that in some families they never get along, and in others they always get along well? I have watched such cases, and have come to a conclusion. In the first instance, nothing seemed to go pleasantly, and after a while there came devastation, domestic disaster, or estrangement. Why? They started wrong. In the other case, although there were hardships and trials and some things that had to be explained, still things went on pleasantly until the very last. Why? They started right.

My second advice to you in your home is, to exercise to the very last possibility of your nature *the law of forbearance*. Prayers in the household will not make up for every thing. Some of the best people in the world are the hardest to get along with. There are people who stand up in prayer-meetings and pray like angels, who at home are uncompromising and cranky. You may not have every thing just as you want it. Sometimes it will be the duty of the husband and sometimes of the wife to yield; but both stand punctiliously on your rights, and you will have a Waterloo with no Blücher coming up at night-fall to decide the conflict.

Never be ashamed to apologize when you have done wrong in domestic affairs. Let that be a law of your household. The best thing I ever heard of my grandfather, whom I never saw, was this: that once having unrighteously rebuked one of his children, he himself having lost his patience, and, perhaps, having been misinformed of the child's doings, found out his mistake, and in the evening of the same day gathered all his family together, and said, "Now, I have one explanation to make, and one thing to say. Thomas, this morning I rebuked you very unfairly. I am very sorry for it. I rebuked you in the presence of the whole family, and now I ask your forgiveness in their presence." It must have taken some courage to do that. It was right, was it not? Never be ashamed to apologize for domestic inaccuracy. Find out the points;

what are the weak points, if I may call them so, of your companion, and then stand aloof from them. Do not carry the fire of your temper too near the gunpowder. If the wife be easily fretted by disorder in the household, let the husband be careful where he throws his slippers. If the husband come home from the store with his patience all exhausted, do not let the wife unnecessarily cross his temper; but both stand up for your rights, and I will promise the everlasting sound of the war-whoop. Your life will be spent in making-up, and marriage will be to you an unmitigated curse. Cowper said,

> "The kindest and the happiest pair
> Will find occasion to forbear;
> And something, every day they live,
> To pity, and perhaps forgive."

I advise, also, that you make your *chief pleasure circle around about that home.* It is unfortunate when it is otherwise. If the husband spend the most of his nights away from home, of choice, and not of necessity, he is not the head of the household; he is only the cashier. If the wife throw the cares of the household into the servant's lap, and then spend five nights of the week at the opera or theatre, she may clothe her children with satins and laces and ribbons that would confound a French milliner, but they are orphans. Oh, it is sad when a child has no one to say its prayers to because mother has gone off to the evening entertainment! In India they bring children and throw them to the crocodiles, and it seems very cruel; but the jaws of New York and Brooklyn dissipation are swallowing down more little children to-day than all the monsters that ever crawled upon the banks of the Ganges!

I have seen the sorrow of a godless mother on the death of a child she had neglected. It was not so much grief that she felt from the fact that the child was dead as the fact that she had neglected it. She said, "If I had only watched over and cared for the child, I know God would not have taken it." The tears came not: it was a dry, blistering tempest—a scorching simoom of the desert. When she wrung her hands, it seemed as if she would twist her fingers from their sockets; when she seized her hair, it seemed as if she had, in wild terror, grasped a coiling serpent with her right hand. No tears! Comrades of the little one came in and wept over the coffin; neighbors came in, and the moment they saw the still face of the child the shower broke. No tears for her. God gives tears as the summer rain to the parched soul; but in all the universe the driest and hottest, the most scorching and consuming thing is a mother's heart if she has neglected her child, when once it is dead. God may forgive her, but she will never forgive herself. The memory will sink the eyes deeper into the sockets, and pinch the face, and whiten the hair, and eat up the heart with vultures that will not be satisfied, forever plunging deeper their iron beaks. Oh, you wanderers from your home, go back to your duty! The brightest flowers in all the earth are those which grow in the garden of a Christian household, clambering over the porch of a Christian home.

I advise you also to *cultivate sympathy of occupation.* Sir James M'Intosh, one of the most eminent and elegant men that ever lived, while standing at the very height of his eminence, said to a great company of scholars, "My wife made me." The wife ought to be the advising partner in every firm. She ought to be interested in all the losses and gains of shop and store. She ought to have a right—she *has* a right—to know every thing. If a man goes into a business transaction that he dare not tell his wife of, you may depend that he is on the way either to bankruptcy or moral ruin. There may be some things which he does not wish to trouble his wife with; but if he *dare* not tell her, he is on the road to discomfiture. On the other hand, the husband ought to be sympathetic with the wife's occupation. It is no easy thing to keep house. Many a woman that could have endured martyrdom as well as Margaret, the Scotch girl, has actually been worn out by house management. There are a thousand martyrs of the kitchen. It is very annoying, after the vexations of the day around the stove or the table, or in the nursery or parlor, to have the husband say, "You know nothing about trouble; you ought to be in the store half an hour." Sympathy of occupation! If the husband's work cover him with the soot of the furnace, or the odors of leather or soap factories, let not the wife be easily disgusted at the begrimed hands or unsavory aroma. Your gains are one, your interests are one, your losses are one; lay hold of the work of life with both hands. Four hands to fight the battles; four eyes to watch for the danger; four shoulders on which to carry the trials. It is a very sad thing when the painter has a wife who does not like pictures. It is a very sad thing for a pianist when she has a husband who does not like music. It is a very sad thing when a wife is not suited unless her husband has what is called a "genteel business." So far as I understand a "genteel business," it is something to which a man goes at ten o'clock in the morning, and from which he comes home at two or three o'clock in the afternoon, and gets a large amount of money for doing nothing. That is, I believe, a "genteel business;" and there has been many a wife who has made the mistake of not being satisfied until the husband has given up the tanning of the hides, or the turning of the banisters, or the building of the walls, and put himself in circles where he has nothing to do but smoke cigars and drink wine, and get himself into habits that upset him, going down in the maelstrom, taking his wife and children with him. There are a good many trains running from earth to destruction. They start all the hours of the day, and all the hours of the night. There are the freight trains; they go very slowly and very heavily: and there are the accommodation trains going on toward destruction, and they stop very often, and let a man get out when he wants to. But genteel idleness is an express train: Satan is the stoker, and death is the engineer; and though one may come out in front of it, and swing the red flag of "danger," or the lantern of God's Word, it makes just one shot into perdition, coming down the embankment with a shout and a wail and a shriek—crash, crash! There are two classes of people sure of destruction: first, those who have nothing to do; secondly, those who have something to do, but who are too lazy or too proud to do it.

I have one more word of advice to give to those who would have a happy home, and that is, *let love preside in it.* When your behavior in the domestic circle becomes a mere matter of calculation; when the caress you give is merely the result of deliberate study of the position you occupy, happiness lies stark dead on the hearth-stone. When the husband's position as head of the household is maintained by loudness of voice, by strength of arm, by fire of temper, the republic of domestic bliss has become a despotism that neither God nor man will abide. Oh, ye who promised to love each other at the altar! how dare you commit perjury? Let no shadow of suspicion come on your affection. It is easier to kill that flower than it is to make it live again. The blast from hell that puts out that light, leaves you in the blackness of darkness forever.

Here are a man and wife; they agree in nothing else, but they agree they will have a home. They will have a splendid house, and they think that if they have a house, they will have a home. Architects make the plan, and the mechanics execute it; the house to cost one hundred thousand dollars. It is done. The carpets are spread; lights are hoisted; curtains are hung; cards of invitation sent out. The horses in gold-plated harness prance at the gate; guests come in and take their places; the flute sounds; the dancers go up and down; and with one grand whirl the wealth and the fashion and the mirth of the great town wheel amidst the pictured walls. Ha! this is happiness. Float it on the smoking viands; sound it in the music; whirl it in the dance; cast it on the snow of sculpture; sound it up the brilliant stair-way; flash it in chandeliers! Happiness, indeed! Let us build on the centre of the parlor floor a throne to Happiness; let all the guests, when come in, bring their flowers and pearls and diamonds, and throw them on this pyramid, and let it be a throne; and then let Happiness, the queen, mount the throne, and we will stand around, and, all chalices lifted, we will say, "Drink, O queen! live forever!" But the guests depart, the flutes are breathless, the last clash of the impatient hoofs is heard in the distance, and the twain of the household come back to see the Queen of Happiness on the throne amidst the parlor floor. But, alas! as they come back, the flowers have faded, the sweet odors have become the smell of a charnel-house, and instead of the Queen of Happiness there sits there the gaunt form of Anguish, with bitten lip and sunken eye, and ashes in her hair. The romp of the dancers who have left seems rumbling yet, like jarring thunders that quake the floor and rattle the glasses of the feast rim to rim. The spilled wine on the floor turns into blood. The wreaths of plush have become wriggling reptiles. Terrors catch tangled in the canopy that overhangs the couch. A strong gust of wind comes through the hall and the drawing-room and the bedchamber, in which all the lights go out. And from the lips of the wine-beakers come the words, "Happiness is not in us!" And the arches respond, "It is not in us!" And the silenced instruments of music, thrummed on by invisible fingers, answer, "Happiness is not in us!" And the frozen lips of Anguish break open, and, seated on the throne of wilted flowers, she strikes her bony hands together, and groans, "It is not in me!"

That very night a clerk with a salary of a thousand dollars a year—only one thousand—goes to his home, set up three months ago, just after the marriage-day. Love meets him at the door; love sits with him at the table; love talks over the work of the day; love takes down the Bible, and reads of Him who came our souls to save; and they kneel, and while they are kneeling—right in that plain room, on that plain carpet—the angels of God build a throne, not out of flowers that perish and fade away, but out of garlands of heaven, wreath on top of wreath, amaranth on amaranth, until the throne is done. Then the harps of God sounded, and suddenly there appeared one who mounted the throne, with eye so bright and brow so fair that the twain knew it was Christian Love. And they knelt at the foot of the throne, and, putting one hand on each head, she blessed them, and said, "Happiness is with me!" And that throne of celestial bloom withered not with the passing years; and the queen left not the throne till one day the married pair felt stricken in years—felt themselves called away, and knew not which way to go, and the queen bounded from the throne, and said, "Follow me, and I will show you the way up to the realm of everlasting love." And so they went up to sing songs of love, and walk on pavements of love, and to live together in mansions of love, and to rejoice forever in the truth that God is love.

THE OLD CORN OF CANAAN.

"And the manna ceased on the morrow after they had eaten of the old corn of the land."—*Joshua* v., 12.

ONLY those who have had something to do with the commissariat of an army know what a job it is to feed and clothe five or six hundred thousand men. Well, there is such a host as that marching across the desert. They are cut off from all army supplies. There are no rail trains bringing down food or blankets. Shall they all perish? No. The Lord comes from heaven to the rescue, and he touches the shoes and the coats which in a year or two would have been worn to rags and tatters, and they become storm-proof and time-proof, so that, after forty years of wearing, the coats and the shoes are as good as new. Besides that, every morning there is a shower of bread, not sour and soggy, for the rising of that bread is made in heaven, and celestial fingers have mixed it, and rolled it into balls, light, flaky, and sweet, as though they were the crumbs thrown out from a heavenly banquet. Two batches of bread made every day in the upper mansion—one for those who sit at the table with the King, and the other for the marching Israelites in the wilderness. I do not very much pity the Israelites for the fact that they had only manna to eat. It was, I suppose, the best food ever provided. I know that the ravens brought food to hungry Elijah; but I should not so well have liked those black waiters. Rather would I have the fare that came down every morning in buckets of dew—clean, sweet, God-provided edibles. But now the Israelites have taken their last bit of it in their fingers, and put the last delicate morsel of it to their lips. They look out, and there is no manna. Why this cessation of heavenly supply? It was because the Israelites had arrived in Canaan, and they smelled the breath of the harvest-fields, and the crowded barns of the country were thrown open to them. All the inhabitants had fled, and in the name of the Lord of hosts the Israelites took possession of every thing. Well, the threshing-floor is cleared, the corn is scattered over it, the oxen are brought around in lazy and perpetual circuit until the corn is trampled loose; then it is winnowed with a fan, and it is ground and it is baked, and, lo! there is enough bread for all the worn-out host. "And the manna ceased on the morrow after they had eaten of the old corn of the land."

The bisection of this subject leads me, first, to speak of especial relief for especial emergency; and, secondly, of the old corn of the Gospel for ordinary circumstances.

If these Israelites crossing the wilderness had not received bread from the heavenly bakeries, there would, first, have been a long line of dead children half buried in the sand; then, there would have been a long line of dead women waiting for the jackals; then, there would have been a long line of dead men unburied, because there would have been no one to bury them. It would have been told in the history of the world that a great company of good people started out from Egypt for Canaan, and were never heard of, as thoroughly lost in the wilderness of sand as the *City of Boston* and the *President* were lost in the wilderness of waters. What use was it to them that there was plenty of corn in Canaan, or plenty of corn in Egypt?

What they wanted was something to eat right there, where there was not so much as a grass-blade. In other words, an especial supply for an especial emergency. That is what some of you want. The ordinary comfort, the ordinary direction, the ordinary counsel, do not seem to meet your case. There are those who feel that they must have an omnipotent and immediate supply, and you shall have it.

Is it pain and physical distress through which you must go? Does not Jesus know all about pain? Did he not suffer it in the most sensitive part of head and hand and foot? He has a mixture of comfort, one drop of which shall cure the worst paroxysm. It is the same grace that soothed Robert Hall when, after writhing on the carpet in physical tortures, he cried out, "Oh! I suffered terribly, but I didn't cry out while I was suffering, did I? Did I cry out?" There is no such nurse as Jesus—his hand the gentlest, his foot the lightest, his arm the strongest. For especial pang especial help.

Is it approaching sorrow? Is it long, shadowing bereavement that you know is coming, because the breath is short, and the voice is faint, and the cheek is pale? Have you been calculating your capacity or incapacity to endure widowhood or childlessness or a disbanded home, and cried, "I can not endure it?" Oh, worried soul, you will wake up amidst all your troubles, and find around about you the sweet consolations of the Gospel as thickly strewed as was the manna around about the Israelitish encampment! Especial solace for especial distress.

Or is it a trouble past, yet present? A silent nursery? A vacant chair opposite you at the table? A musing upon a broken family circle never again to be reunited? A choking sense of loneliness? A blot of grief so large that it extinguishes the light of sun, and puts out bloom of flower, and makes you reckless as to whether you live or die? Especial comfort for that especial trial. Your appetite has failed for every thing else. Oh, try a little of this wilderness manna: "I will never leave thee, I will never forsake thee." "Like as a father pitieth his children, so the Lord pitieth them that fear him." "Can a woman forget her sucking child, that she should not have compassion on the son of her womb? yea, they may forget, yet will I not forget thee."

Or is it the grief of a dissipated companion? There are those here who have it, so I am not speaking in the abstract, but to the point. You have not whispered it, perhaps, to your most intimate friend; but you see your home going away gradually from you, and unless things change soon it will be entirely destroyed. Your grief was well depicted by a woman, presiding at a women's meeting last winter in Ohio, when her intoxicated husband staggered up to the platform, to her overwhelming mortification and the disturbance of the audience, and she pulled a protruding bottle from her husband's pocket, and held it up before the audience, and cried out, "There is the cause of my woe! There are the tears and the life-blood of a drunkard's wife!" And then, looking up to heaven, she said, "How long, O Lord! how long?" and then, looking down to the audience, cried, "Do you wonder I feel strongly on this subject? Sisters, will you help me?" And hundreds of voices responded, "Yes, yes, we will help you." You stand, some of you, in such a tragedy to-day. You can not even ask him to stop drinking. It makes him cross, and he tells you to mind your own business. Is there any relief in such a case? Not such as is found in the rigmarole of comfort ordinarily given in such cases. But there is a relief that drops in manna from the throne of God. Oh, lift up your lacerated soul in prayer, and you will get omnipotent comfort! I do not know in what words the soothing influence may come, but I know that for especial grief there is especial deliverance. I give you two or three passages; try them on; take that which best fits your soul: "Whom the Lord loveth he chasteneth." "All things work together for good to those who love God." "Weeping may endure for a night, but joy cometh in the morning." I know there are those who, when they try to comfort people, always bring the same stale sentiment about the usefulness of trial. Instead of bringing a new plaster for a new wound, and fresh manna for fresh hunger, they rummage their haversack to find some crumb of old consolation, when from horizon to horizon the ground is white with the new-fallen manna of God's help not five minutes old!

But after fourteen thousand six hundred consecutive days of falling manna—Sundays excepted—the manna ceased. Some of them were glad of it. You know they had complained to their leader, and wondered that they had to eat manna instead of onions. Now the fare is changed. Those people in that army under forty years of age had never seen a corn-field, and now, when they hear the leaves rustling and see the tassels waving and the billows of green flowing over the plain as the wind touched them, it must have been a new and lively sensation. "Corn!" cried the old man, as he husked an ear. "Corn!" cried the children, as they counted the shining grains. "Corn!" shouted the vanguard of the host, as they burst open the granaries of the affrighted population, the granaries that had been left in the possession of the victorious Israelites. Then the fire was kindled, and the ears of corn were thrust into it, and, fresh and crisp and tender, were devoured of the hungry victors; and bread was prepared, and many things that can be made out of flour regaled the appetites that had been sharpened by the long march. "And the manna ceased on the morrow after they had eaten of the old corn of the land."

Blessed be God, we stand in just such a field to-day, the luxuriant grain coming above the girdle, the air full of the odors of the ripe old corn of the Gospel Canaan. "Oh!" you say, "the fare is too plain." Then I remember you will soon get tired of a fanciful diet. While I was in Paris, I liked for a while the rare and exquisite cookery; but I soon wished I was home again, and had the plain fare of my native land. So it is a fact that we soon weary of the sirups and the custards and the whipped foam of fanciful religionists, and we cry, "Give us plain bread made out of the old corn of the Gospel Canaan." That is the only food that can quell the soul's hunger.

There are men here this morning who hardly know what is the matter with them. They have tried to get together a fortune and larger account at the bank, and to get investments yielding larger percentages. They are trying to satisfy their soul with a diet of greenbacks and Government securities. There are others here who have been trying to get famous, and have succeeded to a greater or less extent; and they have been trying to satisfy their soul with the chopped feed of magazines and newspapers. All these men are no more happy now than before they made the first thousand dollars; no more happy now than when for the first time they saw their names favorably mentioned. They can not analyze or define their feelings; but I will tell them what is the matter—they are hungry for the old corn of the Gospel. That you must have, or be pinched, and wan, and wasted, and hollow-eyed, and shriveled up with an eternity of famine.

The infidel scientists of this day are offering us a different kind of soul food; but they are, of all men, the most miserable. I have known many of them; but I never knew one of them who came within a thousand miles of being happy. The great John Stuart Mill provided for himself a new kind of porridge; but yet, when he comes to die, he acknowledges that his philosophy never gave him any comfort in days of bereavement, and in a roundabout way he admits that his life was a failure. So it is with all infidel scientists. They are trying to live on telescopes and crucibles and protoplasms, and they charge us with cant, not realizing that there is no such intolerable cant in all the world as this perpetual talk we are hearing about "positive philosophy," and "the absolute," and "the great to be," and "the everlasting no," and "the higher unity," and "the latent potentialities," and "the cathedral of the immensities." I have been translating what these men have been writing, and I have been translating what they have been doing, and I will tell you what it all means—it means that they want to kill God! And my only wonder is that God has not killed them. I have, in other days, tasted of their confections, and I come back and tell you to-day that there is no nutriment or life or health in any thing but the bread made out of the old corn of the Gospel. What do I mean by that? I mean that Christ is the bread of life, and taking him, you live and live forever.

But, you say, corn is of but little practical use unless it

is threshed and ground and baked. I answer, this Gospel corn has gone through that process. When on Calvary all the hoofs of human scorn came down on the heart of Christ, and all the flails of Satanic fury beat him long and fast, was not the corn threshed? When the mills of God's indignation against sin caught Christ between the upper and nether rollers, was not the corn ground? When Jesus descended into hell, and the flames of the lost world wrapped him all about, was not the corn baked? Oh yes! Christ is ready. His pardon all ready; his peace all ready; every thing ready in Christ. Are you ready for him?

You say, "That is such a simple Gospel!" I know it is. You say you thought religion was a strange mixture of elaborate compounds. No; it is so plain that any abecedarian may understand it. In its simplicity is its power. If you could, this morning, realize that Christ died to save from sin and death and hell, not only your minister and your neighbor and your father and your child, but *you*, it would make this hour like the judgment-day for agitations, and, no longer able to keep your seat, you would leap up, crying, "*For me!* FOR ME!" God grant that you, my brother, may see this Gospel with your own eyes, and hear it with your own ears, and feel with your own heart that you are a lost soul, but that Christ comes for your extrication. Can you not take that truth and digest it, and make it a part of your immortal life? It is only bread.

You have noticed that invalids can not take all kinds of food. The food that will do for one will not do for another. There are kinds of food which will produce, in cases of invalidism, very speedy death. But you have noticed that all persons, however weak they may be, can take bread. Oh, soul sick with sin, invalid in your transgressions, I think this Gospel will agree with you! I think if you can not take any thing else, you can take this. Lost—found! Sunken—raised! Condemned—pardoned! Cast out—invited in! That is the old corn of the Gospel.

You have often seen a wheel with spokes of different colors, and when the wheel was rapidly turned all the colors blended into a rainbow of exquisite beauty. I wish I could, this morning, take the peace and the life and the joy and glory of Christ, and turn them before your soul with such speed and strength that you would be enchanted with the revolving splendors of that name which is above every name—the name written once with tears of exile and in blood of martyrdom, but written now in burnished crown and lifted sceptre and transangelic throne.

There is another characteristic about bread, and that is, you never get tired of it. There are people here seventy years of age who find it just as appropriate for their appetite as they did when, in boyhood, their mother cut a slice of it clear around the loaf. You have not got tired of bread, and that is a characteristic of the Gospel. Old Christian man, are you tired of Jesus? If so, let us take his name out of our Bible, and let us with pen and ink erase that name wherever we see it. Let us cast it out of our hymnology, and let "There is a Fountain" and "Rock of Ages" go into forgetfulness. Let us tear down the communion-table where we celebrate his love. Let us dash down the baptismal bowl where we were consecrated to him. Let us hurl Jesus from our heart, and ask some other hero to come in. Let us say, "Go away, Jesus; I want another companion, another friend, than thou art." Could you do it? The years of your past life, aged man, would utter a protest against it, and the graves of your Christian dead would charge you with being an ingrate, and your little grandchildren would say, "Grandfather, don't do that. Jesus is the one to whom we say our prayers at night, and who is to open heaven when we die. Grandfather, don't do that." Tired of Jesus? The Burgundy rose you pluck from the garden is not so fresh and fair and beautiful. Tired of Jesus? As well get weary of the spring morning, and the voices of the mountain runnel, and the quiet of your own home, and the gladness of your own children. Jesus is bread, and the appetite for that is never obliterated.

I notice, in regard to this article of food, you take it three times a day. It is on your table morning, noon, and night; and if it is forgotten, you say, "Where is the bread?" Just so certainly you need Jesus three times a day. Oh, do not start out without him; do not dare to go out of the front door; do not dare to go off the front steps, without first having communed with him! Before noon there may be perils that will destroy body, mind, and soul forever. You can not afford to do without him. You will during the day be amidst sharp hoofs and swift wheels and dangerous scaffoldings threatening the body, and traps for the soul that have taken some who are more wily than you. When they launch a ship they break against the side of it a bottle of wine. That is a sort of superstition among sailors. But oh, on the launching of every day, that we might strike against it at least one earnest prayer for divine protection! That would not be superstition; that would be Christian. Then at the apex of the day, at the tiptop of the hours, equidistant from morning and night, look three ways. Look backward to the forenoon; look ahead to the afternoon; look up to that Saviour who presides over all. You want bread at noon. You may find no place in which to kneel amidst the cotton bales and the tierces of rice; but if Jonah could find room to pray in the whale's belly, most certainly you will never be in such a crowded place that you can not pray. Bread at noon! When the evening hour comes, and your head is buzzing with the day's engagements, and your whole nature is sore from the abrasion of rough life, and you see a great many duties you have neglected, then commune with Christ, asking his pardon, thanking him for his love. That would be a queer evening repast at which there was no bread.

This is the nutriment and life of the plain Gospel that I commend to you. I do not know how some of our ministers make it so intricate and elaborate and mystifying a thing. It seems as if they had a sort of mongrelism, in religion — part humanitarianism, part spiritualism, part nothingarianism; and sometimes you think they are building their temple out of the "Rock of Ages," but you find there is no rock in it at all. It is stucco. The Gospel is plain. It is bread. There are no fogs hovering over this river of life. All the fogs hover over the marsh of human speculation. If you can not tell, when you hear a man preach, whether or not he believes in the plenary inspiration of the Scriptures, it is because he does not believe in it. If, when you hear a man preach, you can not tell whether or not he believes that sin is inborn, it is because he does not think it is congenital. If, when you hear a man talk in pulpit or prayer-meeting, you can not make up your mind whether or not he believes in regeneration, it is because he does not believe in it. If, when you hear a man speak on religious themes, you can not make up your mind whether or not he thinks the righteous and the wicked will come out at the same place, then it is because he really believes their destinies are conterminous. Do not talk to me about a man being doubtful about the doctrines of grace. He is not doubtful to me at all. Bread is bread, and I know it the moment I see it. I had a cornfield which I cultured this summer with my own hand. I did not ask once in all the summer, "Is this corn?" I did not hunt up *The Agriculturist* to get a picture of corn. I was born in sight of a corn-field, and I know all about it. When these Israelites came to Canaan and looked off upon the fields, the cry was "Corn! corn!" And if a man has once tasted of this heavenly bread, he knows it right away. He can tell this corn of the Gospel Canaan from "the chaff which the wind driveth away." I bless God so many have found this Gospel corn. It is the bread of which if a man eat he shall never hunger. I set the gladness of your soul to the tunes of "Ariel" and "Antioch." I ring the wedding-bells, for Christ and your soul are married, and there is no power on earth or in hell to get out letters of divorcement.

But alas for the famine-struck! Enough corn, yet it seems you have no sickle to cut it, no mill to grind it, no fire to bake it, no appetite to eat it. Starving to death, when the plain is golden with a magnificent harvest! My brother, if your friends had acted as crazily about worldly things as you have acted about spiritual things, you would have sent them before this to Bloomingdale Insane Asylum. You do not seem to realize the hunger that is gnawing on your soul, the precipices on the edge of which you walk, the fires into which you run. .Oh, the insanity, the awful madness, of a man that will not take Christ! When I think of the risks you run, it seems as if I must rush from the pulpit, and take you by the shoulder, and tell you of what is coming and how little you are ready for it.

This summer I rode some thirteen miles to see the *Alexander*, a large steamship that was beached near Southampton, Long Island, last winter. It was a splendid vessel. As I walked up and down the decks and in the cabins, I said, "What a pity that this vessel should go to pieces, or be lying here idle!" The coast wreckers had spent thirty thousand dollars trying to get her off, and they succeeded once; but she came back again to the old place. While I was walking on deck, every part of the vessel trembled with the beating of the surf on one side. Since then I heard that that vessel, which was worth two hundred and fifty thousand dollars, has been sold for three thousand five hundred, and is to be knocked to pieces. They had given up the idea of getting her to sail again. How suggestive all that is to me! There are those here who are aground in religious things. Once you started for heaven, but you are now aground. Several times we thought we had started you again heavenward, but you soon got back to the old place, and there is not much prospect you will ever reach the harbors of the blessed. I fear it will be after a while said in regard to some of you, "No use; no use. To be destroyed without remedy." God's wreckers will pronounce you a hopeless case. *Beached for eternity!* And then it will be written in heaven concerning some one of your size, and complexion, and age, and name, that he was invited to be saved, but refused the offer, and starved to death within sight of the fields and granaries full of the Old Corn of Canaan.

ZIKLAG IN ASHES.

"Then David and the people that were with him lifted up their voice and wept, until they had no more power to weep....... David recovered all...... As his part is that goeth down to the battle, so shall his part be that tarrieth by the stuff."—1 *Samuel* xxx., 4, 19, 24.

THERE is intense excitement in the village of Ziklag. David and his men are bidding good-bye to their families, and are off for the wars. In that little village of Ziklag the defenseless ones will be safe until the warriors, flushed with victory, come home. But will the defenseless ones be safe? The soft arms of children are around the necks of the bronzed warriors until they shake themselves free and start, and handkerchiefs and flags are waved and kisses thrown until the armed men vanish beyond the hills. David and his men soon get through with their campaign and start homeward. Every night on their way home, no sooner does the soldier put his head on the knapsack than in his dream he hears the welcome of the wife and the shout of the child. Oh, what long stories they will have to tell their families, of how they dodged the battle-axe! and then will roll up their sleeve and show the half-healed wound. With glad, quick step, they march on, David and his men, for they are marching home. Now they come up to the last hill which overlooks Ziklag, and they expect in a moment to see the dwelling-places of their loved ones. They look, and as they look their cheek turns pale, and their lip quivers, and their hand involuntarily comes down on the hilt of the sword. "Where is Ziklag? Where are our homes?" they cry. Alas! the curling smoke above the ruin tells the tragedy. The Amalekites have come down and consumed the village, and carried the mothers and the wives and the children of David and his men into captivity. The swarthy warriors stand for a few moments transfixed with horror. Then their eyes glance to each other, and they burst into uncontrollable weeping; for when a strong warrior weeps, the grief is appalling. It seems as if the emotion might tear him to pieces. They "wept until they had no more power to weep." But soon their sorrow turns into rage, and David, swinging his sword high in air, cries, "Pursue, for thou shalt overtake them, and without fail recover all." Now the march becomes a "double-quick." Two hundred of David's men stop by the brook Besor, faint with fatigue and grief. They can not go a step farther. They are left there. But the other four hundred men under David, with a sort of panther step, march on in sorrow and in rage. They find by the side of the road a half-dead Egyptian, and they resuscitate him, and compel him to tell the whole story. He says, "Yonder they went, the captors and the captives," pointing in the direction. Forward, ye four hundred brave men of fire! Very soon David and his enraged company come upon the Amalekitish host. Yonder they see their own wives and children and mothers, and under Amalekitish guard. Here are the officers of the Amalekitish army holding a banquet. The cups are full, the music is roused, the dance begins. The Amalekitish host cheer and cheer and cheer over their victory. But, without note of bugle or warning of trumpet, David and his four hundred men burst upon the scene, suddenly as Robert Bruce hurled his

Scotchmen upon the revelers at Bannockburn. David and his men look up, and one glance at their loved ones in captivity and under Amalekitish guard throws them into a very fury of determination; for you know how men will fight when they fight for their wives and children. Ah, there are lightnings in their eye, and every finger is a spear, and their voice is like the shout of the whirlwind! Amidst the upset tankards and the costly viands crushed underfoot, the wounded Amalekites lie (their blood mingling with their wine), shrieking for mercy. No sooner do David and his men win the victory than they throw their swords down into the dust—what do they want with swords now?—and the broken families come together amidst a great shout of joy that makes the parting scene in Ziklag seem very insipid in the comparison. The rough old warrior has to use some persuasion before he can get his child to come to him now after so long an absence; but soon the little finger traces the familiar wrinkle across the scarred face. And then the empty tankards are set up, and they are filled with the best wine from the hills, and David and his men, the husbands, the wives, the brothers, the sisters, drink to the overthrow of the Amalekites and to the rebuilding of Ziklag. So, O Lord, let thine enemies perish!

Now they are coming home, David and his men and their families—a long procession. Men, women, and children, loaded with jewels and robes and with all kinds of trophies that the Amalekites had gathered up in years of conquest—every thing now in the hands of David and his men. When they come by the brook Besor, the place where staid the men sick and incompetent to travel, the jewels and the robes and all kinds of treasures are divided among the sick as well as among the well. Surely, the lame and exhausted ought to have some of the treasures. Here is a robe for this pale-faced warrior. Here is a pillow for this dying man. Here is a handful of gold for the wasted trumpeter. I really think that these men who fainted by the brook Besor may have endured as much as those men who went into the battle. Some mean fellows objected to the sick ones having any of the spoils. The objectors said, "These men did not fight." David, with a magnanimous heart, replies, "As his part is that goeth down to the battle, so shall his part be that tarrieth by the stuff."

This subject is practically suggestive to me. Thank God, in these times a man can go off on a journey, and be gone weeks and months, and come back and see his house untouched of incendiary, and have his family on the step to greet him if by telegram he has foretold the moment of his coming. But there are Amalekitish disasters, and there are Amalekitish diseases, that sometimes come down upon one's home, making as devastating work as the day when Ziklag took fire. There are families in my congregation whose homes have been broken up. No batteringram smote in the door, no iconoclast crumbled the statues, no flame leaped amidst the curtains; but so far as all the joy and merriment that once belonged to that house are concerned, the home has departed. Armed diseases came down upon the quietness of the scene—scarlet fevers, or pleurisies, or consumptions, or undefined disorders came and seized upon some members of that family, and carried them away. Ziklag in ashes! And you go about, sometimes weeping and sometimes enraged, wanting to get back your loved ones as much as David and his men wanted to reconstruct their despoiled households. Ziklag in ashes! Some of you went off from home. You counted the days of your absence. Every day seemed as long as a week. Oh! how glad you were when the time came for you to go aboard the steamboat or rail-car and start for home! You arrived. You went up the street where your dwelling was, and in the night you put your hand on the door-bell, and, behold! it was wrapped with the signal of bereavement, and you found that Amalekitish Death, which has devastated a thousand other households, had blasted yours. You go about weeping amidst the desolation of your once happy home, thinking of the bright eyes closed, and the noble hearts stopped, and the gentle hands folded, and you weep until you have no more power to weep. Ziklag in ashes!

A gentleman went to a friend of mine in the city of Washington, and asked that through him he might get a consulship to some foreign port. My friend said to him, "What do you want to go away from your beautiful home for, into a foreign port?" "Oh," he replied, "my home is gone! My six children are dead. I must get away, sir. I can't stand it in this country any longer." Ziklag in ashes!

Why these long shadows of bereavement across this audience? Why is it that in almost every assemblage black is the predominant color of the apparel? Is it because you do not like saffron or brown or violet? Oh no! You say, "The world is not so bright to us as once it was;" and there is a story of silent voices, and of still feet, and of loved ones gone, and when you look over the hills, expecting only beauty and loveliness, you find only devastation and woe. Ziklag in ashes!

Last Wednesday week, in Ulster County, New York,

the village church was decorated until the fragrance of the flowers was almost bewildering. The maidens of the village had emptied the place of flowers upon one marriage altar. One of their own number was affianced to a minister of Christ, who had come to take her to his own home. With hands joined, amidst a congratulatory audience, the vows were taken. In three days from that time one of those who stood at the altar exchanged earth for heaven. The wedding march broke down into the funeral dirge. There were not enough flowers now for the coffin-lid, because they had all been taken for the bridal hour. The dead minister of Christ is brought to another village. He had gone out from them less than a week before in his strength; now he comes home lifeless. The whole church bewailed him. The solemn procession moved around to look upon the still face that once had beamed with messages of salvation. Little children were lifted up to look at him. And some of those whom he had comforted in days of sorrow, when they passed that silent form, made the place dreadful with their weeping. Another village emptied of its flowers—some of them put in the shape of a cross to symbolize his hope, others put in the shape of a crown to symbolize his triumph. A hundred lights blown out in one strong gust from the open door of a sepulchre. Ziklag in ashes!

I preach this sermon to-day, because I want to rally you, as David rallied his men, for the recovery of the loved and the lost. I want not only to win heaven, but I want all this congregation to go along with me. I feel that somehow I have a responsibility in your arriving at that great city. I have on other Sabbaths used other inducements. I mean, to-day, for the sake of variety, hoping to reach your heart, to try another kind of inducement. Do you really want to join the companionship of your loved ones who have gone? Are you as anxious to join them as David and his men were to join their families? Then I am here, in the name of God, to say that you may, and to tell you how.

I remark, in the first place, if you want to join your loved ones in glory, *you must travel the same way they went.* No sooner had the half-dead Egyptian been resuscitated than he pointed the way the captors and the captives had gone, and David and his men followed after. So our Christian friends have gone into another country, and if we want to reach their companionship we must take the same road. They repented; we must repent. They prayed; we must pray. They trusted in Christ; we must trust in Christ. They lived a religious life; we must live a religious life. They were in some things like ourselves. I know, now that they are gone, there is a halo around their names; but they had their faults. They said and did things they ought never to have said or done. They were sometimes rebellious, sometimes cast down. They were far from being perfect. So I suppose that when we have gone, some things in us that are now only tolerable may be almost resplendent. But as they were like us in deficiencies, we ought to be like them in taking a supernal Christ to make up for the deficits. Had it not been for Jesus, they would have all perished; but Christ confronted them, and said, "I am the way," and they took it.

I have also to say to you that the path that these captives trod *was a troubled path,* and that David and his men had to go over the same difficult way. While these captives were being taken off, they said, "Oh! we are so tired; we are so sick; we are so hungry!" But the men who had charge of them said, "Stop this crying. Go on!" David and his men also found it a hard way. They had to travel it. Our friends have gone into glory, and it is through much tribulation that we are to enter into the kingdom. How our loved ones used to have to struggle! how their old hearts ached! how sometimes they had a tussle for bread! In our childhood we wondered why there were so many wrinkles on their faces. We did not know that what were called "crow's-feet" on their faces were the marks of the black raven of trouble. Did you never hear the old people, seated by the evening stand, talk over their early trials, their hardships, the accidents, the burials, the disappointments, the empty flour-barrel when there were so many hungry ones to feed, the sickness almost unto death, where the next dose of morphine decided between ghastly bereavement and an unbroken home circle? Oh yes! it was trouble that whitened their hair. It was trouble that shook the cup in their hands. It was trouble that washed the lustre from their eyes with the rain of tears until they needed spectacles. It was trouble that made the cane a necessity for their journey. Do you never remember seeing your old mother sitting, on some rainy day, looking out of the window, her elbow on the window-sill, her hand to her brow—looking out, not seeing the falling shower at all (you well knew she was looking into the distant past), until the apron came up to her eyes, because the memory was too much for her?

> "Oft the big, unbidden tear,
>   Stealing down the furrowed cheek,
>   Told in eloquence sincere,
>   Tales of woe they could not speak.

> "But this scene of weeping o'er,
> Past this scene of toil and pain,
> They shall feel distress no more,
> Never, never weep again."

"Who are these under the altar?" the question was asked; and the response came, "These are they which came out of great tribulation, and have washed their robes, and made them white in the blood of the Lamb." Our friends went by a path of tears into glory. Be not surprised if we have to travel the same pathway.

I remark, again, if we want to win the society of our friends in heaven, we will not only have to travel a path of faith and a path of tribulation, but we will also have to positively *battle for their companionship.* David and his men never wanted sharp swords and invulnerable shields and thick breastplates so much as they wanted them on the day when they came down upon the Amalekites. If they had lost that battle, they never would have got their families back. I suppose that one glance at their loved ones in captivity hurled them into the battle with tenfold courage and energy. They said, "We must win it. Every thing depends upon it. Let each one take a man on point of spear or sword. We must win it." And I have to tell you that between us and coming into the companionship of our loved ones who are departed there is an Austerlitz, there is a Gettysburg, there is a Waterloo. War with the world, war with the flesh, war with the devil. We have either to conquer our troubles, or our troubles will conquer us. David will either slay the Amalekites, or the Amalekites will slay David. And yet is not the fort to be taken worth all the pain, all the peril, all the besiegement? Look! Who are they on the bright hills of heaven yonder? There they are, those who sat at your own table, the chair now vacant. There they are, those whom you rocked in infancy in the cradle, or hushed to sleep in your arms. There they are, those in whose life your life was bound up. There they are, their brow more radiant than ever before you saw it, their lips waiting for the kiss of heavenly greeting, their cheek roseate with the health of eternal summer, their hands beckoning you up the steep, their feet bounding with the mirth of heaven. The pallor of their last sickness gone out of their face, never more to be sick, never more to cough, never more to limp, never more to be old, never more to weep. They are watching from those heights to see if through Christ you can take that fort, and whether you will rush in upon them — victors. They know that upon this battle depends whether you will ever join their society. Up! strike harder! Charge more bravely! Remember that every inch you gain puts you so much farther on toward that heavenly reunion.

If this morning while I speak you could hear the cannonade of a foreign navy, coming through the "Narrows," which was to despoil our city, and if they really should succeed in carrying our families away from us, how long would we take before we resolved to go after them? Every weapon, whether fresh from Springfield or old and rusty in the garret, would be brought out; and we would urge on, and, coming in front of the foe, we would look at them, and then look at our families, and the cry would be, "Victory or death!" and when the ammunition was gone, we would take the captors on the point of the bayonet or under the breech of the gun. If you would make such a struggle for the getting-back of your earthly friends, will you not make as much struggle for the gaining of the eternal companionship of your heavenly friends? Oh yes! we must join them. We must sit in their holy society. We must sing with them the song. We must celebrate with them the triumph. Let it never be told on earth or in heaven that David and his men pushed out with braver hearts for the getting-back of their earthly friends for a few years on earth than we to get our departed!

You say that all this implies that our departed Christian friends are alive. Why, had you any idea they were dead? They have only moved. If you should go on the 2d of May to a house where one of your friends lived, and found him gone, you would not think that he was dead. You would inquire next door where he had moved to. Our departed Christian friends have only taken another house. The secret is that they are richer now than they once were, and can afford a better residence. They once drank out of earthenware; they now drink from the King's chalice. "Joseph is yet alive," and Jacob will go up and see him. Living? are they? Why, if a man can live in this damp, dark dungeon of earthly captivity, can he not live where he breathes the bracing atmosphere of the mountains of heaven? Oh yes, they are living!

Do you think that Paul is so near dead now as he was when he was living in the Roman dungeon? Do you think that Frederick Robertson, of Brighton, is as near dead now as he was when, year after year, he slept seated on the floor, his head on the bottom of a chair, because he could find ease in no other position? Do you think that Robert Hall is as near dead now as when, on his couch, he tossed in physical tortures? No. Death gave them the few black drops that cured them. That is all death does to a Christian—cures him. I know that what I have said implies that they are living. There is no question about that. The only question, this morning, is whether you will ever join them.

But I must not forget those two hundred men who fainted by the brook Besor. They could not take another step farther. Their feet were sore; their head ached; their entire nature was exhausted. Besides that, they were broken-hearted because their homes were gone. Ziklag in ashes! And yet David, when he comes up to them, divides the spoils among them! He says they shall have some of the jewels, some of the robes, some of the treasures. I look over this audience this morning, and I find at least two hundred who have fainted by the brook Besor —the brook of tears. You feel as if you could not take another step farther, as though you could never look up again. But I am going to imitate David, and divide among you some glorious trophies. Here is a robe, "All things work together for good, to those who love God." Wrap yourself in that glorious promise. Here is for your neck a string of pearls, made out of crystallized tears, "Weeping may endure for a night, but joy cometh in the morning." Here is a coronet, "Be thou faithful unto death, and I will give thee a crown of life." O ye fainting ones by the brook Besor, dip your blistered feet in the running stream of God's mercy. Bathe your brow at the wells of salvation. Soothe your wounds with the balsam that exudes from trees of life. God will not utterly cast you off, O broken-hearted man, O broken-hearted woman, fainting by the brook Besor.

A shepherd finds that his musical pipe is bruised. He says, "I can't get any more music out of this instrument; so I will just break it, and I will throw this reed away.

Then I will get another reed, and I will play music on that." But God says he will not cast you off because all the music has gone out of your soul. "The bruised reed he will not break." As far as I can tell the diagnosis of your disease, you want Divine nursing, and it is promised you: "As one whom his mother comforteth, so will I comfort you." God will see you all the way through, O troubled soul, and when you come down to the Jordan of death, you will find it to be as thin a brook as Besor; for Dr. Robinson says that, in April, Besor dries up, and there is no brook at all. And in your last moment you will be as placid as the Kentucky minister who recently went up to God, saying, in the dying hour, "Write to my sister Kate, and tell her not to be worried and frightened about the story of the horrors around the death-bed. Tell her there is not a word of truth in it, for I am there now, and Jesus is with me, and I find it a very happy way; not because I am a good man, for I am not; I am nothing but a poor, miserable sinner; but I have an Almighty Saviour, and both of his arms are around me."

May God Almighty, through the blood of the everlasting covenant, bring us into the companionship of our loved ones who have already entered the heavenly land, and into the presence of Christ whom, not having seen, we love, and so David shall recover all, "and as his part is that goeth down to the battle, so shall his part be that tarrieth by the stuff."

THE RELIGION OF GHOSTS.

"Behold, there is a woman that hath a familiar spirit at En-dor. And Saul disguised himself, and put on other raiment, and he went, and two men with him, and they came to the woman by night: and he said, I pray thee, divine unto me by the familiar spirit, and bring me him up whom I shall name unto thee."—1 *Samuel* xxviii., 7, 8.

TROUBLE to the right of him and trouble to the left of him, Saul knew not what to do. As a last resort, he concluded to seek out a spiritual medium, or a witch, or any thing that you please to call her—at any rate, a woman who had communication with the spirits of the eternal world. It was a very difficult thing to do, for Saul had either slain all the witches or compelled them to stop business. A servant one day said to King Saul, "I know of a spiritual medium down at the village of En-dor." "Do you?" said the king. Night falls. Saul, putting off his kingly robes, and putting on the dress of a plain citizen, with two servants goes out to hunt up this spiritual medium. It was no easy thing for Saul to disguise himself, for the tallest people in the country only came up to his shoulder, and, I think, from the strength of the man and the way he bore himself, he must have been well proportioned. It must have been a frightful thing to see a man walking along in the night eight or nine feet high. I suppose, as the people saw him pass, they said, "Who is that? He is as tall as the king"—having no idea that in such a plain dress there really was passing the king. Saul and his servants after a while reach the village, and they say, "I wonder if this is the house;" and they look in, and they see the haggard, weird, and shriveled-up spiritual medium sitting by the light, and on the table sculptured images, and divining-rods, and poisonous herbs, and bottles, and vases. They say, "Yes, this must be the place." One loud rap brings the woman to the door, and as she stands there, holding the candle or lamp above her head and peering out into the darkness, she says, "Who is here?" The tall king informs her that he has come to have his fortune told. When she hears that, she trembles and almost drops the light, for she knows there is no chance for a fortune-teller or spiritual medium in all the land. But Saul having sworn that no harm shall come to her, she says, "Well, whom shall I bring up from the dead?" Saul says, "Bring up Samuel." That was the prophet who had died a little while before. I see her waving a wand, or stirring up some poisonous herbs in a caldron, or hear her muttering over some incantations, or stamping with her foot, as she cries out to the realm of the dead, "Samuel! Samuel!" Lo, the freezing horror! The floor of the tenement opens, and the gray hairs float up; and the forehead, the eyes, the lips, the shoulders, the arms, the feet, the entire body of dead Samuel, wrapped in sepulchral robe, appear to the astonished group, who stagger back, and hold fast, and catch their breath, and shiver with the terror. The dead prophet, white and awful from the tomb, begins to move his ashen lips, and he glares upon King Saul, and cries out, "What did you bring me up for? Why did you break my long sleep? What do you mean, King Saul?" Saul, trying to compose and control himself, makes this stammering and affrighted utterance, as he says to the dead prophet, "The Lord is against me, and I have come to you for help. What shall I do?" The dead prophet stretched forth his finger to King Saul, and said, "Die to-morrow! Come with me into the sepulchre. I am going now. Come, come with me!" And, lo! the floor again opens, and the feet of the dead prophet disappear, and the arms and the shoulders and the forehead. The floor closes. Nothing is left in the room but Saul, and the two servants, and the spiritual medium, and the sculptured images, and the divining-rods, and the bottles, and the vases, and the poisonous herbs. Oh, that was an awful séance!

I learn first from this subject that *spiritualism is a very old religion*. It is natural that people should want to know the origin and the history of a doctrine which is so widespread in all the villages, towns, and cities of the civilized world, getting new converts every day—a doctrine with which many of you are already tinged.

Spiritualism in this country was born in 1847, in Hydesville, Wayne County, New York, when one night there was a loud rap heard against the door of Michael Weekman; a rap a second time, a rap a third time; and all three times, when the door was opened, there was nothing found there, the knocking having been made seemingly by invisible knuckles. In that same house there was a young woman who had a cold hand passed over her face, and, there being seemingly no arm attached to it, ghostly suspicions were excited. After a while, Mr. Fox and his family moved into that house, and then every night there was a banging at the door; and one night Mr. Fox said, "Are you a spirit?" Two raps, answering in the affirmative. "Are you an injured spirit?" Two raps, answering in the affirmative. And so they found out, as they say, that it was the ghost or spirit of a peddler who had been murdered in that house, many years before, for his five hundred dollars. Whether the ghost of the dead peddler had come there to collect his five hundred dollars, or his bones, I can not say, not being a spiritualist; but there was a great racket at the door, so Mr. Weekman declared, and Mrs. Weekman, and Mr. Fox, and Mrs. Fox, and all the little Foxes. The excitement spread. There was a universal rumpus. The Honorable Judge Edmonds declared, in a book, that he had actually seen a bell start from the top shelf of a closet, heard it ring over the people that were standing in the closet; then, swung by invisible hands, it rang over the people in the back parlor, and floated through the folding-doors to the front parlor; rang over the people there, and then dropped on the floor. N. P. Talmage, Senator of the United States, afterward Governor of Wisconsin, had his head completely turned with spiritualistic demonstrations. A man, as he was passing along the road, said that he was lifted up bodily, and carried toward his home through the air at such great speed he could not count the posts on the fence as he passed; and, as he had a hand-saw and a square in his hand, they beat as he passed through the air most delightful music. And the tables tipped, and the stools tilted, and the bedsteads raised, and the chairs upset, and it seemed as if the spirits everywhere had gone into the furniture business! Well, the people said, "We have got something new in this country; it is a new religion." Oh no, my friends. Thousands of years ago we find in our text a spiritualistic séance. Nothing in the spiritualistic circles of our day has been more strange, mysterious, and wonderful than things which have been seen in the past centuries of the world.

In all the ages there have been necromancers, those who consult with the spirits of the departed; charmers, those who put their subjects in a mesmeric state; sorcerers, those who by taking poisonous drugs see every thing, and hear every thing, and tell every thing; dreamers, people who in their sleeping moments can see the future world and hold consultation with spirits; astrologers, who could read a new dispensation in the stars; experts in palmistry, who can tell by the lines in the palm of your hand your origin and your history. From a cave on Mount Parnassus, we are told, there was an exhalation that intoxicated the sheep and the goats that came anywhere near it; and a shepherd approaching it was thrown by that exhalation into an excitement in which he could foretell future events, and hold consultation with the spiritual world. Yea, before the time of Christ the Brahmins went through all the table-moving, all the furniture excitement, which the spirits have exploited in our day; precisely the same thing, over and over again, under the manipulations of the Brahmins. Now, do you say that spiritualism is different from these? I answer, all these delusions I have mentioned belong to the same family. They are exhumations from the unseen world. What does God think of all these delusions? He thinks so severely of them that he never speaks of them but with livid thunders of indignation. He says, "I will be a swift witness against the sorcerer." He says, "Thou shalt not suffer a witch to live." And lest you might make some important distinction between spiritualism and witchcraft, God says, in so many words, "There shall not be among you a consulter of familiar spirits, or a wizard, or a necromancer; for all that do these things are an abomination unto the Lord." And he says again, "The soul that turneth after such as have familiar spirits, and after wizards, to go a whoring after them, I will even set my face against that soul, and will cut him off from among his people." The Lord Almighty, in a score of passages which I have not now time to quote, utters his indignation against all this great family of delusions. After that, be a spiritualist if you dare!

Still further, we learn from this text *how it is that people come to fall into spiritualism.* Saul had enough trouble to kill ten men. He did not know where to go for relief. After a while he resolved to go and see the Witch of En-dor. He expected that somehow she would afford him relief. It was his trouble that drove him there. And I have to tell you now that spiritualism finds its victims in the troubled, the bankrupt, the sick, the bereft. You lose your watch, and you go to the fortune-teller to find where it is. You are sick with a strange disease, and you go to a clairvoyant to find out by a lock of hair what is the matter with you. You lose a friend, you want the spiritual world opened, so that you may have communication with him. In a highly wrought, nervous, and diseased state of mind, you go and put yourself in that communication. That is why I hate spiritualism. It takes advantage of one in a moment of weakness, which may come upon us at any time. We lose a friend. The trial is keen, sharp, suffocating, almost maddening. If we could marshal a host, and storm the eternal world, and recapture our loved one, the host would soon be marshaled. The house is so lonely. The world is so dark. The separation is so insufferable. But spiritualism says, "We will open the future world, and your loved one can come back and talk to you." Though we may not hear his voice, we may

hear the rap of his hand. So, clear the table. Sit down.
Put your hands on the table. Be very quiet. Five minutes gone. Ten minutes. No motion of the table. No response from the future world. Twenty minutes. Thirty minutes. Nervous excitement all the time increasing. Forty minutes. The table shivers. Two raps from the future world. The letters of the alphabet are called over. The departed friend's name is John. At the pronunciation of the letter "J," two raps. At the pronunciation of the letter "O," two raps. At the pronunciation of the letter "H," two raps. At the pronunciation of the letter "N," two raps. There you have the whole name spelled out. J-o-h-n, John. Now, the spirit being present, you say, "John, are you happy?" Two raps give an affirmative answer. Pretty soon the hand of the medium begins to twitch and toss, and begins to write out, after paper and ink are furnished, a message from the eternal world. What is remarkable, the departed spirit, although it has been amidst the illuminations of heaven, can not spell as well as it used to! It has lost all grammatical accuracy, and can not write as distinctly. I received a letter through a medium once. I sent it back. I said, "Just please to tell those ghosts they had better go to school and get improved in their orthography!" Now, just think of spirits that the Bible represents as enthroned in glory coming down to crawl under the table, and break crockery, and ring tea-bells before supper is ready, and rap the window-shutter on a gusty night! Is there any consolation in such poor, miserable work compared with the thought that our departed Christian friends, rid of pain and languishing, are in the radiant society of heaven, and that we shall join them there, not in a stifled and mysterious half-utterance which

makes the hair stand on end and the cold chills creep the back, but in an unhindered and illimitable delight?

> "And none shall murmur or misdoubt,
> When God's great sunrise finds us out."

Yes, my friends, spiritualism comes to those who are in trouble, and sweeps them into its delusions. Saul, in the midst of his disaster, went to the Witch of En-dor. The vast majority of those who have gone to spiritual mediums have been sent there through their misfortunes.

I learn still further from this subject, that *spiritualism and necromancy are affairs of the darkness.* Why did not Saul go in the day-time? He was ashamed to go. Besides that, he knew that this spiritual medium, like all her successors, performed her exploits in the night. The Davenports, the Fowlers, the Foxes, the spiritual mediums of all ages, have chosen the night or a darkened room. Why? The majority of their wonders have been swindles, and deception prospers best in the night.

Some of the performances of spiritual mediums are not to be ascribed to fraud, but to some occult law that after a while may be demonstrated. But I believe that now nine hundred and ninety-nine out of every thousand achievements on the part of spiritual mediums are arrant and unmitigated humbug. The mysterious red letters that used to come out on the medium's arm were found to have been made by an iron pencil that went heavily over the flesh, not tearing it, but disturbing the blood so it came up in great round letters. The witnesses of the séance have locked the door, put the key in their pocket, arrested the operator, and found out by searching the room that hidden levers moved the tables. The sealed letters that were mysteriously read without opening have been found to have been cut at the side, and then afterward slyly put together with gum arabic; and the medium who, with a heavy blanket over his head, could read a book has been found to have had a bottle of phosphoric oil, by the light of which any body can read a book; and ventriloquism, and legerdemain, and sleight-of-hand, and optical delusion account for nearly every thing. Deception being the main staple of spiritualism, no wonder it chooses the darkness.

You have all seen strange and unaccountable things in the night. Almost every man has some time had a touch of hallucination. Some time ago, after I had been overtempted to eat something indigestible before retiring at night, after retiring I saw the president of one of the prominent colleges astride the foot of the bed, while he demanded of me a loan of five cents! When I awakened I had no idea it was any thing supernatural. And I have to advise you, if you hear and see strange things at night, to stop eating hot mince-pie and take a dose of bilious medicine. It is an outraged physical organism, and not a call from the future world. Spiritualism, knowing that it is able to deceive the very elect after sundown, does nearly all its work in the night. The Witch of En-dor held her séances at night; so do all the witches. Away with this religion of spooks!

Still further: I learn from my text that *spiritualism is doom and death to its disciples.* King Saul thought that he would get help from the "medium;" but the first thing that he sees makes him swoon away, and no sooner is he resuscitated than he is told he must die. Spiritualism is doom and death to every one that yields to it. It ruins the body. Look in upon an audience of spiritualists. Cadaverous. Weak. Nervous. Exhausted. Hands clammy and cold. Nothing prospers but long hair—soft marshes yielding rank grass. Spiritualism destroys the physical health. Its disciples are ever hearing startling news from the other world. Strange beings crossing the room in white. Table fidgety, wanting to get its feet loose as if to dance. Voices sepulchral and ominous. Bewildered with raps.

I never knew a confirmed spiritualist who had a healthy nervous system. It is incipient epilepsy and catalepsy. Destroy your nervous system, and you might as well be dead. I have noticed that people who are hearing raps from the future world have but little strength left to bear the hard raps of this world. It is an awful thing to trifle with one's nervous system. It is so delicate, it is so far-reaching, its derangements are so terrible. Get the nervous system a-jangle, and, so far as your body and soul are concerned, the whole universe is a-jangle. Better, in our ignorance, experiment with a chemist's retort that may smite us dead, or with an engineer's steam-boiler that may blow us to atoms, than experiment with the nervous system. A man can live with only one lung or with no eyes, and be happy, as men have been under such afflictions; but woe be to the man whose nerves are shattered! Spiritualism smites first of all and mightily against the nervous system, and so makes life miserable.

I indict spiritualism, also, because *it is a social and marital curse.* The worst deeds of licentiousness and the worst orgies of obscenity have been enacted under its patronage. The story is too vile for me to tell. I will not pollute my tongue nor your ears with the recital. Sometimes the civil law has been evoked to stop the outrage. Families innumerable have been broken up by it. It has pushed off hundreds of young women into a life of profligacy. It talks about "elective affinities," and "affinital relations," and "spiritual matches," and adopts the whole vocabulary of free-lovism. In one of its public journals it declares "marriage is the monster curse of civilization;" that "it is a source of debauchery and intemperance." If spiritualism could have its full swing, it would turn this world into a pandemonium of carnality. It is an unclean, adulterous, damnable religion, and the sooner it drops into the hell from which it rose, the better both for earth and heaven. For the sake of man's honor and woman's purity, I say let the last vestige of it perish forever. I wish I could gather up all the raps it has ever heard from spirits blest or damned, and gather them all on its own head in one thundering rap of annihilation!

I further indict spiritualism for the fact that *it is the cause of much insanity.* There is not an asylum between Bangor and San Francisco which has not the torn and bleeding victims of this delusion. Go into any asylum, I care not where it is, and the presiding doctor, after you have asked him, "What is the matter with that man?" will say, "Spiritualism demented him;" or, "What is the matter with that woman?" he will say, "Spiritualism demented her." It has taken down some of the brightest intellects. It swept off into mental midnight judges, senators, governors, ministers of the Gospel, and one time came near capturing one of the presidents of the United States. At Flushing, near this city, a man became absorbed with it, forsook his family, took his only fifteen thousand dollars, surrendered them to a spiritual medium in New York, attempted three times to put an end to his own life, and then was incarcerated in the State Lunatic

Asylum, where he is to-day a raving maniac. Put your hand in the hand of this Witch of En-dor, and she will lead you to bottomless perdition, where she holds her everlasting séance.

Many years ago the steamer *Atlantic* started from Europe for the United States. Getting mid-ocean, the machinery broke, and she floundered around day after day and week after week; and, for a whole month after she was due, people wondered, and finally gave her up. There was great anguish in the cities, for there were many who had friends aboard that vessel. Some of the women, in their distress, went to the spiritual mediums, and inquired as to the fate of that vessel. The mediums called up the spirits, and the rappings on the table indicated the steamship lost, with all on board. Women went raving mad, and were carried to the lunatic asylum. After a while one day a gun was heard off Quarantine. The flags went up on the shipping, and the bells of the churches were rung. The boys ran through the streets, crying "Extra! The *Atlantic* is safe!" There was the embracing as from the dead, when friends came again to friends; but some of those passengers went up to find their wives in the lunatic asylum, where this cheat of infernal spiritualism had put them. A man in Bellevue Hospital, dying from wounds made by his own hand, was asked why he had tried to commit suicide, and he said, "The spirits told me to." Parents have strangled their children, and when asked why they did it, replied, "Spiritualism demanded it." It is the patronizer and forager for the mad-house. Judge Edmonds, in the Broadway Tabernacle, New York, delivering a lecture in behalf of spiritualism, admitted, in so many words, "There is a fascination about consultation with the spirits of the dead that has a tendency to lead people off from their right judgment, and to instill into them a fanaticism that is revolting to the natural mind."

It not only ruins its disciples, but it ruins the mediums also, only give it time. The Gaderean swine, on the banks of the Lake of Galilee, no sooner became spiritual mediums than down they went in an avalanche of pork, to the consternation of all the herdsmen. The office of a medium is bad for a man, bad for a woman, bad for a beast.

I bring against this delusion a more fearful indictment: *it ruins the soul immortal.* First, it makes a man a quarter of an infidel; then it makes him half an infidel; then it makes him a whole infidel. The entire system, as I conceive it, is founded on the insufficiency of the Word of God as a revelation. God says the Bible is enough for you to know about the future world. You say it is not enough, and there is where you and the Lord differ. You clear the table, you shove aside the Bible, you put your hand on the table, and say, "Now, let spirits of the future world come and tell me something the Bible has not told me." And although the Scriptures say, "Add thou not unto his words, lest he reprove thee, and thou be found a liar," you risk it, and say, "Come back, spirit of my departed father; come back, spirit of my departed mother, of my companion, of my little child, and tell me some things I don't know about you and about the unseen world." If God is ever slapped square in the face it is when a spiritual medium puts down her hand on the table, invoking spirits departed to make a revelation. God has told you all you ought to know, and how dare you be prying into that which is none of your business? You can not keep the Bible in one hand and spiritualism in the other. One or the other will slip out of your grasp, depend upon it. Spiritualism is adverse to the Bible in the fact that it has in these last days called from the future world Christian men to testify against Christianity. Its mediums call back Lorenzo Dow, the celebrated evangelist, and Lorenzo Dow testifies that Christians are idolaters. Spiritualism calls back Tom Paine, and he testifies that he is stopping in the same house in heaven with John Bunyan. They call back John Wesley, and he testifies against the Christian religion which he all his life gloriously preached. Andrew Jackson Davis, the greatest of all the spiritualists, comes to the front and declares that the New Testament is but "the dismal echo of a barbaric age," and the Bible only "one of the pen-and-ink relics of Christianity." They attempt to substitute the writings of Swedenborg, and Andrew Jackson Davis, and other religious balderdash, in the place of this old Bible. I have in my house a book which was used in this very city in the public service of spiritualists. It is well worn with much service. I open that book, and it says, "What is our baptism? Answer, Frequent ablutions of water. What is our inspiration? Plenty of fresh air and sunlight. What is our prayer? Abundant physical exercise. What is our love-feast? A clear conscience and sound sleep." And I find from the same book that the chief item in their public worship is gymnastic exercise; and that whenever they want to rouse up their souls to a very high pitch of devotion they sing page sixty-five, "The night has gathered up her moonlit fringes;" or page sixteen, "Come to the woods, heigh-ho!" You say you are not such a fool as that; but you will be if you keep on in the track in which you have started.

"But," says some one, "wouldn't it be of advantage to hear from the future world? Don't you think it would strengthen Christians? There are a great many materialists who do not believe there are souls; but if spirits from the future world should knock and talk over to us, we would all be persuaded." To that I answer in the ringing words of the Son of God, "If they believe not Moses and the prophets, neither will they be persuaded though one rose from the dead."

Now I believe, under God, that this sermon will save many from disease, insanity, and perdition. I believe these are the days of which the apostle spake when he said, "In the latter times some shall depart from the faith, giving heed to seducing spirits." I think my audience, as well as other audiences in this day, need to have reiterated in their hearing the passages I quoted some minutes ago, "There shall not be among you a consulter of familiar spirits, or a wizard, or a necromancer; for they that do these things are an abomination unto the Lord;" and "The soul that turneth after such as have familiar spirits, and after wizards, I will even set my face against that soul, and will cut him off from among his people."

But I invite you this morning to a Christian séance, a noonday séance. This congregation is only one great family. Here is the church table. Come around the church table, take your seats for this great Christian séance, put your Bible on the table, put your hands on the top of the Bible, and then listen, and hear if there are any voices coming from the eternal world. I think there are. Listen! "Secret things belong unto the Lord our God, but those things which are revealed belong unto us and to our children." Surely that is a voice from the spirit-world! But,

4

before you rise from this Christian séance, I want you to promise me you will be satisfied with the Divine revelation until the light of the Eternal Throne breaks upon your vision. Do not go after the Witch of En-dor. Do not sit down at table-rappings, either in sport or in dead earnest. Have your tables so well made and their legs so even that they will not tip and rattle. If the table must move, let it be under the offices of industrious housewifery. Teach your children there are no ghosts to be seen or heard in this world save those which walk on two feet or four, human or bestial. Remember that spiritualism at the best is a useless thing; for if it tells what the Bible reveals it is a superfluity, and if it tells what the Bible does not reveal it is a lie. Instead of going out to get other people to tell your fortune, tell your own fortune by putting your trust in God and doing the best you can. I will tell your fortune: "All things work together for good to them who love God." Insult not your departed friends by asking them to come down and scrabble under an extension-table. Remember that there is only one Spirit whose dictation you have a right to invoke, and that is the holy, blessed, and omnipotent Spirit of God. Hark! He is rapping now, not on a table or the floor, but rapping on the door of your heart; and every rap is an invitation to Christ and a warning of judgment to come. Oh, grieve him not away! Quench him not. He has been all around you this morning. He was all around you last night. He has been around you all your lives. Hark! There comes a voice dropping through the roof, breaking through the window, filling all this house from door to door and from floor to ceiling with tender and overmastering intonation, saying, "My spirit shall not always strive."

SNOW-WATER AND ALKALI INSUFFICIENT.

"If I wash myself with snow-water, and should I cleanse my hands in alkali, yet shalt thou plunge me in the ditch, and mine own clothes shall abhor me."—*Job* ix., 30, 31.

ALBERT BARNES—honored be his name on earth and in heaven—went straight back to the original writing of my text, and translated it as I have now quoted it, giving substantial reasons for so doing. Athough we know better, the ancients had an idea that in snow-water there was a special power to cleanse, and that a garment washed and rinsed in it would be as clean as clean could be; but if the plain snow-water failed to do its work, then they would take lye or alkali and mix it with oil, and under that preparation they felt that the last impurity would certainly be gone. Job, in my text, in most forceful figure sets forth the idea that all his attempts to make himself pure before God were a dead failure, and that, unless we are abluted by something better than earthly liquids and chemical preparations, we are loathsome and in the ditch. "If I wash myself with snow-water, and should I cleanse my hands in alkali, yet shalt thou plunge me in the ditch, and mine own clothes shall abhor me."

You are now sitting for your picture. I turn the camera obscura of God's word full upon you, and I pray that the sunshine falling through the sky-light may enable me to take you just as you are. Shall it be a flattering picture, or shall it be a true one? You say, "Let it be a true one." The first profile that was ever taken was taken, three hundred and thirty years before Christ, of Antigonus. He had a blind eye, and he compelled the artist to take his profile so as to hide the defect in his vision. But since that invention, three hundred and thirty years before Christ, there have been a great many profiles. Shall I to-night give you a one-sided view of yourselves, a profile? or shall it be a full-length portrait, showing you how you stand before heaven and earth and hell? If God will help me by his almighty grace, I shall give you that last kind of a picture.

When I first entered the ministry, I used to write my sermons all out and read them, and run my hand along the line lest I should lose my place. I have hundreds of those manuscripts. Shall I ever preach them? Never; for in those days I was somehow overmastered with the idea I heard talked all around about of the dignity of human nature, and I adopted the idea, and I evolved it, and I illustrated it, and I argued it; but coming on in life, and having seen more of the world, and studied better my Bible, I find that that early teaching was faulty, and that there is no dignity in human nature, until it is reconstructed by the grace of God. Talk about vessels going to pieces on the Skerries, off Ireland! There never was such a ship-wreck as in the Gihon and the Hiddekel, rivers of Eden, where our first parents foundered. Talk of a steamer going down with five hundred passengers on board! What is that to the shipwreck of twelve hundred million souls? We are by nature a mass of uncleanness and putrefaction, from which it takes all the omnipotence and infinitude of God's grace to extricate us. "If I wash myself with snow-water, and should I cleanse my hands in alkali, yet shalt thou plunge me in the ditch, and mine own clothes shall abhor me."

I remark, in the first place, that some people try to cleanse their soul of sin in the snow-water of *fine apologies.* Here is one man who says, "I am a sinner; I confess that: but I inherited this. My father was a sinner, my grandfather, my great-great-grandfather, and all the way back to Adam, and I couldn't help myself." My brother, have you not, every day in your life, added something to the original estate of sin that was bequeathed to you? Are you not brave enough to confess that you have sometimes surrendered to sin, which you ought to have conquered? I ask you whether it is fair play to put upon our ancestry things for which we ourselves are personally responsible? If your nature was askew when you got it, have you not sometimes given it an additional twist? Will all the tombstones of those who have preceded us make a barricade high enough for eternal defenses? I know a devout man who had blasphemous parentage. I know an honest man whose father was a thief. I know a pure man whose mother was a waif of the street. The hereditary tide may be very strong, but there is such a thing as stemming it. The fact that I have a corrupt nature is no reason why I should yield to it. The deep stains of our soul can never be washed out by the snow-water of such insufficient apology.

Still further, says some one, "If I have gone into sin, it has been through my companions, my comrades, and associates; they ruined me. They taught me to drink. They took me to the gambling-hell. They plunged me into the house of sin. They ruined my soul." I do not believe it. God gave to no one the power to destroy you or me. If a man is destroyed, he is self-destroyed, and that is always so. Why did you not break away from them? If they had tried to steal your purse, you would have knocked them down; if they had tried to purloin your gold watch, you would have riddled them with shot; but when they tried to steal your immortal soul, you placidly submitted to it. Those bad fellows have a cup of fire to drink; do not pour your cup into it. In this matter of the soul, every man for himself. That those persons are not fully responsible for your sin, I prove by the fact that you still consort with them. Your affinities are with them; you stay with them, and there is some prospect that you will stay with them forever. Perhaps you may have adjoining dungeons. Perhaps you may be fastened to opposite ends of the same chain. Perhaps you may carry different parts of the same groan. You can not get off by blaming them. Though you gather up all these apologies; though there were a great flood of them; though they should come down with the force of the melting snows from Lebanon and the Himalayas, they could not wash out one stain of your immortal soul.

Still further, some persons apologize for their sins by saying, "We are a great deal better than some people. You see people all around about us that are a great deal worse than we." You stand up columnar in your integrity, and look down upon those who are prostrate in their habits and crimes. What of that, my brother? If I failed through recklessness and wicked imprudence for ten thousand dollars, is the matter alleviated at all by the fact that somebody else has failed for one hundred thousand dollars, and somebody else for two hundred thousand dollars? Oh no. If I have the neuralgia, shall I refuse medical attendance because my neighbor has virulent typhoid fever? The fact that his disease is worse than mine—does that cure mine? If I, through my foolhardiness, leap off into eternal woe, does it break the fall to know that others leap off a higher cliff into deeper darkness? When the Hudson River rail-train went through the bridge at Spuyten Duyvel, did it alleviate the matter at all that instead of two or three people being hurt there were seventy-five mangled and crushed? Because others are depraved, is that any excuse for my depravity? Am I better than they? Perhaps they had worse temptations than I have had. Perhaps their surroundings in life were more overpowering. Perhaps, O man, if you had been under the same stress of temptation, instead of sitting here to-night, you would have been looking through the bars of a penitentiary. Perhaps, O woman, if you had been under the same power of temptation, instead of sitting here to-night, you would be tramping the street, the laughing-stock of men and the grief of the angels of God, dungeoned, body, mind, and soul, in the blackness of despair. Ah, do not let us solace ourselves with the thought that other people are worse than we. Perhaps in the future, when our fortunes may change, unless God prevents it, we may be worse than they are. Many a man after thirty years, after forty years, after fifty years, after sixty years, has gone to pieces on the sand-bars. Oh! instead of wasting our time in hypercriticism about others, let us ask ourselves the questions, Where do *we* stand? what are *our* sins? what are *our* deficits? what are *our* perils? what *our* hopes? Let each one say to himself, "Where will I be? Shall I range in summery fields, or grind in the mills of a great night? Shall it be anthem or shriek? Shall it be with God or fiends? Where? Where?"

Some winter morning you go out and see a snow-bank in graceful drifts, as though by some heavenly compass it had been curved; and as the sun glints it the lustre is almost insufferable, and it seems as if God had wrapped the earth in a shroud with white plaits woven in looms celestial. And you say, "Was there ever any thing so pure as the snow, so beautiful as the snow?" But you brought a pail of that snow, and put it upon the stove and melted it; and you found that there was a sediment at the bottom, and every drop of that snow-water was riled; and you found that the snow-bank had gathered up the impurity of the field, and that, after all, it was not fit to wash in. And so I say it will be if you try to gather up these contrasts and comparisons with others, and with these apologies attempt to wash out the sins of your heart and life. It will be an unsuccessful ablution. Such snow-water will never wash away a single stain of an immortal soul.

But I hear some one say, "I will try something better than that. I will try the force of a *good resolution.* That will be more pungent, more caustic, more extirpating, more cleansing. The snow-water has failed, and now I will try the alkali of a good, strong resolution." My dear brother, have you any idea that a resolution about the future will liquidate the past? Suppose I owed you five thousand dollars, and I should come to you to-morrow, and say, "Sir, I will never run in debt to you again; if I should live thirty years, I will never run in debt to you again;" will you turn to me and say, "If you will not run in debt in the future, I will forgive you the five thousand dollars." Will you do that? No! Nor will God. We have been running up a long score of indebtedness with God. If for the future we should abstain from sin, that would be no defrayment of past indebtedness. Though you should live from this time forth pure as an archangel before the throne, that would not redeem the past. God, in the Bible, distinctly declares that he "will require that which is past" —past opportunities, past neglects, past wicked words, past impure imaginations, past every thing. The past is a great cemetery, and every day is buried in it. And here is a long row of three hundred and sixty-five graves. They are the dead days of 1873. Here is a long row of three hundred and sixty-five more graves, and they are the dead days of 1872. And here is a long row of three hundred and sixty-five more graves, and they are the dead days of 1871. It is a vast cemetery of the past. But God will rouse them all up with resurrectionary blast, and as the prisoner stands face to face with juror and judge, so you and I will have to come up and look upon those departed days face to face, exulting in their smile or cowering in their frown.

"Murder will out" is a proverb that stops too short. Every sin, however small as well as great, will out. In hard times in England, years ago, it is authentically stated that a manufacturer was on the way, with a bag of money, to pay off his hands. A man infuriated with hunger met him on the road, and took a rail with a nail in it from a paling fence, and struck him down, and the nail entering the skull instantly slew him. Thirty years after that the murderer went back to that place. He passed into the grave-yard, where the sexton was digging a grave, and while he stood there the spade of the sexton turned up a skull, and, lo! the murderer saw a nail protruding from the back part of the skull; and as the sexton turned the skull, it seemed with hollow eyes to glare on the murderer;

and he, first petrified with horror, stood in silence, but soon cried out, "Guilty! guilty! O God!" The mystery of the crime was over. The man was tried and executed. My friends, all the unpardoned sins of our lives, though we may think they are buried out of sight and gone into a mere skeleton of memory, will turn up in the cemetery of the past, and glower upon us with their misdoings. I say all our unpardoned sins. Oh, have you done the preposterous thing of supposing that good resolutions for the future will wipe out the past? Good resolutions, though they may be pungent and caustic as alkali, have no power to neutralize a sin, have no power to wash away a transgression. It wants something more than earthly chemistry to do this. Yea, yea, though "I wash myself with snow-water, and should I cleanse my hands in alkali, yet shalt thou plunge me in the ditch, and mine own clothes shall abhor me."

You see from the last part of this text that Job's idea of sin was very different from that of Lord Byron, or Eugene Sue, or George Sand, or M. J. Michelet, or any of the hundreds of writers who have done up iniquity in mezzotint, and garlanded the wine-cup with eglantine and rosemary, and made the path of the libertine end in bowers of ease instead of on the hot flagging of infernal torture. You see that Job thinks that sin is not a flowery parterre; that it is not a table-land of fine prospects; that it is not music, dulcimer, violoncello, castanet, and Pandean pipes, all making music together. No. He says it is a ditch, long, deep, loathsome, stenchful, and we are all plunged into it, and there we wallow and sink and struggle, not able to get out. Our robes of propriety and robes of worldly profession are saturated in the slime and abomination, and our soul, covered over with transgression, hates its covering, and the covering hates the soul, until we are plunged into the ditch, and our own clothes abhor us.

I know that some modern religionists caricature sorrow for sin, and they make out an easier path than the "pilgrim's progress" that John Bunyan dreamed of. The road they travel does not start where John's did, at the city of Destruction, but at the gate of the university; and I am very certain that it will not come out where John's did, under the shining ramparts of the celestial city. No repentance, no pardon. If you do not, my brother, feel that you are down in the ditch, what do you want of Christ to lift you out? If you have no appreciation of the fact that you are astray, what do you want of Him who came to seek and save that which was lost? Yonder is the *Scotia*, the swiftest of the Cunarders, coming across the Atlantic. The wind is abaft, so that she has not only her engines at work, but all sails up. I am on board the *Spain*, of the National line. The boat-davits are swung around. The boat is lowered. I get into it with a red flag, and cross over to where the *Scotia* is coming, and I wave the flag. The captain looks off from the bridge, and says, "What do you want?" I reply, "I come to take some of your passengers across to the other vessel; I think they will be safer and happier there." The captain would look down with indignation and say, "Get out of the way, or I will run you down." And then I would back oars, amidst the jeering of two or three hundred people looking over the taffrail. But the *Spain* and the *Scotia* meet under different circumstances after a while. The *Scotia* is coming out of a cyclone; the life-boats all smashed; the bulwarks gone; the wheel off; the vessel rapidly going down.

The boatswain gives his last whistle of despairing command. The passengers run up and down the deck, and some pray, and all make a great outcry. The captain says, "You have about fifteen minutes now to prepare for the next world." "No hope!" sounds from stem to stern, and from the ratlines down to the cabin. I see the distress. I am let down by the side of the *Spain*. I push off as fast as I can toward the sinking *Scotia*. Before I come up, people are leaping into the water in their anxiety to get to the boat, and when I have swung up under the side of the *Scotia*, the frenzied passengers rush through the gangway until the officers, with axe and clubs and pistols, try to keep back the crowd, each wanting his turn to come next. There is but one life-boat, and they all want to get into it, and the cry is, "Me next! me next!" You see the application before I make it. As long as a man going on in his sin feels that all is well, that he is coming out at a beautiful port, and has all sail set, he wants no Christ, he wants no help, he wants no rescue; but if under the flash of God's convicting spirit he shall see that by reason of sin he is dismasted and water-logged, and going down into the trough of a sea where he can not live, how soon he puts the sea-glass to his eye and sweeps the horizon, and at the first sign of help cries out, "I want to be saved. I want to be saved now. I want to be saved forever." No sense of danger, no application for rescue.

Oh that God's eternal spirit would flash upon us a sense of our sinfulness! The Bible tells the story in letters of fire, but we get used to it. We joke about sin. We make merry over it. What is sin? Is it a trifling thing? Sin is a vampire that is sucking out the life-blood of your immortal nature. Sin? It is a Bastile that no earthly key ever unlocked. Sin? It is expatriation from God and heaven. Sin? It is grand larceny against the Almighty, for the Bible asks the question, "Will a man rob God?" answering it in the affirmative. This Gospel is a writ of replevin to recover property unlawfully detained from God.

The bell at the gate of Greenwood tolls. The procession goes through, and ropes are wrapped around the casket, and the casket lowered five or six feet; but the body inside the casket is no more dead than is every man until he has been regenerated by the grace of God. It is not my say so, but the Bible, which pronounces us *dead*, dead in trespasses and in sins. The maniac who puts around his brow a bunch of straw, and thinks it is a crown, and holds in his hand a stick, and thinks it is a sceptre, and gathers up some pebbles, and thinks they are diamonds, is no more beside himself than is every one who has not accepted the Lord Jesus Christ as his personal Saviour; for the Bible, in the parable, intimates that every prodigal is beside himself, in phantasia, in delirium, in madness.

In the Shetland Islands there is a man with leprosy. The hollow of the foot has swollen until it is flat on the ground. The joints begin to fall away. The ankle thickens until it looks like the foot of a wild beast. A stare unnatural comes to the eye. The nostril is constricted. The voice drops to an almost inaudible hoarseness. Tubercles blotch the whole body, and from them there comes an exudation that is unbearable to the beholder. That is leprosy, and we have all got it unless cleansed by the grace of God. See Leviticus. See Second Kings. See Mark. See Luke. See fifty Bible allusions and confirmations. If these things be so, should I not tell you?

The Bible is not complimentary in its language. It does not speak mincingly about our sins. It does not talk apologetically. There is no vermilion in its style. It does not cover up our transgressions with blooming metaphor. It does not sing about them in weak falsetto; but it thunders out, "The imagination of man's heart is evil from his youth." "Every one has gone back. He has altogether become filthy. He is abominable and filthy, and drinketh in iniquity like water." And then the Lord Jesus Christ flings down at our feet this humiliating catalogue, "Out of the heart of men proceed evil thoughts, adulteries, fornication, murders, thefts, blasphemy." There is a text for your rationalist to preach from! Oh, the dignity of human nature! There is an element of your science of man that the anthropologist never has had the courage yet to touch; and the Bible, in all the ins and outs of the most forceful style, sets forth our natural pollution, and represents iniquity as a frightful thing, as an exhausting thing, as a loathsome thing. It is not a mere bemiring of the feet, it is not a mere befouling of the hands; it is going down, head and ears under, in a ditch until our own clothes abhor us.

My brethren, shall we stay down where sin thrusts us? I shall not, if you do. We can not afford to. I have, to-night, to tell you that there is something purer than snow-water, something more pungent than alkali, and that is the blood of Jesus Christ that cleanseth from all sin. Ay, the river of salvation, bright, crystalline, and heaven-born, rushes through this audience with billowy tide strong enough to wash your sins completely and forever away. O Jesus! let the dam that holds it back now break, and the floods of salvation roll over us.

> "Let the water and the blood,
> From thy side a healing flood,
> Be of sin the double cure,
> Save from wrath and make me pure."

O sinner! get down on both knees and bathe in that flood of mercy. Ay, strike out with both hands, and try to swim to the other shore of this river of God's grace. To you is the word of this salvation sent. Take this largess of the Divine bounty. Though you have gone down in the deepest ditch of libidinous desire and corrupt behavior, though you have sworn all blasphemies until there is not one sinful word left for you to speak, though you have been submerged by the transgressions of a life-time, though you are so far down in your sin that no earthly help can touch your case—the Lord Jesus Christ bends over you to-night, and offers you his right hand, proposing to lift you up, first making you whiter than snow, and then raising you to glories that never die. "Billy," said a Christian boot-black to another, "when we come up to heaven it won't make any difference that we've been boot-blacks here, for we shall get in, not somehow or other, but, Billy, we shall get straight through the gate." Oh, if you only knew how full and free and tender is the offer of Christ, this night you would all take him without one single exception; and if all the doors of this house were locked save one, and you were compelled to make egress by only one door, and I stood there and questioned you, and the Gospel of Christ had made the right impression upon your heart to-night, you would answer me as you went out, one and all, "Jesus is mine, and I am his!" Oh, that this might be the night when you would receive him! It is not a Gospel merely for foot-pads and vagrants and buccaneers; it is for the highly polished and the educated and the refined as well. "Except a man be born again, he can not see the kingdom of God." Whatever may be your associations, and whatever your worldly refinements, I must tell you, as before God I expect to answer in the last day, that if you are not changed by the grace of God, you are still down in the ditch of sin, in the ditch of sorrow, in the ditch of condemnation; a ditch that empties into a deeper ditch, the ditch of the lost. But blessed be God for the lifting, cleansing, lustrating power of his Gospel.

> "The voice of free grace cries, Escape to the mountain;
> For all that believe Christ has opened a fountain.
> Hallelujah! to the Lamb who hath bought us our pardon;
> We'll praise him again when we pass over Jordan."

STRIPPING THE SLAIN.

"And it came to pass on the morrow, when the Philistines came to strip the slain, that they found Saul and his three sons fallen in Mount Gilboa."— 1 *Samuel* xxxi., 8.

SOME of you were at South Mountain, or Shiloh, or Ball's Bluff, or Gettysburg, and I ask you if there is any sadder sight than a battle-field after the guns have stopped firing? I walked across the field of Antietam just after the conflict. The scene was so sickening I shall not describe it. Every valuable thing had been taken from the bodies of the dead, for there are always vultures hovering over and around about an army, and they pick up the watches, and the memorandum-books, and the letters, and the daguerreotypes, and the hats, and the coats, applying them to their own uses. The dead make no resistance. So there are always camp followers going on after an army, as when Scott went down into Mexico, as when Napoleon marched up toward Moscow, as when Von Moltke went to Sedan. There is a similar scene in my text. Saul and his army had been horribly cut to pieces. Mount Gilboa was ghastly with the dead. On the morrow the stragglers came on to the field, and they lifted the latchet of the helmet from under the chin of the dead, and they picked up the swords and bent them on their knee to test the temper of the metal, and they opened the wallets and counted the coin. Saul lay dead along the ground, eight or nine feet in length, and I suppose the cowardly

Philistines, to show their bravery, leaped upon the trunk of his carcass, and jeered at the fallen slain, and whistled through the mouth of the helmet. Before night, those cormorants had taken every thing valuable from the field. "And it came to pass on the morrow, when the Philistines came to strip the slain, that they found Saul and his three sons fallen in Mount Gilboa."

Before I get through to-night, I will show you that the same process is going on all the world over, and every day; and that when men have fallen, Satan and the world, so far from pitying them or helping them, go to work remorselessly to take what little is left, thus *stripping the slain.*

There are tens of thousands of young men every year coming from the country to our great cities. They come with brave hearts and grand expectations. They think they will be Rufus Choates in the law, or Drapers in chemistry, or A. T. Stewarts in merchandise. The country lads sit down in the village grocery, with their feet on the iron rod around the red-hot stove in the evening, talking over the prospects of the young man who has gone off to the city. Two or three of them think that perhaps he may get along very well and succeed, but the most of them prophesy failure; for it is very hard to think that those whom we knew in boyhood will ever make any stir in the world. But our young man has a fine position in a drygoods store. The month is over. He gets his wages. He is not accustomed to have so much money belonging to himself. He is a little excited, and does not exactly know what to do with it, and he spends it in some places where he ought not. Soon there come up new companions and acquaintances from the bar-rooms and the saloons of the city. Soon that young man begins to waver in the battle of temptation, and soon his soul goes down. In a few months, or few years, he has fallen. He is morally dead. He is a mere corpse of what he once was. The harpies of sin snuff up the taint and come on the field. His garments gradually give out. He has pawned his watch. His health is failing him. His credit perishes. He is too poor to stay in the city, and he is too poor to pay his way home to the country. Down! down! Why do the low fellows of the city now stick to him so closely? Is it to help him back to a moral and spiritual life? Oh no. I will tell you why they stay; they are the Philistines stripping the slain.

Do not look where I point, but yonder stands a man who once had a beautiful home in this city. His house had elegant furniture, his children were beautifully clad, his name was synonymous with honor and usefulness; but evil habit knocked at his front door, knocked at his back door, knocked at his parlor door, knocked at his bedroom door. Where is the piano? Sold to pay the rent. Where is the hat-rack? Sold to meet the butcher's bill. Where are the carpets? Sold to get bread. Where is the wardrobe? Sold to get rum. Where are the daughters? Working their fingers off in trying to keep the family together. Worse and worse, until every thing is gone. Who is that going up the front steps of that house? That is a creditor, hoping to find some chair or bed that has not been levied upon. Who are those two gentlemen now going up the front steps? The one is a constable, the other is the sheriff. Why do they go there? The unfortunate is morally dead, socially dead, financially dead. Why do they go there? I will tell you why the creditors and the constables and the sheriffs go there. They are, some on their own account and some on account of the law, stripping the slain.

An ex-member of Congress, one of the most eloquent men that ever stood in the House of Representatives, said, in his last moments, "This is the end. I am dying—dying on a borrowed bed, covered by a borrowed sheet, in a house built by public charity. Bury me under that tree in the middle of the field, where I shall not be crowded, for I have been crowded all my life." Where were the jolly politicians and the dissipating comrades who had been with him, laughing at his jokes, applauding his eloquence, and plunging him into sin? They have left. Why? His money is gone, his reputation is gone, his wit is gone, his clothes are gone, every thing is gone. Why should they stay any longer? They have completed their work. They have stripped the slain.

There is another way, however, of doing that same work. Here is a man who, through his sin, is prostrate. He acknowledges that he has done wrong. Now is the time for you to go to that man, and say, "Thousands of people have been as far astray as you are, and got back." Now is the time for you to go to that man, and tell him of the omnipotent grace of God that is sufficient for any poor soul. Now is the time to go to tell him how swearing John Bunyan, through the grace of God, afterward came to the celestial city. Now is the time to go to that man and tell him how profligate Newton came, through conversion, to be a world-renowned preacher of righteousness. Now is the time to tell that man that multitudes who have been pounded with all the flails of sin, and dragged through all the sewers of pollution, at last have risen to positive dominion of moral power. You do not tell him that, do you? No. You say to him, "Loan you money! No. You are down. You will have to go to the dogs. Lend you a shilling! I would not lend you two cents to keep you from the gallows. You are debauched. Get out of my sight now! Down; you will have to stay down." And thus these bruised and battered men are sometimes accosted by those who ought to lift them up. Thus the last vestige of hope is taken from them. Thus those who ought to go and lift and save them are guilty of stripping the slain.

The point I want to make is this: *sin is hard, cruel, and merciless.* Instead of helping a man up, it helps him down; and when, like Saul and his comrades, you lie on the field, it will come and steal your sword and helmet and shield, leaving you to the jackal and the crow.

But the world and Satan do not do all their work with the outcast and abandoned. A respectable, impenitent man comes to die. He is flat on his back. He could not get up if the house were on fire. Adroitest medical skill and gentlest nursing have been a failure. He has come to his last hour. What does Satan do for such a man? Why, he fetches up all the inapt, disagreeable, and harrowing things in his life. He says, "Do you remember those chances you had for heaven, and missed them? Do you remember all those lapses in conduct? Do you remember all those opprobrious words and thoughts and actions? Don't remember them, eh? I'll make you remember them." And then he takes all the past and empties it on that death-bed, as the mail-bags are emptied on the post-office floor. The man is sick. He can not get away from them. Then the man says to Satan, "You have deceived me. You told me that all would be well. You said there would be no trouble at the last. You told me if I did so and so, you would do so and so. Now you corner me, and hedge me up, and submerge me in every thing evil." "Ha! ha!" says Satan, "I was only fooling you. It is mirth for me to see you suffer. I have been for thirty years plotting to get you just where you are. It is hard for you now—it will be worse for you after a while. It pleases me. Lie still, sir. Don't flinch or shudder. Come, now, I will tear off from you the last rag of expectation. I will rend away from your soul the last hope. I will leave you bare for the beating of the storm. It is my business to strip the slain."

While men are in robust health, and their digestion is good, and their nerves are strong, they think their physical strength will get them safely through the last exigency. They say it is only cowardly women who are afraid at the last, and cry out for God. "Wait till I come to die. I will show you. You won't hear me pray, nor call for a minister, nor want a chapter read me from the Bible." But after the man has been three weeks in a sick-room his nerves are not so steady, and his worldly companions are not anywhere near to cheer him up, and he is persuaded that he must quit life. His physical courage is all gone. He jumps at the fall of a tea-spoon in a saucer. He shivers at the idea of going away. He says, "Wife, I don't think my infidelity is going to take me through. For God's sake, don't bring up the children to do as I have done! If you feel like it, I wish you would read a verse or two out of Fanny's Sabbath-school hymn-book or New Testament." But Satan breaks in, and says, "You have always thought religion trash and a lie; don't give up at the last. Besides that, you can not, in the hour you have to live, get off on that track. Die as you lived. With my great black wings I shut out that light. Die in darkness. I rend away from you that last vestige of hope. It is my business to strip the slain."

A man who had rejected Christianity, and thought it all trash, came to die. He was in the sweat of a great agony, and his wife said, "We had better have some prayer." "Mary, not a breath of that!" he said. "The lightest word of prayer would roll back on me like rocks on a drowning man. I have come to the hour of test. I had a chance, and I forfeited it. I believed in a liar, and he has left me in the lurch. Mary, bring me Tom Paine, the book that I swore by and lived by, and pitch it into the fire, and let it burn and burn as I myself shall soon burn." And then, with the foam on his lip, and his hands tossing wildly in the air, he cried out, "Blackness of darkness! Oh, my God, too late!" And the spirits of darkness whistled up from the depth, and wheeled around and around him, stripping the slain.

Sin is a luxury now; it is exhilaration now; it is victory now. But after a while it is collision; it is defeat; it is extermination; it is jackalism; it is robbing the dead; it is stripping the slain.

Give it up to-night; give it up! Oh, how you have been cheated on, my brother, from one thing to another! All these years you have been under an evil mastery that you understood not. What have your companions done for you? What have they done for your health? Nearly ruined it by carousal. What have they done for your fortune? Almost scattered it by spendthrift behavior. What have they done for your reputation? Almost ruined it with good men. What have they done for your immortal soul? Almost insured its overthrow. You are hastening on toward the consummation of all that is sad. To-night you stop and think, but it is only for a moment, and then you will tramp on, and at the close of this service you will go out, and the question will be, "How did you like the sermon?" and one man will say, "I liked it very well;" and another man will say, "I didn't like it at all;" but neither of the answers will touch the tremendous fact that, if impenitent, you are going at eighteen knots an hour toward shipwreck! Yea, you are in a battle where you will fall; and while your surviving relatives will take your remaining estate, and Greenwood will take your body, the messengers of darkness will take your soul, and come and go about you for the next ten million years, stripping the slain.

Many are crying out, "I admit I am slain, I admit it." On what battle-field, my brothers? By what weapon? "Polluted imagination," says one man. "Intoxicating liquor," says another man. "My own hard heart," says another man. Do you realize this? Then I come to tell you that the omnipotent Christ is ready to walk across this battle-field, and revive and resuscitate and resurrect your dead soul. Let him take your hand, and rub away the numbness; your head, and bathe off the aching; your heart, and stop its wild throb. He brought Lazarus to life; he brought Jairus's daughter to life; he brought the young man of Nain to life, and these are three proofs anyhow that he can bring you to life.

When the Philistines came down on the field, they stepped between the corpses, and they rolled over the dead, and they took away every thing that was valuable; and so it was with the people that followed after our army at

Chancellorsville, and at Pittsburg Landing, and at Stone River, and at Atlanta, stripping the slain; but the Northern and Southern women—God bless them—came on the field with basins, and pads, and towels, and lint, and cordials, and Christian encouragement, and the poor fellows that lay there lifted up their arms and said, "Oh, how good that does feel since you dressed it!" and others looked up, and said, "Oh, how you make me think of my mother!" and others said, "Tell the folks at home I died thinking about them;" and another looked up and said, "Miss, won't you sing me a verse of 'Home, Sweet Home' before I die?" And then the tattoo was sounded, and the hats were off, and the service was read, "I am the resurrection and the life;" and in honor of the departed the muskets were loaded and the command given, "Take aim—fire!" And there was a shingle set up at the head of the grave, with the epitaph of "Lieutenant ——, in the Fourteenth Massachusetts Volunteers," or "Captain ——, in the Fifteenth Regiment of South Carolina Volunteers." And so to-night, across this great field of moral and spiritual battle, the angels of God come walking among the slain, and there are voices of comfort, and voices of hope, and voices of resurrection, and voices of heaven.

Oh, the slain! the slain! Christ is ready to give life to the dead. He will make the deaf ear to hear, the blind eye to see, the pulseless heart to beat, and the damp walls of your spiritual charnel-house will crash into ruin at his cry, "Come forth!" I verily believe there are souls in this house who are now dead in sin, who in half an hour will be alive forever. There was a thrilling dream, a glorious dream—you may have heard of it. Ezekiel closed his eyes, and he saw two mountains, and a valley between the mountains. That valley looked as though there had been a great battle there, and a whole army had been slain, and they had been unburied; and the heat of the land, and the vultures coming there, soon the bones were exposed to the sun, and they looked like thousands of snow-drifts all through the valley. Frightful spectacle! The bleaching skeletons of a host! But Ezekiel still kept his eyes shut; and, lo! there were four currents of wind that struck that battle-field, and where those four currents of wind met, the bones began to rattle; and the foot came to the ankle, and the hand came to the wrist, and the jaws clashed together, and the spinal column gathered up the ganglions and the nervous fibre, and all the valley wriggled, and writhed, and throbbed, and rocked, and rose up. There, a man coming to life. There, a hundred men. There, a thousand; and all falling into line, waiting for the shout of their commander. Ten thousand bleached skeletons springing up into ten thousand warriors, panting for the fray. I hope that instead of being a dream it may be a prophecy of what we shall see here to-night. Let this north wall be one of the mountains, and the south wall be taken for another of the mountains, and let all the aisles and the pews be the valley between, for there are thousands here to-night without one pulsation of spiritual life. I look off in one direction, and they are dead. I look off in another direction, and they are dead. Who will bring them to life? Who shall rouse them up? If I should halloo at the top of my voice, I could not wake them.

Wait a moment! Listen! There is a rustling. There is a gale from heaven. It comes from the north, and from the south, and from the east, and from the west. It shuts us in. It blows upon the slain. There, a soul begins to move in spiritual life; there, ten souls; there, a score of souls; there, a hundred souls. The nostril throbbing in divine respiration, the hands lifted as though to take hold of heaven, the tongue moving as in prayer and adoration. Life! immortal life coming into the slain. Ten men for God—fifty—a hundred—a regiment—an army for God. Oh that we might have such a scene here to-night! In Ezekiel's words, and in almost a frenzy of prayer, I cry, "Come from the four winds, O breath, and breathe upon the slain."

You will have to surrender your heart to-night to God. You can not take the responsibility of fighting against the Spirit in this crisis, which will decide whether you are to go to heaven or to hell—to join the hallelujahs of the saved, or the howlings of the damned. You must pray. You must repent. You must this night fling your sinful soul on the pardoning mercy of God. *You must!* I see your resolution against God giving way. Your determination wavering. I break through the breach in the wall, and follow up the advantage gained, hoping to rout your last opposition to Christ, and make you " ground arms" at the feet of the Divine Conqueror. Oh, you must! You must! The moon does not ask the tides of the Atlantic Ocean to rise. It only stoops down with two great hands of light, the one at the European beach and the other at the American beach, and then lifts the great laver of molten silver. And God, it seems to me, is now going to lift this audience to newness of life. Do you not feel the swellings of the great oceanic tides of Divine mercy? My heart is in anguish to have you saved. For this I pray and preach and long, glad to be called a fool for Christ's sake and your salvation. Some one replies, "Dear me, I do wish I could have these matters arranged with my God. I want to be saved. God knows I want to be saved; but you stand there talking about this matter, and you don't show me how." My dear brother, the work has all been done. Christ did it with his own torn hand and lacerated foot and bleeding side. He took your place and died your death, if you would only believe it, only accept him as your substitute. "But," you say, "how am I to get up to that feeling?" I reply, the Holy Spirit is ready to help you up to that feeling, if you will only ask him here and now.

What an amazing pity that any man should go from this house unblessed, when such a large blessing is offered him at less cost than you would pay for a pin—"without money and without price!" I have driven down to-night with the Lord's ambulance to the battle-field where your soul lies exposed to the darkness and the storm, and I want to lift you in and drive off with you toward heaven. Oh, Christians! by your prayers help lift these wounded souls into the ambulance. God forbid that any should be left on the field, and that at last eternal sorrow and remorse and despair should come up around their souls like the bandit Philistines to the field of Gilboa, stripping the slain.

A SUM IN GOSPEL ARITHMETIC.

"What shall it profit a man, if he shall gain the whole world, and lose his own soul?"—*Mark* viii., 36.

I AM accustomed, Sabbath by Sabbath, to stand before an audience of bargain-makers. There may be men in all occupations sitting before me, yet the vast majority of them, I am very well aware, are engaged from Monday morning to Saturday night in the store. In many of the families of my congregation, across the breakfast-table and the tea-table are discussed questions of loss and gain. You are every day asking yourself, "What is the value of this? What is the value of that?" You would not think of giving something of greater value for that which is of lesser value. You would not think of selling that which cost you ten dollars for five dollars. If you had a property that was worth fifteen thousand dollars, you would not sell it for four thousand dollars. You are intelligent in all matters of bargain-making. Are you as wise in the things that pertain to the matters of the soul? Christ adapted his instructions to the circumstances of those to whom he spoke. When he talked to fishermen, he spoke of the Gospel net. When he talked to the farmers, he said, "A sower went forth to sow." When he talked to the shepherds, he told the parable of the lost sheep. And am I not right when speaking this morning to an audience made up of bargain-makers, that I address them in the words of my text, asking, "What shall it profit a man, if he shall gain the whole world, and lose his own soul?"

I propose, as far as possible, to estimate and compare the value of two properties.

First, I have to say that the world is a *very grand property*. Its flowers are God's thoughts in bloom. Its rocks are God's thoughts in stone. Its dew-drops are God's thoughts in pearl. This world is God's child—a wayward child indeed: it has wandered off through the heavens. But about eighteen hundred and seventy-four or eighteen hundred and seventy-five years ago, one Christmas night, God sent out a sister world to call that wanderer back, and it hung over Bethlehem only long enough to get the promise of the wanderer's return, and now that lost world, with soft feet of light, comes treading back through the heavens. The hills, how beautiful they billow up, the edge of the wave white with the foam of crocuses! How beautiful the rainbow, the arched bridge on which heaven and earth come and talk to each other in tears, after the storm is over! How nimble the feet of the lamp-lighters that in a few minutes set all the dome of the night ablaze with brackets of fire! How bright the oar of the saffron cloud that rows across the deep sea of heaven! How beautiful the Spring, with bridal blossoms in her hair! I wonder who it is that beats time on a June morning for the bird orchestra. How gently the harebell tolls its fragrance on the air! There may be grander worlds, swarthier worlds, larger worlds than this; but I think that this is a most exquisite world—a mignonnette on the bosom of immensity! "Oh," you say, "take my soul! give me that world! I am willing to take it in exchange. I am ready now for the bargain. It is so beautiful a world, so sweet a world, so grand a world!"

But let us look more minutely into the value of this world. You will not buy property unless you can get a good title to it. After you have looked at the property and found out that it suits you, you send an attorney to the public office, and he examines the book of deeds, and the book of mortgages, and the book of judgments, and the book of liens, and he decides whether the title is good before you will have any thing to do with it. There might be a splendid property, and in every way exactly suited to your want; but if you can not get a good title, you will not take it. Now, I am here this morning to say that it is impossible to get a good title to this world. If I settle down upon it, in the very year I so settle down upon it as a permanent possession, I may be driven away from it. Ay, in five minutes after I give up my soul for the world I may have to part with the world; and what kind of a title do you call that? There is only one way in which I can hold an earthly possession, and that is through the senses. All beautiful sights through the eye, but the eye may be blotted out; all captivating sounds through the ear, but my ear may be deafened; all lusciousness of fruits and viands through my taste, but my taste may be destroyed; all appreciation of culture and of art through my mind, but I may lose my mind. What a frail hold, then, I have upon any earthly possession!

In courts of law, if you want to get a man off a property, you must serve upon him a writ of ejectment, giving him a certain time to vacate the premises; but when Death comes to us and serves a writ of ejectment, he does not give us one second of forewarning. He says, "Off of this place!

You have no right any longer to the possession." We might cry out, "I gave you a hundred thousand dollars for that property;" the plea would be of no avail. We might say, "We have a warrantee deed for that property;" the plea would be of no avail. We might say, "We have a lien on that store-house;" that would do us no good. Death is blind, and he can not see a seal, and can not read an indenture. So that, first and last, I want to tell you that when you propose that I give up my soul for the world, you can not give me the first item of title.

Having examined the title of a property, your next question is about insurance. You would not be silly enough to buy a large warehouse that could not possibly be insured. You would not have any thing to do with such a property. Now, I ask you what assurance can you give me that this world is not going to be burned up? Absolutely none. Geologists tell us that it is already on fire; that the heart of the world is one great living coal; that it is just like a ship on fire at sea, the flames not bursting out because the hatches are kept down. And yet you propose to palm off on me, in return for my soul, a world for which, in the first place, you give no title, and in the second place, for which you can give no insurance. "Oh," you say, "the water of the oceans will wash over all the land and put out the fire." Oh no. There are inflammable elements in the water, hydrogen and oxygen. Call off the hydrogen, and then the Atlantic and the Pacific oceans would blaze like heaps of shavings. You want me to take this world, for which you can give no possible insurance.

Astronomers have swept their telescopes through the sky, and have found out that there have been thirteen worlds, in the last two centuries, that have disappeared.

At first, they looked just like other worlds. Then they got deeply red—they were on fire. Then they got ashen, showing they were burned down. Then they disappeared, showing that even the ashes were scattered. And if the geologist be right in his prophecy, then our world is to go in the same way. And yet you want me to exchange my soul for it. Ah no; it is a world that is burning now. Suppose you brought an insurance agent to look at your property for the purpose of giving you a policy upon it, and while he stood in front of the house, he should say, "That house is on fire now in the basement," you could not get any insurance upon it. Yet you talk about this world as though it were a safe investment, as though you could get some insurance upon it, when down in the basement it is on fire.

I remark, also, that this world is a property, with which every body who has taken it as a possession has had trouble. Now, between my house and this church there is a reach of land which is not built on. I ask what is the matter, and they reply that every body who has had any thing to do with that property got into trouble about it. It is just so with this world: every body that has had any thing to do with it, as a possession, has been in perplexity. How was it with Lord Byron? Did he not sell his immortal soul for the purpose of getting the world? Was he satisfied with the possession? Alas! alas! the poem graphically describes his case when it says:

> "Drank every cup of joy,
> Heard every trump of fame;
> Drank early, deeply drank,
> Drank draughts which common millions might have quenched.
> Then died of thirst, because there was no more to drink."

Oh yes, he had trouble with it; and so did Napoleon. After conquering nations by the force of the sword, he lies down to die, his entire possession the military boots that he insisted on having upon his feet while he was dying. So it has been with men who had better ambition. Thackeray, one of the most genial and lovable souls, after he had won the applause of all intelligent lands through his wonderful genius, sits down in a restaurant in Paris, looks to the other end of the room, and wonders whose that forlorn and wretched face is; rising up after a while, he finds that it is Thackeray in the mirror. Oh yes, this world is a cheat. Talk about a man gaining the world! Who ever gained half of the world? Who ever owned a hemisphere? Who ever gained a continent? Who ever owned Asia? Who ever gained a city? Who ever owned Brooklyn? Talk about gaining the world! No man ever gained it, or the hundred-thousandth part of it. You are demanding that I sell my soul, not for the world, but for a fragment of it. Here is a man who has had a large estate for forty or fifty years. He lies down to die. You say, "That man is worth millions and millions of dollars." Is he? You call up a surveyor, with his compass and chains, and you say, "There is a property extending three miles in one direction, and three miles in another direction." Is that the way to measure that man's property? No! You do not want any surveyor, with his compass and chains. That is not the way you want to measure that man's property now. It is an undertaker that you need, who will come and put his finger in his vest-pocket, and take out a tape-line, and he will measure five feet nine inches one way, and two feet and a half the other way. That is the man's property. Oh no, I forgot; not so much as that, for he does not own even the place in which he lies in the cemetery. The deed to that belongs to the executors and the heirs. Oh, what a property you propose to give me for my soul! If you sell a bill of goods, you go into the counting-room, and say to your partner, "Do you think that man is good for this bill? Can he give proper security? Will he meet this payment?" Now, when you are offered this world as a possession, I want you to test the matter. I do not want you to go into this bargain blindly. I want you to ask about the title, about the insurance, about whether men have ever had any trouble with it, about whether you can keep it, about whether you can get all, or the ten-thousandth, or one-hundred-thousandth part of it.

There is the world now. I shall say no more about it. Make up your mind for yourself, as I shall, before God, have to make up my mind for myself, about the value of this world. I can not afford to make a mistake for my soul, and you can not afford to make a mistake for your soul.

Now, let us look at the other property—the soul. We can not make a bargain without seeing the comparative value. The soul! How shall I estimate the value of it? Well, by its exquisite organization. It is the most wonderful piece of mechanism ever put together. Machinery is of value in proportion as it is mighty and silent at the same time. You look at the engine and the machinery in the Philadelphia Mint, and, as you see it performing its wonderful work, you will be surprised to find how silently it goes. Machinery that roars and tears soon destroys itself; but silent machinery is often most effective. Now, so it is with the soul of man, with all its tremendous faculties—it moves in silence. Judgment, without any racket, lifting its scales; memory, without any noise, bringing down all its treasures; conscience taking its judgment-seat without any excitement; the understanding and the will all doing their work. Velocity, majesty, might; but silence—silence. You listen at the door of your heart. You can hear no sound. The soul is all quiet. It is so delicate an instrument that no human hand can touch it. You break a bone, and with splinters and bandages the surgeon sets it; the eye becomes inflamed, the apothecary's wash cools it; but a soul off the track, unbalanced, no human power can re-adjust it. With one sweep of its wing it circles the universe, and overvaults the throne of God. Why, in the hour of death the soul is so mighty, it throws aside the body as though it were a toy. It drives back medical skill as impotent. It breaks through the circle of loved ones who stand around the dying couch. With one leap, it springs beyond star, and moon, and sun, and chasms of immensity. Oh, it is a soul superior to all material things! No fire can consume it; no floods can drown it; no rocks can crush it; no walls can impede it; no time can exhaust it. It wants no bridge on which to cross a chasm. It wants no plummet with which to sound a depth. A soul so mighty, so swift, so silent, must be a priceless soul.

I calculate the value of the soul, also, by its capacity for happiness. How much joy it can get in this world, out of friendships, out of books, out of clouds, out of the sea, out of flowers, out of ten thousand things; and yet all the joy it has here does' not test its capacity. You are in a concert before the curtain hoists, and you hear the instruments preparing—the sharp snap of the broken string, the scraping of the bow across the viol. "There is no music in that," you say. It is only getting ready for the music.

And all the enjoyment of the soul in this world, the enjoyment we think is real enjoyment, is only preparative; it is only anticipative; it is only the first stages of the thing; it is only the entrance, the beginning of that which shall be the orchestral harmonies and splendors of the redeemed.

You can not test the full power of the soul for happiness in this world. How much power the soul has here to find enjoyment in friendships! but oh, the grander friendships for the soul in the skies! How sweet the flowers here! but how much sweeter they will be there! I do not think that when flowers die on earth, they die forever. I think that the fragrance of the flowers is the spirit being wafted away into glory. God says there are palm-trees in heaven and fruits in heaven. If so, why not the spirits of the dead flowers? In the sunny valleys of heaven, shall not the marigold creep? On the hills of heaven, will not the amaranth bloom? On the amethystine walls of heaven, will not the jasmine climb? "My beloved is come down into his garden to gather lilies." No flowers in heaven? Where, then, do they get their garlands for the brows of the righteous?

Christ is glorious to our souls now, but how much grander our appreciation after a while! A conqueror comes back after the battle. He has been fighting for us. He comes upon the platform. He has one arm in a sling, and the other arm holds a crutch. As he mounts the platform, oh, the enthusiasm of the audience! They say, "That man fought for us, and imperiled his life for us;" and how wild the huzza that follows huzza! When the Lord Jesus Christ shall at last stand out before the multitudes of the redeemed of heaven, and we meet him face to face, and feel that he was wounded in the head, and wounded in the hands, and wounded in the feet, and wounded in the side for us, methinks we will be overwhelmed. We will sit some time gazing in silence, until some leader amidst the white-robed choir shall lift the baton of light, and give the signal that it is time to wake the song of jubilee; and all heaven then will break forth into, "Hosanna! hosanna! hosanna! Worthy is the Lamb that was slain."

I calculate further the value of the soul by the price that has been paid for it. In St. Petersburg there is a diamond that the Government paid two hundred thousand dollars for: "Well," you say, "it must have been very valuable, or the Government would not have paid two hundred thousand dollars for it." I want to see what my soul is worth, and what your soul is worth, by seeing what has been paid for it. For that immortal soul, the richest blood that was ever shed, the deepest groan that was ever uttered, all the griefs of earth compressed into one tear, all the sufferings of earth gathered into one rapier of pain and struck through his holy heart. Does it not imply tremendous value?

I argue, also, the value of the soul from the home that has been fitted up for it in the future. One would have thought that a street of adamant would have done. No; it is a street of gold. One would have thought that a wall of granite would have done. No; it is the flame of sardonyx mingling with the green of emerald. One would have thought that an occasional doxology would have done. No; it is a perpetual song. If the ages of heaven marched in a straight line, some day the last regiment, perhaps, might pass out of sight; but no, the ages of heaven do not march in a straight line, but in a circle around about the throne of God; forever, forever, tramp, tramp! A soul so bought, so equipped, so provided for, must be a priceless soul, a majestic soul, a tremendous soul.

Now, you have seen the two properties—the world, the soul. One perishable, the other immortal. One unsatisfying, the other capable of ever-increasing felicity. Will you trade? Will you trade even? Remember, it is the only investment you can make. If a man sell a bill of goods worth five thousand dollars, and he is cheated out of it, he may get five thousand dollars somewhere else; but a man who invests his soul, invests all. Losing that, he loses all. Saving that, he saves all. In the light of my text, it seems to me as if you were this morning offering your soul to the highest bidder; and I hear you say, "What is bid for it, my deathless spirit? What is bid for it?" Satan says, "I'll bid the world." You say, "Begone! that is no equivalent. Sell my soul for the world? No! Begone!" But there is some one else in the audience not so wise as that. He says, "What is bid for my immortal soul?" Satan says, "I'll bid the world." "The world? Going at that, going at that, going! Gone!" Gone forever!

> "What is the thing of greatest price,
> The whole creation round?
> That which was lost in paradise,
> That which in Christ is found.
>
> "Then let us gather round the cross,
> That knowledge to obtain;
> Not by the soul's eternal loss,
> But everlasting gain."

Well, there are a great many people in the house who say, "I will not sell my soul for the world. I find the world is an unsatisfying portion." What, then, will you do with your soul? Some one whispers here, "I will give my soul to Christ." Will you? That is the wisest resolution you ever made. Will you give it to Christ? When? To-morrow? No; now. I congratulate you if you have come to such a decision. Oh, if this morning the eternal Spirit of God would come down upon this audience, and show you the vanity of this world, and the immense importance of Christ's religion, and the infinite value of your own immortal souls, what a house this would be! what an hour this would be! what a moment this would be! Do you know that Christ has bought your soul? Do you know that he has paid an infinite price for it? Do you know that he is worthy of it? Will you give it to him now?

I was reading this morning of a sailor who had just got ashore, and was telling about his last experience at sea. He said, "The last time I crossed the ocean, we had a terrific time. After we had been out three or four days, the machinery got disarranged, and the steam began to escape, and the captain, gathering the people and the crew on deck, said, "Unless some one shall go down and shut off that steam, and arrange that machinery at the peril of his life, we must all be destroyed." He was not willing to go down himself. No one seemed willing to go. The passengers gathered at one end of the steamer waiting for their fate. The captain said, "I give you a last warning. If there is no one here willing to imperil his life and go down and fix that machinery, we must all be lost." A plain sailor said, "I'll go, sir;" and he wrapped himself in a coarse piece of canvas and went down, and was gone but a few moments, when the escaping steam stopped, and the machinery was corrected. The captain cried out to the passengers, "All saved! Let us go down below and see what has become of the poor fellow." They went down. There he lay dead. Vicarious suffering! Died for all! Oh! do you suppose that those people on the ship ever forgot, ever can forget that poor fellow? "No!" they say; "it was through his sacrifice that I got ashore." The time came when our whole race must die unless some one should endure torture and sorrow and shame. Who shall come to the rescue? Shall it be one of the seraphim? Not one. Shall it be one of the cherubim? Not one. Shall it be an inhabitant of some pure and unfallen world? Not one. Then Christ said, "Lo! I come to do thy will, O God;" and he went down through the dark stairs of our sin, and wretchedness, and misery; and woe, and he stopped the peril, and he died, that you and I might be free. Oh, the love! oh, the endurance! oh, the horrors of the sacrifice! Shall not our souls this morning go out toward him, saying, "Lord Jesus Christ, take my soul: Thou art worthy to have it. Thou hast died to save it."

God help you this morning rightly to cipher out this sum in Gospel arithmetic: "What shall it profit a man, if he shall gain the whole world, and lose his own soul?"

SWIMMING FOR LIFE.

"He shall spread forth his hands in the midst of them, as he that swimmeth spreadeth forth his hands to swim."—*Isaiah* xxv., 11.

THE fisherman seeks out unfrequented nooks. You stand all day on the bank of a wide river in the broiling sun, and fling out your line, and catch nothing; while the expert angler breaks through the jungle, and goes by the shadow of the solitary rock, and, in a place where no fisherman has been for ten years, throws out his line, and comes home at night, his face shining and his basket full. I do not know why we ministers of the Gospel need always be fishing in the same stream, and preaching from the same texts that other people preach from. I can not understand the policy of the minister who, in Blackfriars, London, England, every week for thirty years preached from the Epistle to the Hebrews. It is an exhilaration to me when I can come across a theme which I feel has not yet been treated, and my text is one of that kind. There are paths in God's Word that are well beaten by Christian feet. When men want to quote Scripture, they quote the old passages that every body has heard. When they want a chapter read, they read a chapter that all the other people have been reading, so that the church to-day is ignorant of three-fourths of the Bible. You go into the Louvre, at Paris. You confine yourself to one corridor of that opulent gallery of paintings. As you come out your friend says to you, "Did you see that Rembrandt?" "No."

"Did you see that Rubens?" "No." "Did you see that Titian?" "No." "Did you see that Raphael?" "No." "Well," says your friend, "then you didn't see the Louvre." Now, my friends, I think we are too much apt to confine ourselves to one of the great corridors of this gallery of Scripture truth, and so much so that there are not three persons in the house to-night who have ever noticed the all-suggestive and powerful picture in the words of my text.

This text represents God as a strong swimmer striking out to push down iniquity and to save the souls of men. "He shall spread forth his hands in the midst of them, as he that swimmeth spreadeth forth his hands to swim." The figure is bold and many-sided. Most of you know how to swim. Some of you learned it in the city school, where this art is taught; some of you in boyhood, in the river near your father's house; some of you since you came to manhood or womanhood, while summering on the beach of the sea. You step down in the wave, you throw your head back, you bring your elbows to the chest, you put the palms of your hands downward and the soles of your feet outward, and you push through the water as though you had been born aquatic. It is a grand thing to know how to swim, not only for yourself, but because you will after a while, perhaps, have to help others. I do not know any thing more stirring or sublime than to see some man like Norman M'Kenzie leaping from the ship *Madras* into the sea to save Charles Turner, who had dropped from the royal-yard while trying to loosen the sail, bringing him back to the deck amidst the cheering of the passengers and the crew. If a man has not enthusiasm enough to hurra in such circumstances, he deserves himself to drop into the sea and have no one help him. The Royal Humane Society of England was established in 1774, its object to applaud and reward those who should pluck up life from the deep. Any one who has performed such a deed of daring has all the particulars of that bravery put down in a public record, and on his breast a medal done in blue and gold and bronze, anchor and monogram and inscription telling to future generations the bravery of the man or woman who had saved a soul from drowning. But, my friends, if it is such a worthy thing to save a body from the deep, I ask you if it is not a worthier thing to save an immortal soul? And you shall see, to-night, the Son of God step forth for this achievement. "He shall spread forth his hands in the midst of them, as he that swimmeth spreadeth forth his hands to swim."

In order to understand the full force of this figure, you need to realize, first of all, that our race is in a sinking condition. You sometimes hear people talking of what they consider the most beautiful words in our language. One man says it is "home;" another man says it is the word "mother;" another says it is the word "Jesus;" but I will tell you the bitterest word in all our language, the word most angry and baleful, the word saturated with the most trouble, the word that accounts for all the loathsomeness, and the pang, and the outrage, and the harrowing; and that word is "Sin." You spell it with three letters, and yet those three letters describe the circumference and pierce the diameter of every thing bad on earth and in perdition. Sin! it is a sibilant word. You can not pronounce it without giving the siss of the flame or the hiss of the serpent. Sin! And, then, if you add three letters to that word, it describes every person in this house, and every one in the world—sinner. That is you and me. We have outraged the law of God; not occasionally, or now and then, but perpetually. The Bible declares it. Hark! it thunders, two claps, "The heart is deceitful above all things, and desperately wicked." "The soul that sinneth, it shall die." What the Bible says our own conscience affirms. After Judge Morgan had sentenced Lady Jane Grey to death, his conscience troubled him so much for the deed that he became insane, and all through his insanity he kept saying, "Take her away from me! Lady Jane Grey. Take her away! Lady Jane Grey." It was the voice of his conscience. And no man ever does anything wrong, however great or small, but his conscience brings that matter before him, and at every step of his misbehavior it says, "Wrong, wrong."

Sin is a leprosy, sin is a paralysis, sin is a consumption, sin is pollution, sin is death. Give it a fair chance, and it will swamp you, body, mind, and soul, forever. In this world it only gives a faint intimation of its virulence; but after for a thousand quadrillion of years it has ransacked your soul—what then? You see a patient in the first stages of typhoid fever. The cheek is somewhat flushed, the hands somewhat hot, preceded by a slight chill. "Why," you say, "typhoid fever does not seem to be much of a disease." But wait until the patient has been six weeks under it, and all his energies have been wrung out, and he is too weak to lift his little finger, and his intellect is gone, then you see the full havoc of the disease. Now, sin in this world is an ailment which is only in its very first stages; but after the grave, it is rending, blasting, all-devouring, all-consuming, eternal typhoid. Oh, if we could see our unpardoned sins as God sees them, our teeth would chatter, and our knees would knock together, and our respiration would be choked, and our heart would break! If your sins are unforgiven, they are bearing down on you, and you are sinking, sinking away from happiness, sinking away from God, sinking away from every thing that is good and blessed, sinking forever.

Then what do we want? A swimmer! A strong swimmer! A swift swimmer! And, blessed be God, in my text we have him announced: "He shall spread forth his hands in the midst of them, as he that swimmeth spreadeth forth his hands to swim." You have noticed that when a swimmer goes out to rescue any one, he puts off his heavy apparel. He must not have any such impediment about him if he is going to do this great deed. And when Christ stepped forth to save us, he shook off the sandals of heaven, and his feet were free; and he laid aside the robe of eternal royalty, and his arms were free; and then he stepped down into the wave of our transgression, and it came up over his wounded feet, and it came above the spear-stab in his side—ay, it dashed to the lacerated temple, the high-water mark of his anguish. Then, rising above the flood, "He stretched forth his hands in the midst of them, as he that swimmeth spreadeth forth his hands to swim."

If you have ever watched a swimmer, you notice that his whole body is brought into play. The arms are flexed, the hands drive the water back, the knees are active, the head is tossed back to escape strangulation, the whole body is in propulsion. And when Christ sprung out into the deep to save us, he threw his entire nature into it, all his Godhead, his omniscience, his goodness, his love, his omnipotence—head, heart, eyes, hands, feet. We were so far out on the sea, and so deep down in the waves that nothing short of an entire God could save us. Christ leaped out for our rescue, saying, "Lo! I come to do thy will," and all the surges of human and Satanic hate beat against him; and those who watched him from the gates of heaven feared he would go down under the wave, and, instead of saving others, would himself perish; but, putting his breast to the foam, and shaking the surf from his locks, he came on, on, until he is to-night within the reach of every one here. Eye omniscient, heart infinite, arm omnipotent. Mighty to save, even unto the uttermost. Oh, it was not half a God that trampled down bellowing Gennesaret! It was not a quarter of a God that mastered the demons of Gadara. It was not two-thirds of a God that lifted up Lazarus into the arms of his overjoyed sisters. It was not a fragment of a God that offered pardon and peace to all the race. No. This mighty swimmer threw his grandeur, his glory, his might, his wisdom, his omnipotence, and his eternity into this one act. It took both hands of God to save us, both feet. How do I prove it? On the cross, were not both hands nailed? On the cross, were not both feet nailed? His entire nature involved in our redemption!

If you have lived much by the water, you have noticed also that if any one is going out to rescue the drowning, he must be independent, self-reliant, able to go alone. There may be a time when he must spring out to save one, and he can not get a life-boat; and if he goes out, and he has not strength enough to bear himself up and bear another up, he will sink, and, instead of dragging one corpse out of the torrent, you will have two to drag out. When Christ sprung out into the sea to deliver us, he had no life-buoy.

His Father did not help him. Alone in the wine-press. Alone in the pang. Alone in the darkness. Alone on the mountain. Alone in the sea. If he saves us, he shall have all the credit, for "there was none to help." No oar. No wing. No ladder. When Nathaniel Lyon fell in the battle charge in front of his troops, he had a whole army to cheer him; when Marshal Ney sprung into the contest, and plunged in the spurs till the horse's flanks spurted blood, all France applauded him. But Jesus alone! "Of the people there was none to help." "All forsook him and fled." Oh, it was not a flotilla that sailed down and saved us! It was not a cluster of gondolas that came over the wave. It was one person, independent and alone, "spreading out his hands among us as a swimmer spreadeth forth his hands to swim."

Behold, then, to-night, the spectacle of a drowning soul, and Christ the swimmer. I believe it was in 1848 when there were six English soldiers of the Fifth Fusiliers who were hanging to the bottom of a capsized boat—a boat that had been upset by a squall three miles from shore. It was in the night; but one man swam mightily for the beach, guided by the dark mountains that lifted their top through the night. He came to the beach. He found a shoreman who consented to go with him and save the other men, and they put out. It was some time before they could find the place where the men were; but after a while they heard their cry, "Help! help!" and they bore down to them, and they saved them and brought them to shore. Oh that to-night our cry might be lifted long, loud, and shrill, till Christ the swimmer shall come and take us, lest we drop a thousand fathoms down! for a man who will not pray will perish.

If you have been much by the water, you know very well that when one is in peril help must come very quickly, or it will be of no use. One minute may decide every thing. Immediate help the man wants, or no help at all. Now, that is just the kind of a relief the sinner wants. The case is urgent, imminent, instantaneous. See that soul sinking. Son of God, lay hold of him! It is his last hour of mercy. Be quick! be quick! Oh, I wish you all understood how urgent this Gospel is! There was a man in the navy at sea who had been severely whipped for bad behavior, and he was maddened by it, and he leaped into the sea, and no sooner had he leaped into the sea than, quick as lightning, an albatross swooped upon him. The drowning man, brought to his senses, seized hold of the albatross and held on. The fluttering of the bird kept him on the wave until relief could come. Would that to-night the dove of God's convicting, converting, and saving Spirit might flash from the throne upon your soul, and that you, taking hold of its potent wing, might live, and live forever.

I want to persuade you to-night to lay hold of this strong swimmer. "No," you say, "it is always ruin." There is not a river or a lake but has a calamity resultant from the fact that, when a strong swimmer went out to save a sinking man, the drowning man clutched him, threw his arms around him, pinioned his arms, and they both went down together. When you are saving a man in the water, you do not want to come up by his face; you want to come up by his back. You do not want him to take hold of you while you take hold of him. But, blessed be God, Jesus Christ is so strong a swimmer he comes, not to our back, but to our face, and he asks us to throw around him the arms of our love, and then promises to take us to the beach, and he will do it. Do not trust that plank of good works. Do not trust that shivered spar of your own righteousness. Christ only can give you transportation. Turn your face upon him to-night as the dying martyr did in olden days when he cried out, "None but Christ! None but Christ!" Jesus has taken millions to the land, and he is willing to take you there. Oh, what hardness to shove him back when he has been swimming all the way from the throne of God to where you are to-night, and is ready to swim all the way back again, taking your redeemed spirit!

I have sometimes thought what a spectacle the ocean bed will present when in the last day the water is all drawn off. It will be a line of wrecks from beach to beach. There is where the harpooners went down. There is where the line-of-battle ships went down. There is where the merchantmen went down. There is where the steamers went down. What a spectacle in the last day when the water is drawn off! But oh, how much more solemn if we had an eye to see the spiritual wrecks and the places where they foundered! You would find thousands along these streets. Coming here to-night, if you had such superb eyesight, standing at the door while yet this room was empty, you might then have seen thousands of such marks of wrecks scattered all through these pews, the places where on other Sabbaths immortal men were invited to heaven, and refused it. Christ came down in their awful catastrophe, putting out for their soul, "spreading forth his hands as a swimmer spreadeth forth his hands to swim;" but they thrust him in the sore heart, and they smote his fair cheek, and they perished; the storm and the darkness swallowing them up. Are there any here now who feel that they are sinking? Do they feel the need of a Divine arm? Christ is ready now to step out for their present and their eternal salvation. I ask you to lay hold of this Christ, and lay hold of him now. You will sink without him. Oh that God this moment would break the madness of those who will not have the mercy and the favor of that Christ who is the only Saviour the world ever has had, or ever will have! Say, do you want to die? Do you covet ruin? Do you despise heaven? Have you lifted the poniard with which to stab the life of your immortal soul? Sinner, thou knowest not where thou art! On the verge of what woe. On the waves of what sea. Sinking. Sinking. Sinking. From horizon to horizon not one sail in sight. Only one strong swimmer, with head flung back and arms outspread as "he that swimmeth spreadeth forth his hands to swim." I pray God that he will lead you into the peace and hope of the Gospel! You will never have so fair a chance as this very one in which to accept of the Lord Jesus Christ.

I hear a great many in the audience saying, "Well, I would like to be a Christian to-night. I am going to work to become a Christian." My brother, you begin wrong. When a man is drowning, and a strong swimmer comes out to help him, he says to the man, "Now, be quiet. Put your arm on my arm or on my shoulder, but don't struggle, don't try to help yourself, and I'll take you ashore. The more you struggle and the more you try to help yourself, the more you impede me. Now, be quiet, and I'll take you ashore." When Christ, the strong swimmer, comes out to save a soul, the sinner says, "That's right. I am glad to see Jesus, and I am going to help him. I am going to do this, that, and the other thing that will help him;

and I am going to pray more, and that will help him; and I am going to weep extravagantly over my sins, and that will help him." No, my brother, it will not. Stop your doing. Christ will do all or none. You can not lift an ounce, you can not move an inch, in this matter of your redemption. This is the difficulty which keeps thousands of souls out of the kingdom of heaven. It is because they can not consent to let Jesus Christ begin and complete the work of their redemption. "Why," you say, "then is there nothing for me to do?" Only one thing have you to do, and that is, to lay hold of Christ, and let him achieve your salvation, and achieve it all. I do not know whether I make the matter plain or not. I simply want to show you that man can not save himself, but that the Almighty Son of God can do it, and will do it, if you ask him. Oh, fling your two arms, the arms of your trust and love, around this omnipotent swimmer of the cross!

My sermon is about ended, and the stenographer has taken it down with his pencil. Oh that the Holy Spirit might write it on all your hearts! How many will be saved through this particular service? How many will be lost? These are the two questions with which I came upon this platform. After the benediction there will be two strong currents, one current bearing mightily toward heaven, the other bearing mightily toward hell; and in one or the other of these currents you will be caught. In the one you will be carried out to where it empties into the ocean whose waves are fire, and whose ships are fire, and whose beach is fire, or you will be carried into a current which will empty into a sea whose surges beat eternal music against the throne of God. Oh, it is a solemn minute! Have you ever seen them trying to resuscitate a half-drowned person? You remember the manipulation. You remember they tried every possible art. You remember how they knelt down and put their lips to the lips of the insensible patient, and breathed and breathed, trying to get the lungs to work; and at last, when he just gave one feeble sigh, they shouted all around the room, "He lives! he lives!" And now, to-night, your drowning soul, O sinner, I hope, is by the grace of Christ to be resuscitated. We have gathered around you. Would that this might be the hour when you begin to live! The Lord Jesus Christ steps down, he gets on his knee, he puts his lip to your lip, and would breathe pardon and life and heaven into your immortal soul. God grant that this hour there may be thousands of souls resuscitated from this awful spiritual drowning. I stand on the deck of the old Gospel ship amidst a crowd of passengers, and yet my soul is wrung with sorrow because I see some of you overboard, and I can not help you. May the living Christ this hour put out for your rescue, "spreading forth his hands in the midst of you, as a swimmer spreadeth forth his hands to swim." Oh that salvation might come to your house this night! You want religion yourselves, and your families need the same religion. Another opportunity for heaven is closing, closing, closing.

> "Ye sinners, seek his grace,
> His wrath ye can not bear;
> Fly to the shelter of his love,
> And find salvation there."

THE CHRISTIAN AT THE BALLOT-BOX.

"Some therefore cried one thing, and some another: for the assembly was confused; and the more part knew not wherefore they were come together. And they drew Alexander out of the multitude, the Jews putting him forward. And Alexander beckoned with the hand, and would have made his defense unto the people. But when they knew that he was a Jew, all with one voice about the space of two hours cried out, Great is Diana of the Ephesians."—*Acts* xix., 32, 33, 34.

EPHESUS was upside down. A manufacturer of silver boxes for holding heathen images had called his laborers together to discuss the behavior of one Paul, who had been in public places assaulting image-worship, and consequently very much damaging that particular business. There was great excitement in the city. People stood in knots along the streets, violently gesticulating, and calling each other hard names. Some of the people favored the policy of the silversmith; other people favored the policy of Paul. There were great moral questions involved; but these did not bother them at all. The only question about which they seemed to be interested was concerning the wages and the salaried positions. The silversmith and his compeers had put up factories at great expense for the making of these silver boxes; and now, if this new policy is to be inaugurated, the business will go down, the laborers will be thrown out of employment, and the whole city will suffer. Well, what is to be done? "Call a convention," says some one; for in all ages a convention has been a panacea for public evils. The convention is called, and, as they want the largest room in the city, they take the theatre. Having there assembled, they all want to get the floor, and they all want to talk at once. You know what excitement that always makes in a convention, where a great many people want to talk at once. Some cried one thing, some cried another. Some wanted to denounce, some wanted to resolve. After a while a prominent man gets the floor, and he begins to speak; but they very soon hiss him down, and then the confusion rises into worse uproar, and they begin to shout, all of them together, and they keep on until they are red in the face and hoarse in the throat, for two long hours crying out, "Great is Diana of the Ephesians! Great is Diana of the Ephesians!"

The whole scene reminds me of the excitement we have almost every autumn at the elections. While that goddess Diana has lost her worshipers, and her temples have gone into the dust, our American people want to set up a god in place of it, and they want us all to bow down before it; and that god is Political Party. Considering our superior civilization, I have to declare to you that the Ephesian idolatry was less offensive in the sight of God than is this all-absorbing American partisanship.

While there are honest men, true men, Christian men, who stand in both political parties, and who come into the autumnal elections resolving to serve their city or their State or the nation in the best possible way, I have noticed also that with many it is a mere contest between the ins and the outs—those who are in trying to stay in and keep the outs out, and those who are out trying to get in and thrust the ins out. And one party cries, "Great is Diana of the Ephesians!" and the other party cries, "Great is

Diana of the Ephesians!" neither of them honest enough to say, "Great is my pocket-book!"

Once or twice a year it is my custom to talk to the people about public affairs from what I call a Christian standpoint, and this morning I have chosen for that duty. I hope to say a practical word. History tells us of a sermon once preached amidst the Highlands of Scotland—a sermon two hours long—on the sin of luxury, where there were not more than three pairs of shoes in the audience; and during our last war a good man went into a hospital distributing tracts, and gave a tract on "The Sin of Dancing" to a man both of whose legs had been amputated! But I hope this morning to present an appropriate and adapted word, as next Tuesday, at the ballot-box, great affairs are to be settled. The Rev. Dr. Emmons, in the early history of our country, in Massachusetts, preached about the election of Thomas Jefferson to the Presidency. The Rev. Dr. Mayhew, of Boston, in the early days of our republic, preached about the repeal of the Stamp Act. There are times when ministers of Christ must look off upon public affairs and discuss them. We need go back to no example. Every man is, before God, responsible for his own duty. If the Norwegian boasts of his home of rocks, and the Siberian is pleased with his land of perpetual snow; if the Roman thought that the muddy Tiber was the favored river in the sight of heaven, and if the Laplander shivers out his eulogy of his native clime, and if the Chinese have pity for any body born outside the "flowery kingdom," shall not we, born under these fair skies, and standing day by day amidst these glorious civil and religious liberties, be public-spirited? I propose to tell the people very plainly what I consider to be their Christian duty at the ballot-box.

First, *set yourselves against all political falsehood.* The most monstrous lies ever told in this country are during the elections. I stop at the door of a Democratic meeting and listen, and hear that the Republicans are thieves. I stop at the door of a Republican meeting and listen, and hear that the Democrats are scoundrels. Our public men microscopized, and the truth distorted. Who believes a tenth part of what he reads or hears in the autumnal elections? Men who at other seasons of the year are very careful in their speech become peddlers of scandal.

In the Far East there is a place where, once a year, they let the people do as they please and say what they please, and the place is full of uproar, misrule, and wickedness, and they call it the "Devil's day." The nearest approximation to that in this country has been the first Tuesday in November. The community at such times seem to say, "Go to, now; let us have a good time at lying." Prominent candidates for office are denounced as renegade and inebriate. A small lie will start in the corner of a country newspaper, and keep on running until it has captured the printing-presses of the whole continent. What garbling of speeches! What misinterpretation of motives! What misrepresentation of individual antecedents! To capture the unwary you shall have a ticket with Democratic heading and Republican names following, and then a Republican heading with Democratic names following; and the poor man will stand at the polls bewildered, at last, perhaps, voting for those whom he has been three weeks vociferously denouncing. O Christian men! frown upon this political falsehood! Remember that a political lie is as black as any other kind of a lie. God has recorded all the falsehoods that have been told at the city, State, or national elections since the foundation of this Government; and, though the perpetrators and their victims may have gone into the dust, in the last day judgment will be awarded. The falsehoods that Aaron Burr breathed into the ear of Blennerhasset, the slanders that Lieutenant-general Gage proclaimed about George Washington, the misrepresentations in regard to James Monroe, are as fresh on God's book to-day as the lie that was printed last week about Samuel J. Tilden or Governor Dix. "And all liars shall have their part in the lake which burneth with fire and brimstone: which is the second death."

Again, *I counsel you as Christian men to set yourselves against the misuse of money in political campaigns.* Of the tens of thousands of dollars already spent this autumn, how much of the amount do you suppose has been properly used? You have a right to spend money for the publishing of political tracts, for the establishment of organizations for the carrying-out of what you consider to be the best; you have a right to appeal to the reason of men by argument and statistics and by facts; but he who puts a bribe into the hand of a voter, or plies weak men with mercenary and corrupt motives, commits a sin against God and the nation. Bribery is one of the most appalling sins of this country. God says, "Fires shall consume the tabernacles of bribery." Have nothing to do with such a sin, O Christian man! Fling it from the ballot-box. Hand over to the police the man who attempts to tamper with your vote, and remember that elections that can not be carried without bribes ought never to be carried at all.

Again, *I ask you as Christian men to set yourselves against the dissipations that hover over the ballot-box.* Let me say that no man can afford to go into political life who is not a teetotaler. Hot political discussion somehow creates an unnatural thirst, and hundreds of thousands of men have gone down into drunkenness through political life. After an exciting canvass through the evening you must "take something;" and rising in the morning with less animation than usual, you must "take something;" and going off among your comrades through the forenoon, you meet political friends, and you must "take something;" and in the afternoon you meet other political friends, and you must "take something;" and before night has come something has taken you. There are but few cases where men have been able to stand up against the dissipations of political life. Joseph was a politician, but he maintained his integrity. Daniel was a politician, but he was a teetotaler to the last. Abraham was a politician, but he was always characterized as the father of the faithful. Moses was a politician, the grandest of them; but he honored God more than he did the Pharaohs. And there are hundreds of Christian men now in the political parties, maintaining their integrity, even when they are obliged to stand amidst the blasted, lecherous, and loathsome crew that sometimes surround the ballot-box; these Christian men doing their political duty, and then coming back to the prayer-meetings and Christian circles as pure as when they went out. But that is not the ordinary circumstance; that is the exception. How often you see men coming back from the political conflict, and their eye is glazed, and their cheek has an unnatural flush, and they talk louder than they usually do, and at the least provocation they will bet, and you say they are convivial, or they are exceedingly vivacious, or you apply some other sweet name to them; but God knows they are drunk! Some of you, a month or six weeks ago, had no more religion than you ought to have, and after the elections are over, to calculate how much religion you have left will be a sum in vulgar fractions. Oh, the pressure is tremendous!

How many mighty intellects have gone down under the dissipation of politics! I think of one who came from the West. He was able to stand out against the whole American Senate. God had given him faculties enough to govern a kingdom, or to frame a constitution. His voice was terrible to his country's enemies, and a mighty inspiration in the day of national peril. He was in a fair way to become our President; but twenty glasses of strong drink a day were his usual allowance, and he went down into the habits of a confirmed inebriate. Alas for him! Though a costly monument has been reared over his resting-place, and though in the presence of the laying of the corner-stone there stood military and ecclesiastical dignitaries, the young men of this country shall not be denied the awful lesson that the agency by which the world was robbed of one of its mightiest intellects, and our country of one of its ablest constitutional defenders, was the dissipation of political life. You want to know who I mean? Young man, ask your father when you get home. The adverse tide is fearful, and I warn you against it!

You need not go far off to find the worn-out politician. Here he is, stumbling along the highway, his limbs hardly able to hold him up. Bent over and pale with exhausting sickness. Surly to any body who accosts him. His last decent article of apparel pawned for strong drink. Glad if, when going by a grocery, some low acquaintance invites him in to take a sip of ale, and then wiping his lip with his greasy sleeve. Kicked off the steps by men who once were proud to be his constituents. Manhood obliterated. Lip blistered with a curse. Scars of brutal assault on cheek and brow. Foul-mouthed. A crouching, staggering, wheezing wretch. No friends. No God. No hope. No heaven. That is your worn-out politician. That is what some of you will become unless by this morning's warning, and the mercy of God, your steps are arrested. Oh, there are no words enough potent, enough portentous, enough consuming, enough damning, to describe the horrible drunkenness that has rolled over this land, and that has bent down the necks of some of the mightiest intellects, until they have been compelled to drink out of the trough of bestiality and abomination! I warn young men against political life, unless they are teetotalers and consecrated Christian men.

Again, I counsel you that, when you go to the ballot-box at the city or the State or the national elections, *you recognize God, and appeal to him for his blessing.* There is a power higher than the ballot-box, than the Gubernatorial chair, than the Presidential White House. It is high time that we put less confidence in political platforms and more confidence in God. See what a weak thing is human foresight. How little our wise men seem to know! See how, every autumn, thousands of men who are clambering up for higher positions are turned under. God upsets them. Every man, every party, every nation, has a mission to perform. Failing to perform it, down he goes.

God said to the House of Bourbon, "Remodel France, and establish equity." House of Bourbon would not do it. Down it went. God said to the House of Stuart, "Make the English people free, God-fearing, and happy." House of Stuart would not do it. Down it went. God said to the House of Hapsburg, "Rule Austria in righteousness, and open the prison-houses until the captives shall go free." House of Hapsburg refuses to do it. Down it goes. God says to the political parties in this day, "By the principles of Christianity remodel, govern, educate, save the people." Failing to do that, down they go, burying in their ruins their disciples and advocates. God can spare all the political intriguers of this day, and can raise up another generation who shall do justice and love mercy. If God could spare Luther before the Reformation was done; and if he could spare Washington before free government had been fully tested; and if he could spare Howard before more than one out of a thousand dungeons had been alleviated; and if he could spare Robert M'Cheyne just as Scotland was gathering to his burning utterances; and if he could spare Thomas Clarkson while yet millions of his fellow-men had chains rusting to the bone — then he can spare any man, and he can spare any party. That man who, through cowardice or blind idolatry of party, forsakes the cause of righteousness, goes down, and the armed battalions of God march over him.

O Christian men! take out your Bible this afternoon, and in the light of that word make up your mind as to what is your duty as citizens. Remember that the highest kind of a patriot is a Christian patriot. Consecrate yourselves first to God, then you will know how to consecrate yourselves to your country. All these political excitements will be gone. Ballot-boxes and Gubernatorial chairs and continents will smoke in the final conflagration; but those who love God and do their best shall come to lustrous dominion after the stars have ceased their shining, and the ocean has heaved its last billow, and the closing thunder of the judgment-day shall toll at the funeral of a world! Oh, prepare for that day! Next Tuesday questions of the State will be settled; but there comes a day when the questions of eternity will be decided. You may vote right, and may get the victory at the ballot-box, and yet suffer eternal defeat. After you have cast your last vote, where will you go to? In this country there are two parties. You belong to the one or the other of them. Likewise in eternity there will be two parties, and only two. " These shall go away into everlasting punishment; but the righteous into life eternal." To which party will you belong? God grant that, while you look after the welfare of the land in which God has graciously cast your lot, you may not forget to look after your soul — blood-bought, judgment-bound, immortal! God save the people!

THE OVERFLOWING CUP.

"My cup runneth over."—*Psalm* xxiii., 5.

EVERY few years we have people critical of the Thanksgiving proclamation. They say, "We have nothing to be thankful for. Commerce down; manufactures dull; commercial prospects blasted. Better have a day for fasting than a day for feasting." Indeed, have you nothing to be thankful for? Does your heart beat? Do your eyes see? Do your ears hear? Did you breakfast this morning? Did you sleep last night? Are the glorious heavens above your head? Is the solid earth beneath your feet? Have you a Bible, a Christ, a proffered heaven? Ay, those of us who are the worst off have more blessings than we appreciate, and "our cup runneth over."

There is a table spread to-day across the top of the two great ranges of mountains which ridge this continent—a table which reaches from the Atlantic to the Pacific seas. It is the Thanksgiving-table of the nation. They come from the East and the West and the North and the South, and sit at it. On it are smoking the products of all lands, birds of every aviary, cattle from every pasture, fish from every lake, feathered spoils from every farm. The fruit-baskets bend down under the products plucked from the peach-fields of New Jersey, the apple-orchards of Western New York, the orange-groves of Florida, the vineyards of Ohio, and the nuts threshed from New England woods.

The bread is white from the wheat-fields of Illinois and Michigan, the banqueters are adorned with California gold, and the table is agleam with Nevada silver, and the feast is warmed with the fire-grates heaped up with Pennsylvania coal. The hall is spread with carpets from Lowell mills, and to-night the lights will flash from bronzed brackets of Philadelphia manufacture. The fingers of Massachusetts girls have hung the embroidery; the music is the drumming of ten thousand mills, accompanied by the shout of children let loose for play, and the gladness of harvesters driving barnward the loads of sheaves, and the thanksgivings of the nation which crowd the celestial gates with doxologies, until the oldest harper of heaven can not tell where the terrestrial song ends and the celestial song begins.

Welcome, Thanksgiving-day! Whatever we may think of New England theology, we all like New England Thanksgiving-day. What meant the rush last night to the dépôts, and the long rail trains darting their lanterns along the tracks of the Stonington and Providence, Boston and Lowell, New Haven and Springfield, Plymouth and South Braintree railroads? Ask the happy group in the New England farm-house. Ask the rustics in the cabin among the Green Mountains. Ask the New England villagers whose song of praise this morning comes over the Berkshire hills. Oh, it is a great day of national festivity! Clap your hands, ye people, and shout aloud for joy! Through the organ-pipes let there come down the thunder of a nation's rejoicing. Blow the cornet! Wave the palm branches! Oh that men would praise the Lord for his goodness, and for his wonderful works to the children of men! "My cup runneth over!"

I propose to speak to you this morning about thanksgiving in the house, thanksgiving in the hovels of the poor, thanksgiving in the church, thanksgiving in the city, thanksgiving in the nation.

Without stopping to ring your door-bell, I come into your house, and I look around and see what God has been doing for you during the past year. You say, "Come in. I am very glad to see you. Sit down in this arm-chair or on this sofa, and make yourself at home." No, my friends, I can not stop. I just want to look around, and see what God has been doing for you in your home. "Oh," you say, "our house is not so large now as the one we used to have." I answer, What of that? It is a great deal of trouble to keep a large house clean. Besides that, a small house is cozy. Besides that, it is a bad thing for children to have a luxuriant starting, for when they get out in the world and are married, then they begin to talk about the way they used to have it, and say, "I haven't been accustomed to such cramped-up apartments." Bless God if you have a real snug, cozy home. But I step into your parlor, and I find there the evidences of refinement and culture and friendship. The sofas and chairs are not always empty. Sympathizing friends sit here when you have trouble. Mirthful friends sit here when you are in good cheer. This chandelier will flash down upon social gatherings, and upon Christmas-tree, and upon merry-making. These keys have often been thrummed by your children, and there is in the port-folio on the music-rack many a well-worn song of "Old Oaken Bucket" and "Old Arm-chair;" and while your grandfathers entertained their guests under rough-hewn rafters and on bare floors, you have a parlor in which are the evidences of painter's pencil and engraver's knife and sculptor's chisel, and I stand in the midst of all this refinement and elegance of your parlor and demand your thanksgiving unto the Lord.

I go on to the next room, and step into your nursery, and I am greeted with the shout and laughter of your children. They romp; they hide; they clap their hands. I get down on the floor and play with them. What bright eyes! What merry hearts! What swift feet! God bless them! Their little troubles dissolve in a tear. Their little enmities are gone after a minute's pouting. Busy all day, without fatigues, they fall asleep chattering, and wake up singing. And the little baby has its realm, waving its sceptre over the parental heart, and you look down in its wondering eyes and see whole worlds of promise there, and think to yourself, "Those little hands will smooth my locks when they get gray, and those little feet will run for me when I am sick, and those eyes will weep for me when I am gone." Oh, hush him to sleep with a holy song! Let him know the name of Jesus long before he can pronounce it. Thank God to-day that upon your home has come the brightness of childhood, and drop a tear of grief for those who weep over a despoiled cradle, and toys that never will be caught up again by little hands now still, alas, forever!

I step from this room into the dining-hall. You have not invited me to dine with you; but I come right in without invitation, and sit down at your table to-day. I do not see any signs of starving around here, although you talk so much about hard times. Besides that, it seems to me you have all the world waiting upon you. The cabinet-makers have prepared with great toil the furniture; the farmers worried themselves almost to death in raising the wheat from which this bread was made; the sailor was lashed to the mast to bring you those foreign luxuries; whole herds and flocks, at different times, have fallen under the knife of the butcher to please your palate; the miners toiled in damp and darkness to get the coal that warms your dining-room to-day. Summer sun and driving snow and howling tempest have sent their contributions to your table to-day. None of your children are crying for bread in vain. The barrel of meal has not wasted; the cruse of oil has not failed. Bread enough and to spare, while many have perished with hunger. Oh, do not, to-day, draw your knife across the sharpening steel until you have sent up one word of thanksgiving to the Lord who has given you all these mercies! And if you are not accustomed to asking a blessing at the table, I think this day will be a good one in which to begin, and if you can not think of any thing else to say, then take the words of my text, "My cup runneth over!"

I step out from the dining-hall into your library, and see your table covered with books and magazines and newspapers fresh from the publishing houses. It seems to me really as if the historians, and the fabulists, and the pamphleteers, and the philosophers of the world were waiting your bidding. Here, on this historic shelf of your library, you have Bancroft and Prescott and Macaulay to tell you the rude story of early America, or describe the wonders of Mexican scenery, or call back the eloquence of the old Parliaments that death long ago dissolved with more than the imperiousness of Cromwell. And here is your poetic shelf, on which stand Dr. Young with his weeping harp, and Walter Scott sounding the Highland bagpipe, and Longfellow ringing out the war-whoop through "Hiawatha," and William Cullen Bryant mingling the moan of the wild woods with the call of the brown thresher. And here is the shelf that Dickens has all to himself, from "Oliver Twist" to "Edwin Drood," avenging the world's sorrows, weeping the world's sins, exposing the world's hypocrisies, winning the world's applause. What a pity that, by high living, he went away so soon! Moan out the grief, O bells of Westminster. Thank God for books—plenty of them—books to make you study, books to waft you into reverie, books to make you weep, books to make you laugh, books in cloth, books in morocco, in satin, in gold; books of travel, of anecdote, of memoir, of legend; books scrolled and starred and wreathed and columned; books about insects, about birds, about shells, about every thing; books for the young, books for the old. "Oh," says some one, "I have not all these luxuries; I have not all these comforts of the parlor, of the nursery, of the dining-hall, of the library." But, my brother, most certainly you know something of the height and depth and length and breadth of that sweet, tender, joyous, triumphant word, *home!* Do not look at it as a place merely to stay in, as the lion looks at his lair, or the fox his burrow, or the eagle his eyric. Do not call it your apartments, or your lodgings, or your domicile, but—by all the memory of those who are gone; by the memory of the old people, whether here or there; for the sake of childhood; for the sake of all that is good, and pure, and true, and blessed—call it *home.* Gather your families together to-day! If you have a musical instrument, open it; if you have not, open your heart—the best of all musical instruments—and while the Lord listens, and the memory of the past rushes through your soul, "Oh, give thanks unto the Lord; for he is good; for his mercy endureth forever;" and let each one clap his hands, and say for himself, "My cup runneth over!"

I pass on now to look at Thanksgiving in the hovels of the poor. No banquet smoking on their table. It is a sad thing to see a poor man, the evening before Thanksgiving, looking into a full grocery-window, while he thinks of his destitute home. It is hard to be hungry in a world with ripe orchards and luxuriant harvests and herds of cattle driven to the slaughtering! It is hard to be cold in a world where the forests are waiting for the axe-man and the mines are waiting for the miners. It is a hard thing to be unclad in a world where there are so many swift cylinders in motion, so many manufactories of goods, and where the fox, and the beaver, and the Arctic bear, and the Siberian squirrel are dying in order that men may have their furs. To-day do not stuff yourself to surfeiting without thinking of those who are gaunt with hunger; do not put your feet up by the warm register without thinking, at least once, of those whose last scuttle of coal is gone. When, to-night, you turn on the gas full head, and it glitters along the wall in bubbles of fire, do not forget to think of those whose last candle has hissed in the socket. If you have nothing better than an old jacket, or a worn-out pair of shoes, or a coat that has been patched until it has become "a coat of many colors," give something this day to the poor. There are two things that I should like to have my Lord Jesus Christ say to me in the last day: "I was hungry, and ye fed me." "I was naked, and ye clothed me." God help the poor!

But I pass on now, and look at Thanksgiving in the church. Last Thanksgiving we were churchless. We had

a wall partly up, a pile of bricks, a heap of lumber. That
was about our position. It was a doleful day to me. I
wandered about with my coat-collar up, and rubbing my
frost-bitten right ear, and there was not, in all the day, any
thing that looked like Thanksgiving save the dinner, and
that was not so good as usual. We felt like the Israelites
in captivity, and would, like them, have hung our harps
on the willows, but for the reason our organ was burned
up, and we had no harp, and no willows to hang it on.
But where are we to-day? Is this our roof? Are these
our altars? Is this our spiritual home? How goodly are
thy tents, O Jacob! "Walk about Zion, and go round
about her: tell the towers thereof. Mark ye well her bul-
warks, consider her palaces; that ye may tell it to the gen-
eration following. For this God is our God for ever and
ever; he will be our guide even unto death." With organ,
with cornet, with multitudinous shout of great congrega-
tion, express this day your praise to God, "Our cup run-
neth over." But better than all material structure is the
spiritual blessing that descended, and the multitude of souls
who, during these nine months, have stood up at this altar,
connecting themselves with our membership—the blessing
still hovering—and at every service immortal souls saved.
"Bless the Lord, O my soul!" I know there are those
who think the Church is a museum of antediluvian fossils.
They think it did very well once, but it is behind the times.
That is not your opinion. You love, first, your home, and
next, your church. O ye descendants of the men who were
hounded amidst the Highlands of Scotland, and who fell
at Bothwell Bridge! O ye sons and daughters of the men
who came across wintry seas to build their log churches in
the American wilderness! O ye sons and daughters of

those who stood in the awful siege of Leyden, and shouted the martyr's triumph in the horrors of the Brussels marketplace! O ye descendants of the men whose garments were dyed in the wine-press of Saint Bartholomew Massacre! ye sons and daughters of the fire! what do you think, to-day, of a quiet church, and a free pulpit, and a Gospel winged with mercy and salvation? What imperial edict forbids our convocation? What sword thirsts for our blood? What fires are kindled for our torture? None. Defended by the law, invited by the Gospel, baptized by the Spirit, we are here to-day free men of the State, free men of God. Glorious Church! "Twelve wells of water, and three-score-and-ten palm-trees." "My cup runneth over." Oh, this day bring the richest Thanksgiving garland, and put it upon the brow of Him who bought the Church, died for your sins, and prepared for you a grand and glorious inheritance. Thanks be unto God for the unspeakable gift of a Saviour.

But I pass on and consider Thanksgiving in the city. It is five years since I came to live in this city. I have seen many cities on both sides the sea, but I have never seen any I like quite so well as this. What quiet Sabbaths! What large and beautiful churches! What costly and magnificent Mercantile Library! What a glory our Academy of Music! What institutions of learning—Packer, the Polytechnic, the Adelphi, and our glorious common schools with the Bible in them! Our long lines of streets, beautifully shaded. Our Park, with its arborescent drives, and its affluence of flowers, and its sculptured bridges, and its exquisite lake. Prospered city. Our Mayor honorable. Our judges just. Our police efficient. Beautiful Brooklyn. Blessed forever be her great population! When we get the bridge done, we will go over and make New York just like it. But, after all, I think New York is as moral a city as there is under the sun, considering the number of its population. We are one city, after all, on both sides of the East River. There are a great many people who think that the worst city on earth is the combined city of New York and Brooklyn; and I do not know but that some people, from the exaggeration in regard to it, may land at the foot of Cortlandt Street, and rush up to the Hudson River Railroad Dépôt, telling the hackman all the way to whip up the horses, lest some scourge come upon them before they get through the town. I do not know but that some countrymen coming to our city, from the stories that have been told about us, may keep looking over both shoulders lest they be garroted somewhere between Fulton Ferry and the City Hall. I think the politicians are responsible for that exaggerated statement of the way things are in this city. I really think it is a grand city, a beautiful city, to live in. Under different administrations of politics it is. We have tried all kinds—the one, perhaps, as good as the other; the chief difference between the two parties, I have found out, being that that one steals most which has the longest opportunity to steal, the change of administration often being the relief which a man gets when he changes from rheumatism to neuralgia! Still, notwithstanding all these things, I think this a fair city to live in; I do not think there is a better city under the sun. Thank God you live here, and that you can to-day boast, as Paul did, that you are the inhabitant of no mean city.

I pass on once more to look at Thanksgiving in the nation. Peace all through the land. The Indians quiet in the plains. No foreign guns coming up through the "Narrows." Insurrection in New Orleans conquered by a revolution at the ballot-box. The South at last satisfied that the wrongs of the last six years will be righted. No American slavery to fight about. By a revolution in national politics, both political parties put upon their good behavior; that party which does the most for the people in the next year and a half winning the Presidential chair and the national supremacy. In our own State and in our own time we have had a wonderful thing occur in this very month, when the question was who should be Governor, as between two men, both of them honorable and Christian men—a good man going out and a good man coming in. John A. Dix followed by Samuel J. Tilden. So also with our financial prospects, they are all brightening.

We have all been compelled to economize; and you well know that economy is the primordial element in national prosperity. If a man should make ten thousand dollars a year and spend eleven thousand dollars, he is not so well off as the man who makes one thousand dollars a year and spends nine hundred dollars. That process of economy going on all through the land has been a healthy process, and we shall feel the good results of it after a while. Superfluous railroads have ceased building; commercial balloons have lost their gas. We have almost a certain prospect of a speedy resumption of specie payments; and the day will soon come when a dollar will mean a dollar, and not something else. The ragged currency will be ended. We have wandered about, supposing we had our pockets full of money, when they turned out to be only the *cartes-de-visite* of some celebrated member of the Cabinet; Mr. Spinner, in awful chirography at the bottom of the bill, certifying that it was a good picture of Hugh M'Culloch or Mr. Boutwell.

Now, all these things are brightening prospects. "Oh," say some, "we never can get out of this financial depression." Why, my brethren, men of business, we have had dark days before this. In 1857 there were four thousand two hundred and fifty-seven failures, to the amount of two hundred and sixty-five million eight hundred and eighteen thousand dollars. People said, "We'll never get out of it." Yet in two years there was not a vestige left of that great commercial disaster. The wheels flew and the feet of American enterprise tramped on, and we soon got over it. Then came the dark days of 1861, when there were five thousand nine hundred and thirty-five business failures, amounting to one hundred and seventy-eight million six hundred and thirty-two thousand one hundred and seventy dollars. Then people threw up their hands, and said, "We shall never get over this." And yet the largest fortunes of the country have been made since then, and our national prosperity has increased beyond the capacity of any arithmetic to state it. If God brought us out of the trouble of 1857 and out of the misfortunes of 1861, is he not strong enough to bring us out of the troubles of 1874? He will. He will. I believe the prosperities that are yet to come will soon put out of sight all our past national accumulations. Our national debt is rapidly dwindling. Added to all, the fact that we have one hundred and sixty-two thousand square miles of coal, and another one hundred and sixty-two thousand square miles of iron, it seems to me that the metals of the earth are to-day, as with the golden lips of California and the silver tongue of Nevada, promising the fact that there shall be no end to our national resources.

But look at the harvests. I do not suppose that for

more than three or four times within the memory of any body here there have been such harvests as we have had this year. The grain-fields have passed their harvests above the veto of drought and deluge. The freight cars are not large enough to bring down the grain to the seaboard. The canal-boats are crowded with bread-stuffs. Hark to the rushing of the wheat through the great Chicago corn "elevators." Hark to the rolling of the hogsheads of the Cincinnati pork-packers! Enough to eat, and at cheap prices. Enough to wear, and of home manufacture. If some have and some have not, then may God help those who have to hand over something to those who have not! Clear the track for the rail trains that come down, bringing the wheat, and the barley, and the oats, and the hops, and the lumber, and the leather, and every thing for man and every thing for beast.

I can not, I dare not, detain you any longer from the home group. The housekeepers will be angry with me if I keep you until the viands are cold. Set the chairs to the table—the easy-chairs for grandfather and grandmother, if they be still alive; the high chair for the youngest and the least. Then put out your hand to take the full cup of thanksgiving; bring it toward your lips, your hands trembling with emotion; and if the chalice shall spill on the cloth, do not be chagrined, but look up thankfully to heaven, and say, "My cup runneth over!"

THE WRECK OF THE "SCHILLER."

"They ran the ship aground; and the forepart stuck fast, and remained unmovable, but the hinder part was broken with the violence of the waves."
—*Acts* xxvii., 41.

CAUGHT in a typhoon! Before yet the chronometer was invented, a vessel is cracking to pieces on the coast of a Mediterranean island. The cargo of corn is spoiled, and, worse than that, two hundred and seventy-six passengers are beside themselves with terror. At the first bump of the ship, every thing was in consternation. She went on, bow first, and the waves cried, "Come, let us tear this old hulk to pieces!" The sea beat against the stern, and dashed the spray clear over the deck, crowded with affrighted passengers. Rudder, yards, mast, bulwark, knocked away. Every thing going to demolition. "They ran the ship aground; and the forepart stuck fast, and remained unmovable, but the hinder part was broken with the violence of the waves."

There are some points of striking analogy between that wreck and the one which stunned our ears a few days ago. Both vessels carried freight and passengers. Both were crowded with people—the one with two hundred and seventy-six on board, the other with three hundred and eighty-five on board. Both were caught in the grip of a tempest. From both the sailors tried to escape in small boats, giving no chance to the passengers. Both lost their reckoning. Both went aground in the night.

The *Schiller* started from our port on the 28th of April, bound for Plymouth, England, and Hamburg, Germany. It was the popular season for transatlantic voyage, and the people went on the ship: invalids in search of health, pleasurists expecting merriment in foreign capitals, merchants on commercial errand, artists bound for the picture-galleries of Dresden and Florence, adopted citizens going back to visit the land of their nativity and the graves of their fathers. They had gone three thousand miles of voyage successfully, and expected on the morrow to wake up in the calm English harbor. Some of them were sleeping, and dreaming of home, of wife, of child, and others of mountains and cities beyond the sea. A dense mist comes upon the ocean. The storm hallooes amidst the rigging. Yet all seems safe. Two men on the lookout. Two men at the wheel. Two men pacing the captain's bridge. Yet all the time making for the rocks. Oh, stop her before she strikes! One turn of the wheel will save the ship. The howl of the storm drowns the tolling of the fog-bell in Bishop Rock Light-house. Still on and on, until, without a moment in which to give warning, or wake up the passengers from their berths, or swing the small boats from their davits, that vessel of three thousand six hundred tons burden strikes the rock, once, twice, three times, four times, and goes down! Between the first plunge and the last the rockets are flung, and the guns are sounded, and a few passengers clamber up in the rigging; but there is no safe retreat there, for soon the mast, with its cluster of precious human life tangled in the cordage, begins to bend and reel in the gale, and then cracks, and with awful plunge dashes into the sea. Meanwhile the captain makes a brave attempt with loaded and firing pistol to keep the life-boats for the passengers. He gathers some of them up on his bridge; but, after having done all he could for the saving of the people on the ship, he wraps himself in a winding-sheet of surf, and lies down beside them in that great democracy of sepulture. Beautiful women and swarthy men and sweet children, side by side, are dead. There she lies, the *Schiller*, under a mound of blue seas, the jutting reef the tombstone, buried in the place where lie the skeletons of the *Thames* steamer, and the *Duro*, and the English *Admiral*, waiting for the day when the sea shall give up its dead. Let the waves tramp up the sad beach in solemn procession, and two continents uncover the brow over this burial of the *Schiller* with three hundred and forty-two passengers, without any warning gone out to meet their God.

Let us learn, first, from this disaster what a *sad thing it is for people to lose their reckoning*. Captain Thomas, through the report from the log-book, which recorded the distances and courses sailed, judged that he was at least two miles off from the Scilly rocks; but he did not really know where he was. He mistook, and that mistake flung hundreds of souls into the eternal world, and the whole civilized world into mourning. So there are those here to-day who have lost their reckoning. They know not where they are. They say, "So many miles have I voyaged since I was launched on the ocean of life, and so many miles more will I voyage before I get to the coast of eternity." Part of their calculation is right, and part of their calculation is wrong, and they have lost their reckoning. They know not how they stand toward God or their Bible, or their duty or heaven. They are sailing on thoughtlessly, when they may be within two minutes of the reef. Alas that men should make a mistake for eternity! now running on one rock, now running on the other rock; and, with the quadrant of God's Word in their hand, by which they might have calculated the latitude, in an evil hour, their watchfulness asleep in the cabin, like the corn ship of the text, or the *Schiller* of last week, going aground, one shivering horror. Oh, slow your engines! Throw out your bower anchor! Stop stock-still until you find out where you are —near what reef, by what coast, on the verge of what shipwreck! There is only one channel leading into the celestial harbor, and that is not a wide channel. "Narrow is the way which leadeth unto life, and few there be that find it." God forbid that any one of us should lose our reckoning.

Again, I see in this disaster *what a dense fog can do.* This calamity was only half a mile from Bishop Rock Lighthouse. It is a granite structure, one hundred and forty-seven feet high, and has one of the best and brightest dioptric lights, a multiplication of refracted rays. When the sun sets, the keeper strikes that light, and it blazes all through the darkness, and in ordinary weather throws out its glow fourteen miles upon the sea. "Well," you say, "there might have been some excuse for a vessel going on those rocks in Queen Anne's time, as the vessels did under the brave Sir Cloudsley Shovel, when nine ships of the line broke to pieces, and two thousand soldiers perished, for then there were no lights on the rock. But how was it possible," says one not conversant with all the circumstances, "that a steamer should have been ruined there within half a mile of Bishop Rock Light-house?" Oh, there was a fog on the sea. Captain Thomas, and First-officer Hillers, and Second-officer Pollman could not see a quarter of the length of that steamer, and if there had been fifty light-houses on the rock they would not have done any good.

Here I get a hint of the way men lose their souls, driving into ruin; for there are scores of men in this day, and institutions, whose whole business seems to be to create a great spiritual fog. Men and women do not go on to death a-purpose; it is because they are cheated, they are deceived, they are mystified, they are befogged. We have in this day the Herbert Spencer fog about life, which, he says, is "the combination of heterogeneous changes, both simultaneous and successive, in correspondences with external co-existences and sequences!" We have the Huxley fog about protoplasm. We have the Darwinian fog about the anthropomorphous origin of our race, and our dear old grandfathers, the gorilla and the chimpanzee. The fog of Materialism, the fog of Pantheism, the fog of Rationalism, the fog that Strauss and Shenkel and Renan have thrown all around the head of Christ. Any thing but believe that God, by his power, made the worlds, and that the Bible is plenarily inspired, and that Christ is the omnipotent Son of God come to save sinners. There is one funeral that these wiseacres would like to attend, and be both pall-bearers and grave-diggers, and that is the decease and burial of the Lord God Almighty. They do not think the universe is large enough for Him and them, and so they are trying to crowd Him back, and crowd Him off the precipices of the universe, and, in trying to do so, they create a great spiritual fog, and the hundreds who went down on the *Schiller* were as nothing compared with the thousands and the hundreds of thousands who, in this great philosophical vaporing, have been wrecked suddenly and forever. One hour after the vessel spoken of struck in the English Channel, the fog lifted, and the survivors saw Bishop Rock Lighthouse; and I would that to-day a fresh gale from heaven might sweep earth and sky of all philosophical obscurations, and that the dioptric light of God's Word might flash its illumination across all kingdoms. Oh, come out of the speculative fog, man! Take the Bible for all you ought to know and can know. Come out of the darkness, and sit in the sunlight of our glorious Christianity. Stop your religious guessing. When in this day I see people all around me drenched and soaked and floundering in the dense mist of modern skepticism, I am put more in love than ever before with the comfortable religion of the Lord Jesus Christ. Oh that these wiseacres would come and sit down for half an hour, and study and absorb the three first questions and answers of Brown's "Shorter Catechism,"— which some of us learned at four years of age!—"Who made you? God. Who redeemed you? Christ. Who sanctified you? The Holy Ghost." May the Sun of righteousness scatter the fog.

Again, in the recent disaster I find an *illustration of what is vicarious sacrifice*. Captain Thomas might have got off to the land safely, in all probability. There were two small boats that reached the shore. Why did he not take one of them at the very beginning of the disaster? Why did he not take some buoyant part of the ship and float to a place of safety? He might have said, "No man can reimburse me for the loss of my life. This is a time when every man must look out for himself." No. He staid there amidst the hurricane, pistol in hand, determined that the women and the children should get into those lifeboats, and no one else. And I hear the crack, crack, of the fire-arms, and I hear him crying out, "Stand back now, and let the passengers be saved! Stand back!" And then I see him gathering some of the sufferers on his bridge, and then I see him going down for still another errand in their behalf, when a wild surge sweeps him off into the merciless Atlantic. All the survivors agree in stating that a brave man perished that night. Come, ye who do not know what the pulpits mean when they talk about vicarious sacrifice. It means one dying for others. It means Captain Thomas dying for the survivors of the *Schiller*. It means the Lord Jesus Christ dying for you and me. Christ knew that we must go down without His interposition. He might have gone safely back to heaven, saying, "I have done enough for that race. I can not afford to die on that wretched cross;" and the angels of God would have taken him by the arms and lifted him into the sky. But no. There he stands in the midnight hurricane of God's wrath against sin, looking off upon our foundering souls, and he launches the life-boat, and tells us to be off for the shore, while he expires. Christ sinking, that we might rise; Christ dying, that we might live. For the first ten million years heaven will not get through talking about it. And yet—amazing fact!—we will not get into the life-boat, though it has come; and we see the oars pulling away, taking from us our last chance, and we will not leap into it. The tears and the sufferings and the dying anguish of the Son of God, so far as we are concerned, a dead failure; and, instead of pleading for us at the last, because of our outrage thereof, demanding our complete and eternal overthrow! It is marvelous that Jesus died. There is only one marvel that comes anywhere near equaling it, and that is our rejection of his mercy. Oh that, this morning, God's Spirit would show the people of this audience how thorough is the ruin of a man who will not have Christ!

The present Eddystone Light-house stands very firmly, but that was not the character of the first structure that stood on that dangerous point. There was an eccentric man by the name of Henry Winstanley, who built a very fantastic light-house at that point in 1696; and, when it was nearly done, he felt so confident that it was strong, that he expressed the wish that he might be in it in the roughest hurricane that ever blew in the face of heaven. And he got his wish. One November night, in 1703, he and his workmen were in that light-house, when there came down the most raging tempest that had ever been known in that region. On the following morning the people came down to see about the light-house. Not a vestige of the wall, not a vestige of the men. Only two twisted iron bolts, showing where the light-house had stood. So there are men building up their fantastic hopes, and plans, and enterprises, and expectations, thinking they will stand forever, saying, "We don't want any of the defenses of the Gospel. We can stand for ourselves. We are not afraid. We take all the risks, and we defy every thing;" and suddenly the Lord blows upon them, and they are gone. Only two things left—a grave and a lost soul.

But I learn, also, from this sad providence *how near people can come to a happy destination, and yet not reach it.* They expected next day to be in Plymouth harbor. Only a few more pacings of the deck by the captain, and then the four blades of the screw would cease their revolutions, and the steamer would stop. Almost in, and yet those people did not live to see Plymouth harbor. They landed at the bottom of the sea. So men sometimes come very near the harbor of God's mercy, but do not quite get into it. They expected to land; we expected they would land; but they strike on some fatal hinderance, and perish. Last Sabbath there were in this house persons who were almost Christians who never will be fully Christians. They got along just so far, and then some violent jerk of resolution stopped them. They thought religion would not be dignified to them, or they thought that it might disorganize their worldly business, or they thought they might compromise their reputation among some of their friends, or they thought they had got on so far toward the religious hope that they were saved. No, no. Remember the *Schiller!* Paul saw two boats, and one was called *Altogether*, and the other was called *Almost*, and he saw the *Altogether* go into port, flags flying, and he saw the *Almost* founder at sea. Not quite a Christian, is to be no Christian at all. To lift one's hand toward Christ, and yet not to take hold of him, is to be a castaway. Some of you, some time ago, wept over sin. I saw anxiety on some of your countenances. Your lips moved as if in prayer. I thought you were going to be saved. I have changed my mind. You disastrously stopped. You struck a reef. Remember the *Schiller!*

Again, I learn that *when our time is up we have to go.* Those people were sure of a safe arrival. Every thing promised it. They were in as stout an iron steamer as ever goes across the Atlantic. It had seven water-tight compartments. There were eight small boats on the side. They had a skillful and long-experienced commander. Yet the Lord decided that between ten o'clock at night and five o'clock in the morning three hundred and forty-two souls should pass out of life, and he executed that decision. And so the time of our exit out of this life is appointed. You can not tell mine, nor I yours. The whole thing is uncertain, and I am glad it is. If we knew the year and the day when we were to leave this life, we would be disqualified for work, and we would be saying, "Now we have another year less to live, and another week less to live, and another day less to live," and we would be nervous and morbid, and a nuisance to ourselves and to others. But while it is uncertain to us, it is not uncertain to God. He has appointed the time. The utmost prudence on our part can not avert it. When that moment comes, we may be on the land, we may be on the sea; but a message from the next world will be put into our hand, and though nobody else can see it, we will see it, and read it, and respond to it, and tramp away. The call will be so inexorable that we must be off. And yet we act as though we had an infallible life-belt that would hold us up in any wave. We act as if we were more invulnerable than Achilles, even the heel encased. We do not realize that our final moment is coming toward us as straight as a bird ever flies. We feel cool and unconcerned and indifferent, as though we had a thousand years to live on earth, and the nine hundred and ninety-ninth would be as favorable for this work as any of its predecessors. Meanwhile, our comrades and best friends are dropping around us like slacked lime — every afternoon, between two and five o'clock, the processions going toward the cemeteries, and we not realizing that we will, after a while, be silent leaders in some such procession. So near eternity, and yet no fittedness. Startling warnings passing out of mind. The shriek of the *Schiller*, like that of the *Arctic* and the *Atlantic* and the *Ville du Havre*, forgotten. The trouble is, we do not realize that the very poorest hour in which to equip ourselves for eternity is the last hour. Of all the thousands and thousands of hours in our whole life, there is not one so poorly fitted for this work as the closing hour; and yet we choose the poorest out of all for this preparation. What chance had those people to pray on that vessel, awakened suddenly out of sleep, the waves of the ocean dashing through the gaping sides of the steamer? Some of them, indeed, got a few moments by clambering up into the rigging; but, alas if they put off the work of the soul's salvation till that moment when, in undress, they swung in the ratlines on the careening ship until the smoke-stack fell, and the foremast fell, and the mainmast fell, and there was a plash, and a gurgle, and all was over! How much better, my brother, it would be for you to prepare now for that eternity which may any moment break in upon you as suddenly as it did upon them! Unless your heart is radically changed by the grace of God, and Christ is your personal Saviour, the plunge of the *Schiller* in the English Channel was only a feeble type of the deeper going-down of your immortal spirit. Why not now repent and believe, and pray and live? This disaster demands your arousal. Wake before it be too late. Remember the *Schiller!*

EXASPERATING COMFORTERS.

"Miserable comforters are ye all."—*Job* xvi., 2.

THE man of Uz had a great many trials; the loss of his family, the loss of his property, the loss of his health; but the most exasperating thing that came upon him was the tantalizing talk of those who ought to have sympathized with him. And looking around upon them, and weighing what they had said, he utters the words of my text.

Why did God let sin come into the world? It is a question I often hear discussed, but never satisfactorily answered. God made the world fair and beautiful at the start. If our first parents had not sinned in Eden, they might have gone out of that garden, and found fifty paradises all around the earth — Europe, Asia, Africa, North and South America—so many flower-gardens or orchards of fruit, redolent and luscious. I suppose that when God poured out the Gihon and the Hiddekel, he poured out, at the same time, the Hudson and the Susquehanna; the whole earth was very fair and beautiful to look upon. Why did it not stay so? God had the power to keep back sin and woe. Why did he not keep them back? Why not every cloud roseate, and every step a joy, and every sound music, and all the ages a long jubilee of sinless men and sinless women? God can make a rose as easily as he can make a thorn. Why, then, the predominance of thorns? He can make good, fair, ripe fruit as well as gnarled and sour fruit. Why so much, then, that is gnarled and sour? He can make men robust in health. Why, then, are there so many invalids? Why not have for our whole race perpetual leisure, instead of this tug and toil and tussle for a livelihood? I will tell you why God let sin come into the world—when I get on the other side of the River of Death. That is the place where such questions will be answered and such mysteries solved. He who this side that river attempts to answer the question, only illustrates his own ignorance and incompetency. All I know is one great fact, and that is, that a herd of woes have come in upon us, trampling down every thing fair and beautiful. A sword at the gate of Eden, and a sword at every gate. More people under the ground than on it. The grave-yards in vast majority. The six thousand winters have made more scars than the six thousand summers can cover up. Trouble has taken the tender heart of this world in its two rough hands, and pinched it until the nations wail with the agony. If all the mounds of grave-yards that have been lifted were put side by side, you might step on them and on nothing else, going all around the world, and around again, and around again. These are the facts. And now I have to say that, in a world like this, the grandest occupation is that of giving condolence. This holy science of imparting comfort to the troubled we ought all of us to study. There are many of you who could look around upon some of your very best friends who wish you well and are very intelligent, and yet be able truthfully to say to them in your days of trouble, "Miserable comforters are ye all."

I remark, in the first place, that *very voluble people are incompetent for the work of giving comfort.* Bildad and Eliphaz had the gift of language, and with their words almost bothered Job's life out. Alas for these voluble people that go among the houses of the afflicted and talk, and talk, and talk, and talk! They rehearse their own sorrows, and then they tell the poor sufferers that they feel badly now, but they will feel worse after a while. Silence! Do you expect, with a thin court-plaster of words, to heal a wound deep as the soul? Step very gently around about a broken heart. Talk very softly around those whom God has bereft. Then go your way. Deep sympathy has not much to say. A firm grasp of the hand, a compassionate look, just one word that means as much as a whole dictionary, and you have given, perhaps, all the comfort that a soul needs. A man has a terrible wound in his arm. The surgeon comes and binds it up. "Now," he says, "carry that arm in a sling, and be very careful of it. Let no one touch it." But the neighbors have heard of the accident, and they come in, and they say, "Let us see it." And the bandage is pulled off, and this one and that one must feel it, and see how much it is swollen; and there is irritation, and inflammation, and exasperation, where there ought to be healing and cooling. The surgeon comes in, and says, "What does all this mean? You have no business to touch those bandages. That wound will never heal unless you let it alone." So there are souls broken down in sorrow. What they most want is rest, or very careful and gentle treatment; but the neighbors have heard of the bereavement or of the loss, and they come in to sympathize, and they say, "Show us now the wound. What were his last words? Rehearse now the whole scene. How did you feel when you found you were an orphan?" Tearing off the bandages here, and pulling them off there, leaving a ghastly wound that the balm of God's grace had already begun to heal. Oh, let no loquacious people, with ever-rattling tongues, go into the homes of the distressed!

Again I remark, that all those persons are incompetent to give any kind of comfort who act merely as *worldly philosophers*. They come in and say, "Why, this is what you ought to have expected. The laws of nature must have their way;" and then they get eloquent over something they have seen in *post-mortem* examinations. Now, away with all human philosophy at such a time! What difference does it make to that father and mother what disease their son died of? He is dead, and it makes no difference whether the trouble was in the epigastric or hypogastric region. If the philosopher be of the stoical school he will come and say, "You ought to control your feelings. You must not cry so. You must cultivate a cooler temperament. You must have self-reliance, self-government, self-control;" an iceberg reproving a hyacinth for having a drop of dew in its eye. A violinist has his instrument, and he sweeps his fingers across the strings, now evoking strains of joy, and now strains of sadness. He can not play all the tunes on one string. The human soul is an instrument of a thousand strings, and all sorts of emotions were made to play on it. Now an anthem, now a dirge. It is no evidence of weakness when one is overcome of sorrow. Edmund Burke was found in the pasture-field with his arms around a horse's neck, caressing him, and some one said, "Why, the great man has lost his mind!" No; that horse belonged to his son who had recently died, and his great heart broke over the grief. It is no sign of weakness that men are overcome of their sorrows. Thank God for the relief of tears. Have you never been in trouble when you could not weep, and you would have given any thing for a good cry? David did well when he mourned for Absalom, Abraham did well when he bemoaned Sarah, Christ did well when he wept for Lazarus; and the last man that I want to see come anywhere near me when I have any kind of trouble is a worldly philosopher.

Again I remark, that those persons are incompetent for the work of comfort-bearing who have *nothing but cant to offer*. There are those who have the idea that you must groan over the distressed and afflicted. There are times in grief when one cheerful face dawning upon a man's soul is worth a thousand dollars to him. Do not whine over the afflicted. Take the promises of the Gospel, and utter them in a manly tone. Do not be afraid to smile if you feel like it. Do not drive any more hearses through that poor soul. Do not tell him the trouble was foreordained; it will not be any comfort to know it was a million years coming. If you want to find splints for a broken bone, do not take cast-iron. Do not tell them it is God's justice that weighs out grief. They want now to hear of God's tender mercy. In other words, do not give them aqua fortis when they need valerian.

Again I remark, that those persons are poor comforters *who have never had any trouble themselves*. A larkspur can not lecture on the nature of a snow-flake—it never saw a snow-flake; and those people who have always lived in the summer of prosperity can not talk to those who are frozen in disaster. God keeps aged people in the world, I think, for this very work of sympathy. They have been through all these trials. They know all that which irritates and all that which soothes. If there are men and women here who have old people in the house, or near at hand so that they can easily reach them, I congratulate them. Some of us have had trials in life, and although we have had many friends around about us, we have wished that father and mother were still alive that we might go and tell them. Perhaps they could not say much, but it would have been such a comfort to have them around. These aged ones who have been all through the trials of life know how to give condolence. Cherish them; let them lean on your arm—these aged people. If, when you speak to them, they can not hear just what you say the first time, and you have to say it a second time, when you say it the second time, do not say it sharply. If you do, you will be sorry for it on the day when you take the last look and brush back the silvery locks from the wrinkled brow just before they screw the lid on. Blessed be God for the old people! They may not have much strength to go around, but they are God's appointed ministers of comfort to a broken heart.

People who have not had trial themselves can not give comfort to others. They may talk very beautifully, and they may give you a great deal of poetic sentiment; but while poetry is perfume that smells sweet, it makes a very poor salve. If you have a grave in your pathway, and somebody comes and covers it all over with flowers, it is a grave yet. Those who have not had grief themselves know not the mystery of a broken heart. They know not the meaning of childlessness, and the having no one to put to bed at night, or the standing in a room where every book and picture and door is full of memories—the door-mat where she sat, the cup out of which she drank—the place where she stood at the door and clapped her hands—the odd figures that she scribbled—the blocks she built into a house. Ah no, you must have trouble yourself before you can comfort trouble in others. But come all ye who have been bereft and ye who have been comforted in your sorrows, and stand around these afflicted souls, and say to them, "I had that very sorrow myself. God comforted me, and he will comfort you;" and that will go right to the spot. In other words, to comfort others, we must have faith in God, practical experience, and good, sound common sense.

But there are three or four considerations that I will bring this morning to those who are sorrowful and distressed, and that we can always bring to them, knowing that they will effect a cure. And the first consideration is, that God sends our troubles in love. I often hear people in their troubles say, "Why, I wonder what God has against me!" They seem to think God has some grudge against them because trouble and misfortune have come. Oh no. Do you not remember that passage of Scripture, "Whom the Lord loveth he chasteneth?" A child comes in with a very bad splinter in its hand, and you try to extract it. It is a very painful operation. The child draws back from you, but you persist. You are going to take that splinter out, so you take the child with a gentle but firm grasp; for although there may be pain in it, the splinter must come out. And it is love that dictates it, and makes you persist. My friends, I really think that nearly all our sorrows in this world are only the hand of our Father extracting some thorn. If all these sorrows were sent by enemies, I would say, arm yourselves against them; and, as in tropical climes, when a tiger comes down from the mountains and carries off a child from the village, the neighbors band together and go into the forest and hunt the monster, so I would have you, if I thought these misfortunes were sent by an enemy, go out and battle against them. But no; they come from a Father so kind, so loving, so gentle, that the prophet, speaking of his tenderness and mercy, drops the idea of a father, and says, "As one whom his mother comforteth, so will I comfort you."

Again I remark, there is comfort in the thought that God, by all this process, *is going to make you useful.* Do you know that those who accomplish the most for God and heaven have all been under the harrow? Show me a man that has done any thing for Christ in this day, in a public or private place, who has had no trouble and whose path has been smooth. Ah no. Go this afternoon at three o'clock into that beautiful parlor in the city of Philadelphia, and see some twenty outcast children there, and ask the history of that home, and why it is that that Christian woman every Sabbath afternoon gathers in these outcasts and talks with them, and prays with them, and tells them of Jesus, and is getting them, by the grace of God, prepared for heaven. You want to know the history of that family? I could go back and tell it. She was not always an earnest Christian woman—once a daughter of fashion; but the first day of my pastorate in Philadelphia I confronted her in awful grief. In the next room her only child lay. He had been drowned at Long Branch, and they had just brought him in. Oh, how impotent all human comfort seemed to be there and then! But God comforted and lifted her out of that darkness, and through all that tribulation he blessed her, and by a baptism of tears she was set apart to look after the outcast and the destitute and the abandoned. What useless beings we are until sanctified trouble molds us!

I once went through an axe-factory, and I saw them take the bars of iron and thrust them into the terrible furnaces. Then besweated workmen with long tongs stirred the blaze. Then they brought out a bar of iron and put it into a crushing-machine, and then they put it between jaws that bit it in twain. Then they put it on an anvil, and there were great hammers swung by machinery—each one a half-ton in weight—that went thump! thump! thump! If that iron could have spoken, it would have said, "Why all this beating? Why must I be pounded any more than any other iron?" The workmen would have said, "We want to make axes out of you, keen, sharp axes—axes with which to hew down the forest, and build the ship, and erect houses, and carry on a thousand enterprises of civilization. That's the reason we pound you." Now, God puts a soul into the furnace of trial, and then it is brought out and run through the crushing-machine, and then it comes down on the anvil, and upon it blow after blow, blow after blow, and the soul cries out, "O Lord, what does all this mean?" God says, "I want to make something very useful out of you. You shall be something to hew with and something to build with. It is a practical process through which I am putting you." Yes, my Christian friends, we want more tools in the Church of God. Not more wedges to split with: we have enough of these. Not more bores with which to drill; we have too many bores. What we really want is keen, sharp, well-tempered axes, and if there be any other way of making them than in the hot furnace, and on the hard anvil, and under the heavy hammer, I do not know what it is.

Remember that if God brings any kind of chastisement upon you, it is only to make you useful. Do not sit down discouraged, and say, "I have no more reason for living. I wish I were dead." Oh, there never was so much reason for your living as now! By this ordeal you have been consecrated a priest of the Most High God. Go out and do your whole work for the Master.

Again, there is comfort in the thought that all our *troubles are a revelation.* Have you ever thought of it in that connection? The man who has never been through chastisement is ignorant about a thousand things in his soul he ought to know. For instance, here is a man who prides himself on his cheerfulness of character. He has no patience with any body who is depressed in spirits. Oh, it is easy for him to be cheerful, with his fine house, his filled wardrobe, and well-strung instruments of music, and tapestried parlor, and plenty of money in the bank waiting for some permanent investment. It is easy for him to be cheerful. But suppose his fortune goes to pieces, and his house goes down under the sheriff's hammer, and the banks will not have any thing to do with his paper. Suppose those people who were once elegantly entertained at his table get so short-sighted that they can not recognize him upon the street. How then? Is it so easy to be cheerful? It is easy to be cheerful in the home, after the day's work is done, and the gas is turned on, and the house is full of romping little ones. But suppose the piano is shut because the fingers that played on it will no more touch the keys, and the childish voice that asked so many questions will ask no more. Then is it so easy? When a man wakes up and finds that his resources are all gone, he begins to rebel, and he says, "God is hard; God

is outrageous. He had no business to do this to me."
My friends, those of us who have been through trouble
know what a sinful and rebellious heart we have, and how
much God has to put up with, and how much we need
pardon. It is only in the light of a flaming furnace that
we can learn our own weakness and our own lack of
moral resource.

There is also a great deal of comfort in the fact that
there will be a family reconstruction in a better place. From
Scotland, or England, or Ireland, a child emigrates to this
country. It is very hard parting, but he comes, after a
while writing home as to what a good land it is. Another brother comes, a sister comes, and another, and after a
while the mother comes, and after a while the father comes,
and now they are all here, and they have a time of great
congratulation and a very pleasant reunion. Well, it is
just so with our families: they are emigrating to a better land. Now, one goes out. Oh, how hard it is to part
with him! Another goes. Oh, how hard it is to part
with her! And another, and another, and we ourselves
will after a while go over, and then we will be together.
Oh, what a reunion! Do you believe that? "Yes," you
say. You do not! You do not believe it as you believe
other things. If you did, and with the same emphasis,
why, it would take nine-tenths of your trouble off your
heart. The fact is, heaven to many of us is a great fog.
It is away off somewhere, filled with an uncertain and indefinite population. That is the kind of heaven that many
of us dream about; but it is the most tremendous fact in
all the universe—this heaven of the Gospel. Our departed
friends are not afloat. The residence in which you live is
not so real as the residence in which they stay. *You* are

afloat, you who do not know in the morning what will happen before night. They are housed and safe forever. Do not, therefore, pity your departed friends who have died in Christ. They do not need any of your pity. You might as well send a letter of condolence to Queen Victoria on her obscurity, or to the Rothschilds on their poverty, as to pity those who have won the palm. Do not say of those who are departed, "Poor child!" "Poor father!" "Poor mother!" They are not poor. You are poor—you whose homes have been shattered, not they. You do not dwell much with your families in this world. All day long you are off to business. Will it not be pleasant when you can be together all the while? If you have had four children and one is gone, and any body asks how many children you have, do not be so infidel as to say three. Say four—one in heaven. Do not think that the grave is unfriendly. You go into your room, and dress for some grand entertainment, and you come forth beautifully appareled; and the grave is only the place where we go to dress for the glorious resurrection, and we will come out radiant, radiant, mortality having become immortality. Oh, how much condolence there is in this thought! I expect to see my kindred in heaven; I expect to see them as certainly as I expect to go home to-day. Ay, I shall more certainly see them. Eight or ten will come up from the grave-yard back of Somerville; and one will come up from the mountains back of Amoy, China; and another will come up from the sea off Cape Hatteras; and thirty will come up from Greenwood; and I shall know them better than I ever knew them here. And your friends—they may be across the sea, but the trumpet that sounds here will sound there. You will come up on just the same day. Some morning you have overslept yourself, and you open your eyes, and see that the sun is high in the heavens, and you say, "I have overslept, and I must be up and off." So you will open your eyes on the morning of the resurrection, in the full blaze of God's light, and you will say, "I must be up and away." Oh yes, you will come up, and there will be a reunion, a reconstruction of your family. I like what Halburton, I think it was—good old Mr. Halburton—said in his last moments, "I thank God that I ever lived, and that I have a father in heaven, and a mother in heaven, and brothers in heaven, and sisters in heaven, and I am now going up to see them."

I remark once more: our troubles in this world *are preparative for glory.* What a transition it was for Paul—from the slippery deck of a foundering ship to the calm presence of Jesus! What a transition it was for Latimer—from the stake to a throne! What a transition it was for Robert Hall—from insanity to glory! What a transition it was for Richard Baxter—from the dropsy to the "saint's everlasting rest!" And what a transition it will be for you— from a world of sorrow to a world of joy! John Holland, when he was dying, said, "What means this brightness in the room? Have you lighted the candles?" "No," they replied, "we have not lighted any candles." Then said he, "Welcome, heaven!" the light already beaming upon his pillow. O ye who are persecuted in this world! your enemies will get off the track after a while, and all will speak well of you among the thrones. Ho! ye who are sick now, no medicines to take there. One breath of the eternal hills will thrill you with immortal vigor. And ye who are lonesome now, there will be a thousand spirits to welcome you into their companionship. O ye bereft souls!

there will be no grave-digger's spade that will cleave the side of that hill, and there will be no dirge wailing from that temple. The river of God, deep as the joy of heaven, will roll on between banks odorous with balm, and over depths bright with jewels, and under skies roseate with gladness, argosies of light going down the stream to the stroke of glittering oar and the song of angels! Not one sigh in the wind; not one tear mingling with the waters.

> " There shall I bathe my weary soul
> In seas of heavenly rest,
> And not a wave of trouble roll
> Across my peaceful breast."

A GOOD WOMAN PROMOTED.

"I go to prepare a place for you."—*John* xiv., 2.

AMONG the most startling stories ever recited are those connected with the adventures of the Western emigrant. In the days before the rail train showered its sparks upon the darkness of the wilderness, people put out on foot, or in slow and cumbrous wagons, from their Eastern homes, and in the wild thickets of the Far West sought to clear for their families a home. Ofttimes leaving their tender little ones in the New England village, with blanket and gun and axe, they dared the forest, terrible with bear's bark and panther's scream, and the war-whoop cry of scalping savages. After a while the trees were felled, and the under-brush was burned, and the farm was cleared, and the house was built. Then word came back here saying that every thing was ready. The family would get into the wagon and start on at slow pace for a very long journey. After a while, some evening-tide, the shout of recognition was heard, and by the fire of the great back-log the newly-arrived would recount the exciting experiences of the way.

Well, my friends, we are all about to become emigrants to a far country. This is no place for us to stay. Our older brother, Jesus, he of the scarred brow and the blistered feet, has gone ahead to build our mansion and to clear the way for us; and he sends a letter back, saying he has it all ready, and I break the seal of that letter and read to you these words, "I go to prepare a place for you."

I might put it in another shape. A young man resolves to build a home for himself. He has pledged himself in one of the purest of earthly attachments. He toils no more for himself than for the one who will share with him the results of his industrious accumulation. After a while the fortune is made, the house is built, the right hands are joined, the blessing is invoked, the joy is consummated. So Jesus, the Lover of our souls, has been toiling to make a place for us. He is fitting up our mansion, and is gathering around it every thing that can possibly enchant the soul, and after a while he will say, "It is all ready now," and he will reach down his hand, and take up to his fair residence " the Church, which is the Lamb's wife." "I go to prepare a place for you."

"But," says some one, "that implies that heaven is a place. I have heard a great many people say it was merely a condition, and that wherever the souls of the righteous are, there is heaven." Absurd idea! Christ ascended to heaven, and there must have been a heaven to go to. Elijah went up to heaven, and there must have been a heaven for him to go to. The Bible was not written merely for philologists and hair-splitters, but for common-sense people; and the plain reading of my text implies not only that heaven is a condition, but that it is a glorious locality. "I go to prepare a *place* for you."

Where is heaven? It is the question which every intelligent Christian sometimes asks, and he especially asks it in time of bereavement. When his loved ones go away from him, you say they are in heaven; but he says, "Where is heaven?" You know there are a great many theories in regard to it. The Mohammedans think that the good Moslems, as soon as they leave this life, come to a fragrant pool of water fed by streams from paradise. They drink out of that fragrant pool, and their thirst is assuaged. Then they go into paradise, and the trees have bells hanging on the branches, chiming whenever the air strikes them. They gaze upon the tree of life, which they say has so broad a shadow that it takes a swift horse one hundred years to race across it. They think that there is a river made up of wine and honey, flowing between banks of camphor, over beds of musk. They suppose that every spirit that goes into the future world has many attendants with baskets and with chalices of pure gold. They suppose that the inhabitant of the future world sits down to a great banquet without any satiety, so that, after a hundred years of eating and drinking, the appetite is as good as at the moment the soul sat down. That is the Mohammedan heaven.

The Hindoo thinks that heaven is all around about— merely a change of body. A vulture dies, and his spirit enters a man; the man dies, and his spirit enters the vulture, and after a great many transmigrations of the soul, it is absorbed in the spirit of the great Brahm. Our forefathers thought heaven to be a place of pastimes, heroic strife, and great banqueting; spirits would fight and be wounded, and then come to the celestial streams and wash off their wounds, and they would be well again; then they would sit down at a banquet and drink wine out of the skulls of their enemies, and rise up and romp, and dance and play.

The aborigines of our own country think heaven to be beyond the great mountains. After you get beyond the great mountains, there is a great river; and after you have passed that great river, there is a vast country; and after you have passed that wide country, there is a world of water; and in that world of water there are a thousand isles, beautiful with streams and trees, and there are buffalo and deer there; and all the departed red man has to do is to whistle up his dogs and go a-shooting to all eternity.

I mention these things because I want you to know it is impossible for a man to get any idea of heaven without the Bible, and to kindle in your soul a feeling of gratitude to God that you have this Lamp, not only for your pathway here, but to throw its glories upon the world that is to come. There is, however, among Christian people great difference of opinion as to where heaven is or will be. Some of the best Christian people think that this world is to be the final residence of the righteous. I can see how God could take all the rigors out of our climate, and all repulsions out of our world, and make it fair, and bright, and beautiful, and fit for eternal occupancy. But I can not adopt the theory. It seems to me the world is not large enough for heaven. Considering all the myriads that have gone, and all the myriads that are to go, there would not be room enough on the continents and on the seas for such a great host. Besides that, heaven is already in existence. Tens of thousands of people have gone into it. It can not be that all our departed friends are floating about in space waiting for our world to get filled up, in order that they may have a heaven. Oh no. They are there now. Christ said, "I go to prepare a place for you;" and if, eighteen centuries ago, he began the work, I think it is done now. Besides that, the Bible declares that the world, and all the things that are therein, will be burned up; and if a thing is burned up, you can not repair it, and you can not make

8*

it a fit residence for the righteous. If it is first destroyed, it will be an entirely new world. Besides that, the elements of dissolution are already in our world. I refer not to the coal-mines in the South, which have been twenty years on fire. I refer not to the vapors coming up from the hot springs, showing great heat underneath, but to the common geological idea that the centre of this world is already on fire. Besides, there is all about a subtle fluid which, if decomposed or set loose from other combinations, would shatter this world into pieces so small that nothing but the eye of the infinite God could find the splinters of the wreck. It would destroy mountains and seas and air. So it will require no omnipotent pry to lift up the mountains in the last day. It will not require the blast of the red-hot furnace of God's indignation to set the sea on fire. It will not require the grip of Almightiness to pull down the pillar of this world. God has only to take his hands off it, and it is gone. The mere cessation of operation on God's part would be the cause of the wreck. Besides that, other worlds have burned. Fifteen hundred stars have disappeared. The astronomer, through his telescope, again and again has seen the conflagration of a world. Why not our world burn up? Ay, I adopt the theory that Peter declares in his epistle when he says, "The world and all that is therein shall be burned up."

There are other Christian people who suppose that each sun is to be the heaven of the surrounding system. You know that there are sisterhoods of worlds that join each other in bands of light around some great central orb, and Christian people have supposed that these surrounding worlds were merely schools in which souls went to be prepared for the central light, the central sun; and there is a

Bible intimation that is not at all inconsistent with that idea; for, while planets have day and night, and heat and cold, showing the possibility of growth and dissolution, the sun has no night, and that corresponds with the Bible statement about heaven, "There shall be no night there." Still, I reject the idea, because if the sun of each system were the heaven of the system, we should have a multitude of paradises, and the words of my text could not be true, "I go to prepare a place"—that is, *one* place—"for you."

There is one other theory consonant with the Bible and consonant with science, and I like any thing that is proved by both those books, or is not inharmonious with either of them. Modern discovery shows that the planets go around the sun, and that the sun and the planets—indeed all the celestial systems—go in one direction and in one circle, all going around about some one great central world; a world vast beyond all astronomical calculation; a world vast enough, by power of gravitation, to wheel the whole universe around it. As our sun—our little sun—is five hundred times larger than the earth and the planets, thus wheeling them around it, so, then, I suppose, the great central world of which I speak is five hundred times larger than all the other worlds put together, so as to wheel them around it. You must believe in the existence of such a central world, unless you reject all scientific exploration and deduction. That world, stupendous beyond arithmetic, beyond words, beyond imagination, I believe is heaven. From all parts of the universe the souls of the dead will fly to that centre. That shall gather up all the resources and splendors and glories that God ever created or redeeming love ever achieved. Gradually the worlds will expire; not only ours, but those and these, and, finally, all save two—the one great central world of which I speak, and a world of darkness; the first the residence of the righteous, the other the abode of the wicked. You say this theory makes heaven a great way off. No! No! We calculate distance by the time taken to traverse it, and the departed spirit will not take the millionth part of a second to get there.

But here I have to tell you that I do not much care where heaven is. All I want is to get there myself, and get these people there. Christ is there, and the angels of God are there, and all my Christian kindred who have departed are there.

"No grief can turn that day to night,
The darkness of that land is light."

Into that world how many of our loved ones have gone! We have sent delegations into it. This morning I wish to speak more especially of one who went out from among us—a Christian woman known all the world over. She has just entered into that glorious world, that vast world, that world where Christ is. Among the Hannah Moores, and the Charlotte Elizabeths, and the Mrs. Adoniram Judsons, and the Mrs. Fletchers, Phebe Palmer has taken her place, radiant as any of them—perhaps more radiant than all of them. It seems to me she must have had a very easy entrance. She did not have to crowd through. When half-and-half Christians come up to the gate of heaven, methinks they have to squeeze in; that the gate grazes them on both sides or closes behind them, catching the skirts of their garment. Not so with her. An abundant entrance was administered unto her. I think a mandate went forth, "Lift up your heads, ye everlasting gates, and let her come through." Oh, I should have liked to have stood somewhere near the gate, to have heard the multitudinous shout that greeted her from all the armies of the saved!

I can not, as a minister of the Most High God, allow such a life to be passed and such a death to be witnessed without, as far as I may, prolonging the echo.

I admired her as the discoverer of what is called, rightly or wrongly, "the higher life." Columbus no more certainly discovered our New World than Phebe Palmer discovered that new world of light, and love, and joy, and peace which she spoke of. Columbus did not create this New World; he only pointed it out. Phebe Palmer did not create "the higher life;" she only exhibited it. She showed to the Church of God that there were mountain-peaks of Christian satisfaction that it had never attained, and created in the souls of us who have not reached that elevation a longing for the glorious ascent. For thirty-seven years—longer than the life, perhaps, of the majority of people present to-day—every Tuesday she had a meeting, the sole object of which was the elevation of the standard of Christian holiness; and there were hundreds of Christian ministers who came in, and sat down at her feet, and got her blessing, and went out stronger for Christian combat. It was no rare thing, in her evangelistic meetings in the United States and Europe, to have ministers of the Presbyterian Church, and the Baptist Church, and the Methodist Church, and the Episcopal Church, and all the churches, coming and kneeling down at the altar, bemoaning their unbelief and their coldness, and then rising up, saying, "I have got it—the blessing." Some caricatured, and said there was no such thing as "a higher life" of peace and Christian satisfaction; but she lived long enough to see the whole Christian Church waking up to this doctrine, and thousands and tens of thousands coming on the high table-land where once she stood, she herself having passed on now, higher up, that she may still beckon us on, crying, "Up this way! Up this way!" Glorious soul of Phebe Palmer! Synonym of holiness unto the Lord!

I am also amazed at the number of conversions under her ministry. She was as far removed as possible from those females who go through the land bawling about their rights, neglecting their home duties, having their husbands hold their hats and shawls while they make speeches in behalf of their rights of suffrage, or in behalf of a seat in Congressional halls—those restless women, marriage to whom would be pandemonium. As far as the north pole is from the south pole, Phebe Palmer was from all them. Always accompanied by her husband, she went out to serve Christ, and she wanted no higher right than this, the grandest right ever given to man or woman—the right to commend the Lord Jesus Christ to a dying world. Modestly and in Christian consecration she went forth to serve God. It will take eternal ages to tell the story of her evangelistic labors. Newcastle, Sunderland, Penrith, Macklesfield, Darlington, Isle of Wight, still feel her overmastering influence. In her Christian meetings a young man rose up, and said, "Why, I have got a new nature;" and a timid woman exclaimed, "Do you think Christ will have me?" and the evangelist put her arms around her neck, and said, "Yes, Jesus will have you." And another cried out, "Oh, what a fool I have been all my days, to reject Christ." And the Duke of Wellington's blind soldier, seventy years of age, both eyes put out in battle, was led by a little child to the communion-rail, and while prayer was being offered, on his blasted vision eternal light broke in. And the soldier in the Queen's employ, drafted for India, stood up in the meeting, in the red-jacket uniform, and said, "Pray for me, wherever I go, that I may be faithful. You look at my red jacket; but if you could see under it, you would see a white and blood-washed robe." At Windsor the musicians of the Queen's band, instruments under arm, stopped and looked and listened, and then and there heard the voice of Christ from this woman's lips, and took Christ with them back to the palace. And the police that stood at the door, too, listening, even they surrendered themselves to the Lord who bought them. Places of iniquity cowered before her. At North Shields, a man who kept intoxicating liquors for sale, said, "I don't know why Dr. and Mrs. Palmer came here to bother me. Before they came to this place, I used to draw off half a barrel of beer every night for my customers. Now I scarcely draw off a quart." Sixty souls saved one night in Sunderland under her work. Six hundred souls brought to God at her call in Manchester. One thousand souls, through her, finding redeeming love at Madeley. Three thousand four hundred and forty-four brought to God in the district of Newcastle. Twenty-five thousand souls saved under the instrumentality of Phebe Palmer! What a record for earth and heaven! What an array for the judgment-day! What a doxology for the one hundred and forty and four thousand! What a mountain of coronets flung down at the feet of Jesus!

I am amazed, also, at her power of prayer. We dabble in it once in a while, but do not know much about the art. Phebe Palmer got what she asked for, because she knew how to ask. Sailing up toward Liverpool with her husband, she prays God that some one may meet them on the beach, and welcome them to England. Coming up by the shore there is a man in the garb of a minister, standing. She says, "There is the man who has come to welcome us to England." The boat strikes the dock, and the minister steps on board, and says, "Is this Dr. and Mrs. Palmer? Welcome to the shores of old England!" Worn out physically with her Christian exertions, she asks for strength. God gives it to her. Laboring in some place amidst great obstacles, she asks that that night a great multitude may be saved; and a multitude press into the side-room, repenting, praying, believing, rejoicing. On the way home from England, a man falls overboard. She sees him floating almost a mile away. She cries mightily unto God for that man's rescue, saying, "Save him, and I will point him to Christ, and I will try to have him become a Christian." And she prayed in an agony that he might be saved, and, by what seemed a miraculous effort, he was saved and brought on deck, and the evangelist did her work with him. Starting with the safe belief that the Lord never lies, she found out the secret of all-prevailing and all-conquering prayer. O Thou who hearest prayer, teach us how to pray! I believe that one hundred Phebe Palmers would bring the millennium to-morrow morning.

But the shepherdess, crook in hand, has gone home to rest by the still waters. The loving wife, the gentle sister, the Christian mother, the flaming evangelist, is dead. One would have supposed that, after so useful a life, the Lord would have allowed her to pass off easily. No. Ten weeks of great anguish, a complication of diseases adding pang to pang. It seemed as if Christ had said, "Now, on this death-bed, I will demonstrate that my grace is sufficient for every thing, and can bear up under every thing." It seemed as if Christ had said, "Now, here is a royal gem for a royal place. I have been fifty years busy with it, polishing it and polishing it, and now only a few more cuttings of the chisel and a few more raspings of the file, and it will be as rare a gem as was ever prepared in all the centuries. Ten weeks of pain are nothing before an eternity of jubilation!" At half-past two o'clock on the afternoon of November 2d, God put up his tools and said, "The work of polishing is done. *Let her go now!*"

I open to you to-day another classic. There is no need of your going back any more to saintly death-beds in the last century, when we have had such an exit here. It seems as if the clouds were only now parting. I hear the rumbling of the vanishing wheels. We stand in the light of the opening of the King's gate as she went in. Hear the story of her dying raptures. It seems to have all the quietness of a pastoral, and yet to be blood-stirring as a battle-march. Her life was a song; her death a "Hallelujah Chorus." In her last sickness she said, "I am fully saved. I have not a single doubt. Hallelujah to God and the Lamb! I am within speaking distance of my home in paradise. You have been the kindest of husbands to me, and our love has been abiding, and it shall abide forever." And when blindness came, and she could not see at all, she said, "Oh, what sweet nurses I have! Jesus was left all alone." When they read to her the promises, she said, "Put my name in those promises." And ever after that, when the promises were read, it was with the name of Phebe Palmer attached to them. She said, "Hallelujah!

precious Jesus! I pass through the valley, but without the shadow, trusting in Christ. Oh, so weary! How I should like to go! But Thy will, not mine, be done. I thought, before this, the light of eternal day would dawn upon me, but it has not yet dawned." When a daughter said, "Do you see me, ma?" she said, "I see no one but Jesus, but I shall soon see the King in his beauty. Glory be to the Father! Glory be to the Son! Glory be to the Holy Ghost!" When they bathed her fevered hands, she said, "I shall soon bathe my hands in the life-giving waters." On the last morning, as she woke up, she said, "I thought I saw the chariot! So glorious! glorious! 'O death! where is thy sting? O grave! where is thy victory? Thanks be unto God, who giveth us the victory through our Lord Jesus Christ!'" Then she pronounced the apostolic benediction—a benediction for her husband, for her children, for the Church universal, and for the world whose redemption she had tried to hasten—"May the grace of our Lord Jesus Christ, and the love of God, and the love of the Holy Ghost, be with you all forever. Amen." And Phebe Palmer was dead!

No, no, no—not dead. She lives! she lives! It seems to me as if I could almost see her standing this morning on the battlements of heaven, waving the triumph, calling down to us through this sweet Sabbath air; and I wave back to her. Hail, ransomed spirit! Hallelujah! Hallelujah!

O bereft souls! be comforted. To have had such a wife, and such a sister, and such a mother, is enough honor for one family. Let her memory be to you both exultation and inspiration. Be sure you get on the road she traveled, that you may come out at the same glory. She will be waiting for you, waiting at the foot of the throne, waiting under the trees of life, waiting on the banks of the river, and some day she will cry out, "My husband's coming! my sister's coming! my child's coming. Stand back, ye blessed ones, and let me welcome them in." And the grief of the afternoon of November 2d will be swallowed in the joy of the heavenly reception. Oh, how like old times it will be to get mother back again, sweeter than when you sat upon her lap in infancy, and nestled in her arms, and looked up into her loving face as she leaned over your cradle. But it will be mother without the shortness of breath. Mother without the weary limbs. Mother without the paroxysm of distress. Sainted mother! Glorified mother! Enthroned mother!

Blessed be God that so many of us have mothers in heaven. They may not have moved in as celebrated a sphere as yours; but they were just as dear to us, and their tenderness breaks upon us to-day in a flood that overflows the banks, and we rejoice at the prospect of flinging ourselves into their arms when, tired out with the work of life, we go home. Alas for any man that misses heaven, when he has a Christian mother there!

Oh that the name of Phebe Palmer might be one of the watch-words to rouse up the Church universal! The Methodist Church can not monopolize her name. She belonged to that Church, she lived in it, she died in it, she loved it; but you can not build any denominational wall high enough to shut out that light from our souls. She is mine. She is yours. She belongs to all earth, and all heaven. Eternal God! let the story of her life and death thrill all nations!

Then, when our hands get hot with the last fever, may

we go up to cool them in the fountains; and, when our physical eye-sight fails in death, may we see "the King in his beauty;" and when it is our time to go, let there be a chariot to fetch us home!

Until then, departed spirit, farewell! We can afford to wait for such a grand reunion. Farewell! Farewell! And now may the God who brought again from the dead our Lord Jesus Christ, that great Shepherd of the sheep, through the blood of the everlasting covenant, make you faithful in every good work to do his will.

THE CRIMSON COAT.

"Who is this that cometh from Edom, with dyed garments from Bozrah? this that is glorious in his apparel, traveling in the greatness of his strength?" —*Isaiah* lxiii., 1.

EDOM and Bozrah having been the scene of fierce battle, when those words are used here or in any other part of the Bible they are figures of speech setting forth scenes of severe conflict. As now we often use the word Waterloo to describe a decisive contest of any kind, so the words Bozrah and Edom in this text are figures of speech descriptive of a scene of great slaughter. Whatever else the prophet may have meant to describe, he most certainly meant to depict the Lord Jesus Christ, saying, "Who is this that cometh from Edom, with dyed garments from Bozrah, traveling in the greatness of his strength?"

When a general is about to go out to the wars, a flag and a sword are publicly presented to him, and the maidens bring flowers, and the young men load the cannon, and the train starts amidst a huzza that drowns the thunder of the wheels and the shriek of the whistle. But all this will give no idea of the excitement that there must have been in heaven when Christ started out on the campaign of the world's conquest. If they could have foreseen the siege that would be laid to him, and the maltreatment he would suffer, and the burdens he would have to carry, and the battles he would have to fight, I think there would have been a million volunteers in heaven who would have insisted on coming along with him; but no, they only accompanied him to the gate, their last shout heard clear down to the earth, the space between the two worlds bridged with a great hosanna. You know there is a wide difference between a man's going off to battle and coming back again. When he goes off, it is with epaulets untangled, with banner unspecked, with horses sleek and shining from the groom. All that there is of struggle and pain is to come yet. So it was with Christ. He had not yet fought a battle. He was starting out, and though this world did not give him a warm-hearted greeting, there was a gentle mother who folded him in her arms; and a babe finds no difference between a stable and a palace, between courtiers and camel-drivers. As Jesus stepped on the stage of this world, it was amidst angelic shouts in the galleries and amidst the kindest maternal ministrations. But soon hostile forces began to gather. They deployed from the Sanhedrim. They were detailed from the standing army. They came out from the Cesarean castles. The vagabonds in the street joined the gentlemen of the mansion. Spirits rode up from hell, and in long array there came a force together that threatened to put to rout this newly arrived one from heaven. Jesus now seeing the battle gathering, lifted his own standard; but who gathered about it? How feeble the recruits! A few shoremen, a blind beggar, a woman with an alabaster box, another woman with two mites, and a group of friendless, moneyless, and positionless people came to his standard. What chance was there for him? Nazareth against him. Bethlehem against him. Capernaum against him. Jerusalem against him. Galilee against him. The courts against him. The army against him. The throne against him. The world against him.

All hell against him. No wonder they asked him to surrender. But he could not surrender, he could not apologize, he could not take any back steps. He had come to strike for the deliverance of an enslaved race, and he must do the work. Then they sent out their pickets to watch him. They saw in what house he went, and when he came out. They watched what he ate, and who with; what he drank, and how much. They did not dare to make their final assault, for they knew not but that behind him there might be a reinforcement that was not seen. But at last the battle came. It was to be more fierce than Bozrah, more bloody than Gettysburg, involving more than Austerlitz, more combatants employed than at Chalons, a ghastlier conflict than all the battles of the earth put together, though Edmund Burke's estimate of thirty-five thousand millions of the slain be accurate. The day was Friday. The hour was between twelve and three o'clock. The field was a slight hillock north-west of Jerusalem. The forces engaged were earth and hell, joined as allies on one side, and heaven, represented by a solitary inhabitant, on the other.

The hour came. Oh, what a time it was! I think that that day the universe looked on. The spirits that could be spared from the heavenly temple, and could get conveyance of wing or chariot, came down from above, and spirits getting furlough from furnaces beneath came up; and they listened, and they looked, and they watched. Oh, what an uneven battle! Two worlds armed on one side; an unarmed man on the other. The German regiment of the Roman army at that time stationed at Jerusalem began the attack. They knew how to fight, for they belonged to the most thoroughly drilled army of all the world. With spears glittering in the sun, they charged up the hill. The horses prance and rear amidst the excitement of the populace—the heels of the riders, plunged in the flanks, urging them on. The weapons begin to tell on Christ. See how faint he looks! There the blood starts, and there, and there, and there. If he is to have reinforcements, let him call them up now. No; he must do this work alone—alone. He is dying. Feel for yourself of the wrist; the pulse is feebler. Feel under the arm; the warmth is less. He is dying. Ay, they pronounce him dead. And just at that moment that they pronounced him dead he rallied, and from his wounds he unsheathed a weapon which staggered the Roman legions down the hill, and hurled the Satanic battalions into the pit. It was a weapon of love—infinite love, all-conquering love. Mightier than javelin or spear, it triumphed over all. Put back, ye armies of earth and hell! The tide of battle turns. Jesus hath overcome. Let the people stand apart and make a line, that he may pass down from Calvary to Jerusalem, and thence on and out all around the world. The battle is fought. The victory is achieved. The triumphal march is begun. Hark to the hoofs of the warrior's steed, and the tramping of a great multitude! for he has many friends now. The Hero of earth and heaven advances. Cheer! cheer! "Who is this that cometh from Edom, with dyed garments from Bozrah, traveling in the greatness of his strength?"

We behold here a new revelation of a blessed and startling fact. People talk of Christ as though he were going to do something grand for us after a while. He has done it. People talk as though, ten or twenty years from now, in the closing hours of our life, or in some terrible pass of life, Jesus will help us. He has done the work already. He did it eighteen hundred and forty-two years ago. You might as well talk of Washington as though he were going to achieve our national independence in 1950, as to speak of Christ as though he were going to achieve our salvation in the future. He did it in the year of our Lord 33, eighteen hundred and forty-two years ago, on the field of Bozrah, the Captain of our salvation fighting unto death for your and my emancipation. All we have to do is to accept that fact in our heart of hearts, and we are free for this world, and we are free for the world to come. But, lest we might not accept, Christ comes through here tonight, "traveling in the greatness of his strength," not to tell you that he is going to fight for you some battle in the future, but to tell you that the battle is already fought, and the victory already won.

You have noticed that, when soldiers come home from the wars, they carry on their flags the names of the battlefields where they were distinguished. The Englishman coming back has on his banner Inkermann and Balaklava; the Frenchman, Jena and Eylau; the German, Versailles and Sedan. And Christ has on the banner he carries as conqueror the names of ten thousand battle-fields he won for you and for me. He rides past all our homes of bereavement—by the door-bell swathed in sorrow, by the wardrobe black with woe, by the dismantled fortress of our strength. Come out and greet him to-night, O ye people! See the names of all the battle-passes on his flag. Ye who are poor, read on this ensign the story of Christ's hard crusts and pillowless head. Ye who are persecuted, read here of the ruffians who chased him from his first breath to his last. Mighty to soothe your troubles, mighty to balk your calamities, mighty to tread down your foes, "traveling in the greatness of his strength." Though his horse be brown with the dust of the march, and the fetlocks be wet with the carnage, and the bit be red with the blood of your spiritual foes, he comes up to-night, not exhausted from the battle, but fresh as when he went into it —coming up from Bozrah, "traveling in the greatness of his strength."

You know that when Augustus, and Constantine, and Trajan, and Titus came back from the wars, what a time there was. You know they came on horseback or in chariots, and there were trophies before and there were captives behind, and there were people shouting on all sides, and there were garlands flung from the window, and over the highway a triumphal arch was sprung. The solid masonry to-day at Beneventum, Rimini, and Rome still tell their admiration for those heroes. And shall we to-night let our Conqueror go by without lifting any acclaim? Have we not flowers red enough to depict the carnage, white enough to celebrate the victory, fragrant enough to breathe the joy? Those men of whom I just spoke dragged their victims at the chariot-wheels; but Christ, our Lord, takes those who once were captives and invites them into his chariot to ride, while he puts around them the arm of his strength, saying, "I have loved thee with an everlasting love, and the waters shall not drown it, and the fires shall not burn it, and eternity shall not exhaust it."

If this be true, I can not see how any man can carry his sorrows a great while. If this Conqueror from Bozrah is going to beat back all your griefs, why not trust him? Oh! do you not feel, under this Gospel to-night, your griefs falling back, and your tears drying up, as you hear the tramp of a thousand illustrious promises led on by the Conqueror from Bozrah, "traveling, traveling, in the greatness of his strength?"

On that Friday which the Episcopal Church rightly celebrates, calling it "Good-Friday," your soul and mine were contended for. On that day Jesus proved himself mightier than earth and hell; and when the lances struck him, he gathered them up into a sheaf, as a reaper gathers the grain, and he stacked them. Mounting the horse of the Apocalypse, he rode down through the ages, "traveling in the greatness of his strength." On that day your sin and mine perished, if we will only believe it.

There may be some one in the house who may say, "I don't like the color of this Conqueror's garments. You tell me that his garments were not only spattered with the blood of conflict, but also that they were soaked, that they were saturated, that they were dyed in it." I admit it. You say you do not like that. Then I quote to you two passages of Scripture: Hebrews ix., 22, "Without the shedding of blood there is no remission." Leviticus xvii., 11, "In the blood is the atonement." But it was not your blood. It was his own. Not only enough to redden his garments and to redden the horse, but enough to wash away the sins of the world. Oh, the blood on his brow, the blood on his hands, the blood on his feet, the blood on his side! It seems as if an artery must have been cut.

"There is a fountain filled with blood
 Drawn from Emmanuel's veins,
And sinners plunged beneath that flood
 Lose all their guilty stains."

Some of our modern theologians who want to give God lessons about the best way to save the world, tell us they do not want any blood in their redemption. They want to take this horse by the bit, and hurl him back on his haunches, and tell this rider from Bozrah to go around some other way. Look out, lest ye fall under the flying hoofs of this horse; lest ye go down under the sword of this Conqueror from Bozrah! What meant the blood of the pigeons in the old dispensation? the blood of the bullock? the blood of the heifer? the blood of the lamb? It meant to prophesy the cleansing blood, the pardoning blood, the healing blood of this Conqueror who comes up from Bozrah to-night, "traveling in the greatness of his strength." No interest in that blood, and you die. It was shed for you, if you will accept it; it will plead trumpet-tongued against you, if you refuse it. I catch a handful of the red torrent that rushes out from the heart of the Lord, and I throw it over this audience, hoping that one drop of its cleansing power may come upon your soul. O Jesus! in that crimson tide wash my poor soul! We need it! We die! We die! We accept thy sacrifice! Conqueror of Bozrah, have mercy upon us! We throw our garments in the way! We fall into line! Ride on, Jesus, ride on! "Traveling, traveling in the greatness of thy strength."

But after a while the returning Conqueror will reach the gate, and all the armies of the saved will be with him. I hope you will be there, and I will be there. As we go through the gate and around about the throne for the review, "a great multitude that no man can number"—all heaven can tell without asking, right away, which one is Jesus, not only because of the brightness of his face, but because, while all the other inhabitants in glory are robed in white—saints in white, cherubim in white, seraphim in white—*his* robes shall be scarlet, even the dyed garments of Bozrah. I catch a glimpse of that triumphant joy, but the gate opens and shuts so quickly, I can hear only half a sentence, and it is this, " Unto him who hath washed us in his blood!"

THE SYRACUSE CALAMITY.

"What is your life?"—*James* iv., 14.

THIS day seems oppressive to me with solemnities. About to come up through the "Narrows" of New York harbor is a vessel of the Bremen line, bringing all that remains on earth of the pleasure-party that went out on the 14th of last month, on Lake Geneva, Switzerland. Of the three young men who perished there, only one body has been reclaimed, and parental arms from our city are stretched out to receive it. Welcome back to thy native shores, O loved one! though thou comest asleep. Welcome, though it be amidst a rain of tears and the snapping of heart-strings! Remorseless lake, give back thy dead! We would have them pillowed in our cemeteries.

While meditating upon these things, there comes a more startling and overpowering cry from the central city of our own State. Many whom we knew were in that catastrophe. And now the call from New York harbor, louder than the dash of the wave, and the call from Syracuse, louder than the crackling of the timbers, unite with the call of my text in demanding, "What is your life?"

The anatomist, with knife and skillful analysis, has sought to find out the secret hiding-place of the principle of life; but there is a barred gate-way that he can not enter. No satisfactory definition has ever been given of what life is. In complete swoon, when all muscular action of the heart has stopped and the brain lies dormant, life may still exist, and, rallying its scattered forces, march on to three-score years and ten. But I have a lamp in the light of which I can give an intelligent answer to this question; and so, leaving the anatomist to his curious, fascinating and sublime investigation, I come in the light of the Word of God to answer the question, "What is your life?"

There may be, now and then, in our existence a staccato passage; but, for the most part, our days and years pass in a sort of monotone. We rise in the morning, we breakfast, we go to our daily occupation, we dine, we shake hands, we taste our evening meal, we sleep; and Tuesday is a copy of Monday, and Wednesday is an echo of Tuesday. If you are forty years of age, then you have passed fourteen thousand six hundred days; and yet, without the use of memorandum, you can not give me an account of fifty of them. Our days pass on with even pace, so that we seldom estimate what we are, what we have been, and what we will be. Oh that, this morning, this solemn and overwhelming providence in a sister city might come to our ears, and give startling emphasis to this interlocutory of the apostle, "What is your life?"

In answering this question of my text, I reply, in the first place, *our life is a test.* If you buy goods, you very soon want to find out whether they are really worth what you paid for them. Every new ship must make a trial trip. If you bring a man into some important position, and there is a crisis where his behavior will either make or break you, you say, "Now I will have a chance to find out what he is." Well, every man is on his trial trip. Men, angels, and devils are finding out what is in you, what you are worth, and what your weaknesses are. No man liveth to himself. Every word you speak, every action you perform, has a thousand echoes. Earth and heaven and hell are gazing upon your behavior, and you are passing the trial. You are watching me to see whether I am faithful or unfaithful; I am watching you to see whether you are faithful or unfaithful; and each one of us is going now through the solemn, unmistakable, tremendous test.

I reply still further to the question of my text, that *our life is an apprenticeship*. A man works at a trade four or five years, or he studies for a profession six or ten years, and then he enters what he considers his chief mission. But, my brethren, our entire life on earth is an apprenticeship. Not until death do we begin our chief employment. This world is not our principal workshop. All the inhabitants of heaven are busy forever. The Bible says they rest not day nor night. If to carry on the little business of this world it requires so many hands and feet and minds, who can estimate how many activities will be required to carry on the enterprises of heaven? When our little world is finished and burned up, is the whole universe to stop business? Because one thread-and-needle store on a back alley fails, is all the commerce of a metropolis arrested? Oh no. In heaven there will be no sleeping, no idling. That Christian woman who feeds the sick pauper on the back street will be a queen over an infinite realm of light and joy and glory. And that Christian man who can hardly make his way to church on crutches, will be a ministering spirit, flying to one of the farthest outposts of God's dominion. We do not work in this world; we are only getting ready to work. We are apprentices, and have not served our time out. We are students, and have not got our diplomas. Death is to be graduation. It will be commencement-day.

I go on and answer the question of my text, by saying that *our life is a conflict.* If you have never tried to control your passions, if you have never tried to subdue your temper, if you have never tried to rouse yourselves up to a better manhood or womanhood, you do not know what I mean. But if you have attempted to live a holy life, and to be better and to do better, then you sympathize with the Apostle Paul when he represented our life on earth a war with the world, a war with the flesh, a war with the devil. In addition to the struggle you have within, you have had a thousand outside battles. Sometimes it has been against poverty, against physical distresses, against bad social position, against an unhappy family name. In one case it has been one thing, and in another case it has been another thing; and with many of you, up to this point, it has been a hand-to-hand fight; and so it will be even unto the end. There is no tent for peaceful encampment but the grave. Life a conflict; so the Bible announces it. Life a conflict; so your own experience affirms it.

> "Must I be carried to the skies
> On flowery beds of ease,
> While others fought to win the prize
> And sailed through bloody seas?"

Again I answer the question of the text, by saying that *our life on earth is a prophecy.* By that I mean that what we are in this world we will be in the world to come, only on a larger scale. If a hero here, a hero there. If a cheat here, a cheat there. If a Christian here, a Christian there. I know sometimes there are marvelous changes in the last

9*

hour of life, and the dying thief, repenting, goes into paradise; but that is the exception. The probability is, my brethren, that what you are in the present time you will be in the future—what you now are you will always be, only with wider range. The prophecy is, if you now love that which is unclean and unrighteous, you will always love it. If your highest joy is in God, and your chief ambition to be like him, you are on your way to grandeurs that no dream ever was bright enough to depict. I judge from the blossoms what the fruit is going to be when it sets. He that is filthy shall be filthy still, and he that is holy shall be holy still. On banks of celestial joy walks the consecrated Alfred Cookman. In dungeons of starless night sits John Wilkes Booth.

I reply further to the question of my text, "What is your life?" by saying that *our life is a preparation.* If we are going on a long journey, we want some time to get ready. We must have extra apparel. We want our guide-book. Our comfort on the journey will depend very much upon what we start with. If we are going among bloodthirsty savages, we must take knife and pistol. God has started us out on a journey that will have no terminus, and, once started, we never come back. Are we getting ready? Are we armed? That question you hear to-day; but if I should utter it an hour from now, perhaps you might not hear it. Life is a preparation. If you have any weapons to sharpen, you had better sharpen them now. If you have any lamps to light, you had better light them now. When death once shuts the door of the sepulchre, the angel of repentance never opens it. "As the tree falleth, so it must lie." So far as I can tell your case, your great need is to get rid of your sins. I know of only one way to do it. The blood of Jesus Christ cleanseth from all sin; and though you may this morning count yourself the worst sinner, you may, by the grace of God, become the best saint. "Where sin abounded, grace shall much more abound."

Again, I answer this question of my text by saying *our life is a great uncertainty.* Nobody steps out of life as he expects to. Though a man may have been sick for thirty years, he is surprised at last when he goes. And though you may have known some one in invalidism for a quarter of a century, when you hear he has departed you throw up your hands, and say, "Is it possible?" We can make no calculation about the future. The world is full of temptation and of peril. We do not know how our children will turn out. We do not know what we ourselves might be tempted to do. We resolve on one thing; we do another. Our associations change. Our plans change. Our friends change. We change. And life is such a complete uncertainty, that I would not want to live one hour without the grace of God, and I very certainly would not want to die without it. Blessed be God, I feel under my feet, this morning, a rock firmer than the everlasting hills. That keeps me hopeful and confident. No overbearing autocrat sits on the throne of the universe. My father is King; and the mountains may depart, and the hills be removed, but his goodness and his kindness and his grace, never, never. In this Christian hope I have indulged for about twenty-two years; and while I should be sorry to know that there is any one in this house more unworthy than I have been, still I can tell you that I know enough of this religion to recommend it everywhere and always, and to say that the kindest, the gentlest, the grandest friend a man ever had is Jesus. I know him. I believe in him. I have put all my hope on him. He has never betrayed me. He will never betray you; and the best thing that you can do now is this moment to surrender yourselves to him for time and for eternity. But do not take my experience. It is comparatively brief. There are some, as you look over the audience, who have frost on the brow; ask them what they think of Jesus. Ask them whether he ever betrayed them. In what dark hour? By what grave? In what sickness? Ah, these old people can tell you a better story than I can of how in sickness Christ was their best physician; and how—when they came to give the last kiss to the cold lips that never might speak again, and to stand on the verge of a grave deep enough to bury all—they found Jesus the Comforter; and that this morning their brightest anticipation of the future is the presence of him whom, having not seen, we love; in whom, though now we see him not, yet believing, we rejoice with a joy unspeakable and full of glory.

I thought it best to say some of these things as I stand on the verge of my summer vacation, for I will be absent from you until September. I thought I would give my testimony for Jesus, and then urge you to look after this matter immediately, while I put to you the question of the text, "What is your life?"

There never was a better illustration of its uncertainty than we find in the disaster of our sister city. Some of you think of Syracuse only as a dépôt through which you pass on the way West. Some of you who know it better know it to be one of the most industrious and busy cities on the continent. It is the Golden Gate between the East and the West. Through its heart rolls the tide of a nation's life, beating hard with the motion of the great lakes on the one side, and the ocean on the other. Its convention halls filled with popular assemblages that have come there to decide great questions of philanthropy or politics. On either bank of this rushing stream of life are mansions, counting-rooms, stores, shops—hives where the voices of busy men hum while they gather in the honey of wealth. Feet shuffling, anvils ringing, bridges rumbling, printing-presses rattling. Illumined lyceum, and literary club, and churches lighted for week-night services, and houses swarming with fashionable levee. But it does not appear to me especially in that light. When I think of Syracuse, I think of it as the place of beautiful homes, and warm sympathies, and ardent friendships, and blessed associations. Among the happiest years of my ministry were those spent in that city, and the sorrow comes from there to my heart to-day. The young pastor of that church, the son of the leading minister of his denomination in this country, had only a few months ago gone to his new field; and last Tuesday night, surrounded by his congregation, in a merry festival, every thing going pleasantly and profitably on, with a sudden crash that I have not the heart to depict, many were ushered into the eternal world, and more were taken out half dead. Awful wreck of youth and old age; bride and bridegroom; the distinguished and the unknown. That city to-day is frantic with grief, and already the long processions have gone out to Oaklands, that beautiful cemetery where I have helped to put down some of my very best friends. It is a good place to sleep in. O men and women who know how to pray, pray for those broken hearts! O men and women who have had troubles of your own, cry unto God for that groaning city—for companions bereft, for parents suddenly made childless, for homes where father and mother will never come, for the pastor of that church, that he may come forth from this anguish of soul newly set apart and ordained by the "laying on of hands" of this calamity! Issuing from such a scene, he will be mightily in earnest now, and his cry will ring through the city, "What is your life?" But while we pray for them, let us also pray for ourselves. Be ye also ready. Risk not one moment away from Christ. For all the unregenerate and unpardoned there is not one hour of safety between this and the judgment-day, and after that there will be a tumbling-in of eternal calamities. Your first, your second, your hundredth, your thousandth, your last want is a heart changed by the almighty grace of God. Oh! get it now. Bow your head on the back of the seat in front of you, and be quick in surrendering yourselves to Jesus. He is mighty to save, and he would just as lief do it now as any other time. I do not think that cowardice is a characteristic of my nature, and yet I tell you plainly that I would not dare to walk down the street or cross the ferry were it not for a hope in Christ that whatever happens to my body my immortal soul shall go free. Why, the air is so full of perils, flying this way, flying that, flying before your face, flying behind your back, flying within, flying without, that we need God's promises hovering over us like a canopy, and marshaled all around us like an armed host.

Standing as we do at the beginning of a season when there is more sickness than at other times in the same year, and when many of us will be exposed to additional perils by travel, I thought it this morning better for me to cry out with an emphasis deepened by the calamity at the

West, asking you, "What is your life?" Is it a test? Make a successful experiment. Is it an apprenticeship? Make it an industrious one. Is it a conflict? Fight a brave fight. Is it a prophecy? Let it foretell glorious results. Is it a preparation? Make sure work. Is it an uncertainty? Get a Divine insurance. You say, "I will do this, I will do that. I will go into this city, and I will get gain." Whereas you know not what shall be on the morrow; for "What is your life?" "It is even as a vapor that appeareth for a little season, and then vanisheth away."

THINGS WE NEVER GET OVER.

"All manner of sin and blasphemy shall be forgiven unto men: but the blasphemy against the Holy Ghost shall not be forgiven unto men. And whosoever speaketh a word against the Son of man, it shall be forgiven him: but whosoever speaketh against the Holy Ghost, it shall not be forgiven him, neither in this world, neither in the world to come."—*Matthew* xii., 31, 32.

"He found no place of repentance, though he sought it carefully with tears."—*Hebrews* xii., 17.

LET it be understood at the outset that the Protestant pulpit has no revelation not given to the Protestant pew. The minister of Christ has no right to lord it over the consciences of men. When we preach, we do not utter edicts; we only offer opinions. Let the old Mother of Harlots from the Vatican issue the fiat that makes the people bow down into the dust; but in this land, and in this age, where King James's translation is in almost every hand and in almost every house, let every man understand that he has a right, equally with others, to interpret the Word of God for himself, asking only Divine illumination.

As sometimes you gather the whole family around the evening stand to hear some book read, so to-night we gather—a great Christian family group—to study this text; and now may one and the same Lamp cast its glow on all the circle!

You see from the first passage that I read that there is a sin against the Holy Ghost for which a man is never pardoned. Once having committed it, he is bound hand and foot for the dungeons of despair. Sermons may be preached to him, songs may be sung to him, prayers may be offered in his behalf; but all to no purpose. He is a captive for this world, and a captive for the world that is to come. Do you suppose that there is any one in this house to-night that has committed that sin? All sins are against the Holy Ghost; but my text speaks of *one* especially. It is very clear to my own mind that the sin against the Holy Ghost was the ascribing of the works of the Spirit to the agency of the devil in the time of the apostles. Indeed, the Bible distinctly tells us that. In other words, if a man had sight given to him, or if another was raised from the dead, and some one standing there should say, "This man got his sight by Satanic power; the Holy Spirit did not do this; Beelzebub accomplished it;" or, "This man raised from the dead was raised by Satanic influence," the man who said that dropped down under the curse of the text, and had committed the fatal sin against the Holy Ghost.

Now, I do not think it is possible in this day to commit that sin. I think it was possible only in apostolic times. But it is a very terrible thing ever to say any thing against the Holy Ghost, and it is a marked fact that our race have been marvelously kept back from that profanity. You hear a man swear by the name of the Eternal God, and by the name of Jesus Christ, but you never heard a man swear by the name of the Holy Ghost. There are those in this house who fear they are guilty of the unpardonable sin. Have you such anxiety? Then I have to tell you positively that you have not committed that sin, because the very anxiety is a result of the movement of the gracious Spirit, and your anxiety is proof positive, as certainly as any thing that can be demonstrated in mathematics, that you have not committed the sin that I have been speaking of. I can look off upon this audience and feel that there is salvation for all. It is not like when they put out with those life-boats from the *Loch Earn* for the *Ville du Havre.* They knew there was not room for all the passengers, but they were going to do as well as they could. But to-night we man the life-boat of the Gospel, and we cry out over the sea, "Room for all!" Oh that the Lord Jesus Christ would, this hour, bring you all out of the flood of sin, and plant you on the deck of this glorious old Gospel craft!

But while I have said I do not think it is possible for us to commit the particular sin spoken of in the first text, I have by reason of the second text to call your attention to the fact that there are sins which, though they may be pardoned, are in some respects irrevocable; and you can find no place for repentance, though you seek it carefully with tears. Esau had a birthright given him. In olden times it meant not only temporal but spiritual blessing. One day Esau took this birthright and traded it off for something to eat. Oh, the folly! But let us not be too severe upon him, for some of us have committed the same folly. After he had made the trade, he wanted to get it back. Just as though you to-morrow morning should take all your notes and bonds and Government securities, and should go into a restaurant, and in a fit of recklessness and hunger throw all those securities on the counter and ask for a plate of food, making that exchange. This was the one Esau made. He sold his birthright for a mess of pottage, and he was very sorry about it afterward; but "he found no place for repentance, though he sought it carefully with tears."

There is an impression in almost every man's mind that somewhere in the future there will be a chance where he can correct all his mistakes. Live as we may, if we only repent in time, God will forgive us, and then all will be as well as though we had never committed sin. My discourse shall come in collision with that theory. I shall show you, my friends, as God will help me, that there is such a thing as unsuccessful repentance; that there are things done wrong that always stay wrong, and for them you may seek some place of repentance, and seek it carefully, but never find it.

Belonging to this class of irrevocable mistakes is *the folly of a misspent youth.* We may look back to our college days, and think how we neglected chemistry, or geology, or botany, or mathematics. We may be sorry about it all our days. Can we ever get the discipline or the advantage that we would have had had we attended to those duties in early life? A man wakes up at forty years of age and finds that his youth has been wasted, and he strives to get back his early advantages. Does he get them back—the days of boyhood, the days in college, the days under his father's roof? "Oh," he says, "if I could only get those times back again, how I would improve them!" My brother, you will never get them back. They are gone, gone. You may be very sorry about it, and God may forgive, so that you may at last reach heaven; but you will never get over some of the mishaps that have come to your soul as a result of your neglect of early duty. You may try to undo it; you can not undo it. When you had a boy's arms, and a boy's eyes, and a boy's heart, you ought to have attended to those things. A man says, at fifty years of age, "I do wish I could get over these habits of indolence." When did you get them? At twenty or twenty-five years of age. You can not shake them off. They will hang to you to the very day of your death. If a young man through a long course of evil conduct undermines his physical health, and then repents of it in after-life, the Lord may pardon him; but that does not bring back good physical condition. I said to a minister of the Gospel, last Sabbath night, at the close of the service, "Where are you preaching now?" "Oh," he says, "I am not preaching. I am suffering from the physical effects of early sin. I can't preach now; I am sick." A consecrated man he now is, and he mourns bitterly over early sins; but that does not arrest their bodily effects.

The simple fact is, that men and women often take twenty years of their life to build up influences that require all the rest of their life to break down. Talk about a man beginning life when he is twenty-one years of age; talk about a woman beginning life when she is eighteen years of age! Ah, no! In many respects that is the time they close life. In nine cases out of ten, all the questions of eternity are decided before that. Talk about a majority of men getting their fortunes between thirty and forty! They get or lose fortunes between ten and twenty. When you tell me that a man is just beginning life, I tell you he is just closing it. The next fifty years will not be of as much importance to him as the first twenty.

Now, why do I say this? Is it for the annoyance of those who have only a baleful retrospection? You know that is not my way. I say it for the benefit of these young men and women. I want them to understand that eternity is wrapped up in this hour; that the sins of youth we never get over; that you are now fashioning the mold in which your great future is to run; that a minute, instead of being sixty seconds long, is made up of everlasting ages. You see what dignity and importance this gives to the life of all our young folks. Why, in the light of this subject life is not something to be frittered away, not something to be smirked about, not something to be danced out, but something to be weighed in the balances of eternity. Oh, young man! the sin of last night, the sin of to-night, the sin of to-morrow, will reach over ten thousand years, ay, over the great and unending eternity. You may, after a while, say, "I am very sorry. Now I have got to be thirty or forty years of age, and I do wish I had never committed those sins." What does that amount to? God may pardon you; but undo those things you never will, you never can.

In this same category of irrevocable mistakes I put *all parental neglect.* We begin the education of our children too late. By the time they get to be ten or fifteen we wake up to our mistakes, and try to eradicate this bad habit, and change that; but it is too late. That parent who omits, in the first ten years of the child's life, to make an eternal impression for Christ, never makes it. The child will probably go on with all the disadvantages, which might have been avoided by parental faithfulness. Now you see what a mistake that father or mother makes who puts off to late life adherence to Christ. Here is a man who at fifty years of age says to you, "I must be a Christian;" and he yields his heart to God, and sits in the house of prayer to-night a Christian. None of us can doubt it. He goes home, and he says, "Here at fifty years of age I have given my heart to the Saviour. Now I must establish a family altar." What? Where are your children now? One in Boston; another in Cincinnati; another in

New Orleans; and you, my brother, at your fiftieth year going to establish your family altar. Very well; better late than never; but alas, alas that you did not do it twenty-five years ago!

When I was in Chamouni, Switzerland, I saw in the window of one of the shops a picture that impressed my mind very much. It was a picture of an accident that occurred on the side of one of the Swiss mountains. A company of travelers, with guides, went up some very steep places— places which but few travelers attempted to go up. They were, as all travelers are there, fastened together with cords at the waist, so that if one slipped, the rope would hold him—the rope fastened to the others. Passing along the most dangerous point, one of the guides slipped, and they all started down the precipice; but after a while, one more muscular than the rest struck his heels into the ice and stopped; but the rope broke, and down, hundreds and thousands of feet, the rest went. And so I see whole families bound together by ties of affection, and in many cases walking on slippery places of worldliness and sin. The father knows it, and the mother knows it, and they are bound all together. After a while they begin to slide down steeper and steeper, and the father becomes alarmed, and he stops, planting his feet on the "Rock of Ages." He stops, but the rope breaks, and those who were once tied fast to him by moral and spiritual influences go over the precipice. Oh, there is such a thing as coming to Christ soon enough to save ourselves, but not soon enough to save others!

How many parents wake up in the latter part of life to find out the mistake! The parent says, "I have been too lenient," or, "I have been too severe in the discipline of my children. If I had the little ones around me again, how different I would do!" You will never have them around again. The work is done, the bent to the character is given, the eternity is decided. I say this to young parents—those who are twenty-five or thirty or thirty-five years of age—have the family altar to-night. How do you suppose that father felt as he leaned over the couch of his dying child, and the expiring son said to him, "Father, you have been very good to me. You have given me a fine education, and you have placed me in a fine social position; you have done every thing for me in a worldly sense; but, father, you never told me how to die. Now I am dying, and I am lost!"

In this category of irrevocable mistakes I place, also, *the unkindnesses done the departed.* When I was a boy, my mother used to say to me sometimes, "De Witt, you will be sorry for that when I am gone." And I remember just how she looked, sitting there, with cap and spectacles, and the old Bible in her lap; and she never said a truer thing than that, for I have often been sorry since. While we have our friends with us, we say unguarded things that wound the feelings of those to whom we ought to give nothing but kindness. Perhaps the parent, without inquiring into the matter, boxes the child's ears. The little one, who has fallen in the street, comes in covered with dust, and, as though the first disaster were not enough, she whips it. After a while the child is taken, or the parent is taken, or the companion is taken, and those who are left say, "Oh, if we could only get back those unkind words, those unkind deeds; if we could only recall them!" But you can not get them back. You might bow down over the grave of that loved one, and cry and cry and cry. The white lips would make no answer. The stars shall be plucked out of their sockets, but these influences shall not be torn away. The world shall die, but there are some wrongs immortal. The moral of which is, take care of your friends while you have them; spare the scolding; be economical of the satire; shut up in a dark cave, from which they shall never swarm forth, all the words that have a sting in them. You will wish you had some day— very soon you will—perhaps to-morrow. Oh yes. While with a firm hand you administer parental discipline, also administer it very gently, lest some day there be a little slab in Greenwood, and on it chiseled "Our Willie," or "Our Charlie;" and though you bow down prone in the grave, and seek a place of repentance, and seek it carefully with tears, you can not find it.

There is another sin that I place in the class of irrevocable mistakes, and that is *lost opportunities of getting good*. I never come to a Saturday night but I can see during that week that I have missed opportunities of getting good. I never come to my birthday but I can see that I have wasted many chances of getting better. I never go home on Sabbath from the discussion of a religious theme without feeling that I might have done it in a more successful way. How is it with you? If you take a certain number of bushels of wheat and scatter them over a certain number of acres of land, you expect a harvest in proportion to the amount of seed scattered. And I ask you to-night, have the sheaves of moral and spiritual harvest corresponded with the advantages given? How has it been with you? You may make resolutions for the future, but past opportunities are gone. In the long procession of future years all those past moments will march; but the archangel's trumpet that wakes the dead will not wake up for you one of those privileges. Esau has sold his birthright, and there is not wealth enough in the treasure-houses of heaven to buy it back again. What does that mean? It means that if you are going to get any advantage out of this Sabbath-day, you will have to get it before the hand wheels around on the clock to twelve to-night. It means that every moment of our life has two wings, and that it does not fly, like a hawk, in circles, but in a straight line from eternity to eternity. It means that though other chariots may break down, or drag heavily, this one never drops the brake, and never ceases to run. It means that while at other feasts the cup may be passed to us and we may reject it, and yet after a while take it, the cup-bearers to this feast never give us but one chance at the chalice, and, rejecting that, we shall "find no place for repentance, though we seek it carefully with tears."

There is one more class of sins that I put in this category of irrevocable sins, and that is *lost opportunities of usefulness.* Your business partner is a proud man. In ordinary circumstances, say to him, "Believe in Christ," and he will say, "You mind your business, and I'll mind mine." But there has been affliction in the household. His heart is tender. He is looking around for sympathy and solace. Now is your time. Speak, speak, or forever hold your peace. There is a time in farm-life when you plant the corn and when you sow the seed. Let that go by, and the farmer will wring his hands while other husbandmen are gathering in the sheaves. You are in a religious meeting, and there is an opportunity for you to speak a word for Christ. You say, "I must do it." Your cheek flushes with embarrassment. You rise half way, but you cower before men whose breath is in their nostrils, and you sag back, and the opportunity is gone, and all eternity will feel the effect of your silence. Try to get back that opportunity! You can not find it. You might as well try to find the fleece that Gideon watched, or take in your hand the dew that came down on the locks of the Bethlehem shepherds, or to find the plume of the first robin that went across paradise. It is gone; it is gone forever. When an opportunity for personal repentance or of doing good passes away, you may hunt for it; you can not find it. You may fish for it; it will not take the hook. You may dig for it; you can not bring it up. Remember that there are wrongs and sins that can never be corrected; that our privileges fly not in circles, but in a straight line; that the lightnings have not as swift feet as our privileges when they are gone, and let an opportunity of salvation go by us an inch, the one hundredth part of an inch, the thousandth part of an inch, the millionth part of an inch, and no man can overtake it. Fire-winged seraphim can not come up with it. The eternal God himself can not catch it.

I stand before those who have a glorious birthright. Esau's was not so rich as yours. Sell it once, and you sell it forever. The world wants to buy it. Satan wants to buy it. Listen for a moment to these brilliant offers, and it is gone.

Why do I tell you these truths? I have stood before you year after year telling you these things. Some have yielded their hearts to God, and a glorious crop of souls has been reaped; but this audience of immortal men and women, are they all prepared for the great future? I could stand here and play a sweeter harp. I could talk of the gates of pearl, and the walls of precious stones, and the crowns of light. What is the use of talking of those things to those who have no preparation for that land, and who are on the wrong road?

I remember the story of the lad on the *Arctic* some years ago—the lad Stewart Holland. A vessel crashed into the *Arctic* in the time of a fog, and it was found that the ship must go down. Some of the passengers got off in the lifeboats, some got off on rafts; but three hundred went to the bottom. During all those hours of calamity, Stewart Holland stood at the signal-gun, and it sounded across the sea, boom! boom! The helmsman forsook his place, the engineer was gone, and some fainted and some prayed and some blasphemed, and the powder was gone, and they could no more set off the signal-gun. The lad broke in the magazine and brought out more powder, and again the gun boomed over the sea. Oh, my friends, I behold many of you in immortal peril! Sickness will come down after a while upon you, death will come upon you, judgment will come upon you, eternity will come upon you. Some, having taken the warning, have gone off in the life-boat, and they are safe; but others are not making any attempt to escape. So I stand at this signal-gun of the Gospel, sounding the alarm, Beware! beware! "Now is the accepted time; now is the day of salvation." The wrath to come! The wrath to come! Boom! Boom! Fly to the hope of the Gospel. Jesus waits. He stretches out his arms to all this auditory, and cries to-night with a tenderness I have never heard before, "Come unto me, all ye who are weary and heavy laden, and I will give you rest." That is what you want, sinful, tempted, bruised, and dying soul! May the Lord help you to accept the mercy and the solace and the salvation of the Gospel! Hear it, that your soul may live!

THE BROKEN-UP FUNERAL.

"Now when he came nigh to the gate of the city, behold, there was a dead man carried out, the only son of his mother, and she was a widow; and much people of the city was with her. And when the Lord saw her, he had compassion on her, and said unto her, Weep not. And he came and touched the bier: and they that bare him stood still. And he said, Young man, I say unto thee, Arise. And he that was dead sat up, and began to speak. And he delivered him to his mother."—*Luke* vii., 12-15.

THE text calls us to stand at the gate of the city of Nain. The streets are a-rush with business and gayety, and the ear is deafened with the hammers of mechanism and the wheels of traffic. Work, with its thousand arms and thousand eyes and thousand feet, fills all the street, when suddenly the crowd parts, and a funeral passes. Between the wheels of work and pleasure there comes a long procession of mourning people. Who is it? A trifler says, "Oh, it is nothing but a funeral. It may have come up from the hospital of the city, or the almshouse, or some low place of the town;" but not so says the serious observer. There are so many evidences of tired bereavement that we know at the first glance some one has been taken away greatly beloved; and to our inquiry, "Who is this that is carried out with so many offices of kindness and affection?" the reply comes, "The only son of his mother, and she a widow." Stand back, and let the procession pass out! Hush all the voices of mirth and pleasure! Let every head be uncovered! Weep with this passing procession; and let it be told through all the market-places and bazaars of Nain, that in Galilee to-day the sepulchre hath gathered to itself "the only son of his mother, and she a widow."

There are two or three things that, in my mind, give especial pathos to this scene. The first is, he was *a young man* that was being carried out. To the aged, death becomes beautiful. The old man halts and pants along the road, where once he bounded like the roe. From the midst of immedicable ailments and sorrows, he cries out, "How long, O Lord, how long?" Foot-sore and hardly bestead on the hot journey, he wants to get home. He sits in the church, and sings, with a very tremulous voice, some tune he sung forty years ago, and longs to join the better assemblage of the one hundred and forty and four thousand, and the thousands of thousands who have passed the flood. How sweetly he sleeps the last sleep! Push back the white locks from the wrinkled temples; they will never ache again. Fold the hands over the still heart; they will never toil again. Close gently the eyes; they will never weep again.

But this man that I am speaking of was a young man. He was just putting on the armor of life, and he was exulting to think how his sturdy blows would ring out above the clangor of the battle. I suppose he had a young man's hopes, a young man's ambition, and a young man's courage. He said, "If I live many years, I will feed the hungry and clothe the naked. In this city of Nain, where there are so many bad young men, I will be sober, and honest, and pure, and magnanimous, and my mother shall never be ashamed of me." But all these prospects are blasted in one hour. There he passes lifeless in the procession. Behold all that is left on earth of the high-hearted young man of the city of Nain.

There is another thing that adds very much to this scene, and that is, he was an *only* son. However large the family flock may be, we never could think of sparing one of the lambs. Though they may all have their faults, they all have their excellences that commend them to the parental heart; and if it were peremptorily demanded of you to-day that you should yield up one of your children out of a very large family, you would be confounded, and you could not make a selection. But this was an only son, around whom gathered all the parental expectations. How much care in his education! How much caution in watching his habits! He would carry down the name to other times. He would have entire control of the family property long after the parents had gone to their last reward. He would stand in society a thinker, a worker, a philanthropist, a Christian. No, no. It is all ended. Behold him there. Breath is gone. Life is extinct. The only son of his mother.

There was one other thing that added to the pathos of this scene, and that was, his mother was a widow. The main hope of that home had been broken, and now he was come up to be the staff. The chief light of the household had been extinguished, and this was the only light left. I suppose she often said, looking at him, " There are only two of us." Oh, it is a grand thing to see a young man step out in life, and say to his mother, " Don't be downhearted. I will, as far as possible, take father's place, and as long as I live you shall never want any thing." It is not always that way. Sometimes the young people get tired of the old people. They say they are queer; that they have so many ailments; and they sometimes wish them out of the way. A young man and his wife sat at the table, their little son on the floor playing beneath the table. The old father was very old, and his hand shook so, they said, "You shall no more sit with us at the table." And so they gave him a place in the corner, where day by day he ate out of an earthen bowl—every thing put into that bowl. One day his hand trembled so much, he dropped it, and it broke; and the son, seated at the elegant table in midfloor, said to his wife, "Now, we'll get father a wooden bowl, and that he can't break." So a wooden bowl was obtained, and every day old grandfather ate out of that, sitting in the corner. One day, while the elegant young man and his wife were seated at their table, with chased silver and all the luxuries, and their little son sat upon the floor, they saw the lad whittling, and they said, "My son, what are you doing there with that knife?" "Oh," said he, "I—I'm making a trough for my father and mother to eat out of when they get old!"

But this young man of the text was not of that character. He did not belong to that school. I can tell it from the way they mourned over him. He was to be the companion of his mother. He was to be his mother's protector. He would return now some of the kindnesses he had received in the days of childhood and boyhood. Ay, he would with his strong hand uphold that form already enfeebled with age. Will he do it? No. In one hour all that promise of help and companionship is gone. There is a world of anguish in that one short phrase, "The only son of his mother, and she a widow."

Now, my friends, it was upon this scene that Christ broke. He came in without any introduction. He stopped the procession. He had only two utterances to make; the one to the mourning mother, the other to the dead. He cried out to the mourning one, "Weep not;" and then, touching the bier on which the son lay, he cried out, "Young man, I say unto thee, Arise! And he that was dead sat up."

I learn two or three things from this subject, and, first, that Christ *was a man*. You see how that sorrow played upon all the chords of his heart. I think we forget this too often. Christ was a man more certainly than you are, for he was a perfect man. No sailor ever slept in ship's hammock more soundly than Christ slept in that boat on Gennesaret. In every nerve, and muscle, and bone, and fibre of his body; in every emotion and affection of his heart; in every action and decision of his mind, he was a man. He looked off upon the sea just as you look off upon the waters. He went into Martha's house just as you go into a cottage. He breathed hard when he was tired, just as you do when you are exhausted. He felt after sleeping out a night in the storm just like you do when you have been exposed to a tempest. It was just as humiliating for him to beg bread as it would be for you to become a pauper. He felt just as much insulted by being sold for thirty pieces of silver as you would if you were sold for the price of a dog. From the crown of the head to the sole of the foot he was a man. When the thorns were twisted for his brow, they hurt him just as much as they would hurt your brow, if they were twisted for it. He took not on him the nature of angels; he took on him the seed of Abraham. *Ecce homo!*—Behold the man!

But I must also draw from this subject that *he was a God*. Suppose that a man should now attempt to break up a funeral obsequy: he would be seized by the law, he would be imprisoned, if he were not actually slain by the

mob before the officers could secure him. If Christ had
been a mere mortal, would he have had a right to come
in upon such a procession? Would he have succeeded in
his interruption? He was more than a man, for when
he cried out, "'I say unto thee, Arise!' he that was dead
sat up." What excitement there must have been thereabouts! The body had lain prostrate. It had been mourned
over with agonizing tears, and yet now it begins to move
in the shroud, and to be flushed with life; and, at the
command of Christ, he rises up and looks into the faces
of the astonished spectators. Oh, this was the work of a
God! I hear it in his voice; I see it in the flash of his
eye; I behold it in the snapping of death's shackles; I see
it in the face of the rising slumberer; I hear it in the outcry of all those who were spectators of the scene. If, when
I see my Lord Jesus Christ mourning with the bereaved,
I put my hands on his shoulders, and say, "My brother,"
now that I hear him proclaim supernatural deliverances, I
look up into his face and say with Thomas, "My Lord and
my God." Do you not think he was a God? A great
many people do not believe that, and they compromise the
matter, or they think they compromise it. They say he
was a very good man, but he was not a God. That is impossible. He was either a God or a wretch, and I will
prove it. If a man professes to be that which he is not,
what is he? He is a liar, an impostor, a hypocrite. That
is your unanimous verdict. Now, Christ professed to be a
God. He said over and over again he was a God, took the
attributes of a God, and assumed the works and offices of a
God. Dare you now say he was not? He was a God, or
he was a wretch. Choose ye.

Do you think I can not prove by this Bible that he was

a God? If you do not believe this Bible, of course there is no need of my talking with you. There is no common data from which to start. Suppose you do believe it? Then I can demonstrate that he was divine. I can prove he was creator, John i., 3, "All things were made by him; and without him was not any thing made that was made." He was eternal, Rev. xxii., 13, "I am Alpha and Omega, the beginning and the end, the first and the last." I can prove he was omnipotent, Heb. i., 10, "The heavens are the work of thine hands." I can prove he was omniscient, John ii., 25, "He knew what was in man." Oh yes, he is a God. He cleft the sea. He upheaved the crystalline walls along which the Israelites marched. He planted the mountains. He raises up governments and casts down thrones, and marches across nations and across worlds and across the universe, eternal, omnipotent, unhindered, and unabashed. That hand that was nailed to the cross holds the stars in a leash of love. That head that dropped on the bosom in fainting and death shall make the world quake at its nod. That voice that groaned in the last pang shall swear before the trembling world that time shall be no longer. Oh, do not insult the common sense of the race by telling us that this person was only a man, in whose presence the paralytic arm was thrust out well, and the devils crouched, and the lepers dropped their scales, and the tempests folded their wings, and the boy's sachel of a few loaves made a banquet for five thousand, and the sad procession of my text broke up in congratulation and hosanna!

Again, I learn from this subject *that Christ was a sympathizer*. Mark you, this was a city funeral. In the country, when the bell tolls, they know all about it for five miles around, and they know what was the matter with the man, how old he was, and what were his last experiences. They know with what temporal prospects he has left his family. There is no haste, there is no indecency in the obsequies. There is nothing done as a mere matter of business. Even the children come out as the procession passes, and look sympathetic, and the tree-shadows seem to deepen, and the brooks weep in sympathy as the procession goes by. But, mark you, this that I am speaking of was a city funeral. In great cities the cart jostles the hearse, and there is mirth, and gladness, and indifference as the weeping procession goes by. In this city of Nain it was a common thing to have trouble and bereavement and death. Christ saw it every day there. Perhaps that very hour there were others being carried out; but this frequency of trouble did not harden Christ's heart at all. He stepped right out, and he saw this mourner, and he had compassion on her, and he said, "Weep not."

Now, I have to tell you, O bruised souls, and there are many here to-day (have you ever looked over an audience like this and noticed how many shadows of sorrow there are? You can not, where you sit, see them, but I can from where I stand), I come to all such to-day and say, "Christ meets you, and he has compassion on you, and he says, 'Weep not.'" Perhaps with some it is financial trouble. "Oh," you say, "it is such a silly thing for a man to cry over lost money." Is it? Suppose you had a large fortune, and all luxuries brought to your table, and your wardrobe was full, and your home was beautified by music and sculpture and painting, and thronged by the elegant and educated, and then some rough misfortune should strike you in the face, and trample your treasures, and taunt your children for their faded dress, and send you into commercial circles an underling where once you waved a sceptre of gold, do you think you would cry then? I think you would. But Christ comes and meets all such to-day. He sees all the straits in which you have been thrust. He observes the sneer of that man who once was proud to walk in your shadow, and glad to get your help. He sees the protested note, the uncanceled judgment, the foreclosed mortgage, the heart-breaking exasperation, and he says, "Weep not. I own the cattle on a thousand hills. I will never let you starve. From my hand the fowls of heaven peck all their food. And will I let you starve? Never— no, my child, never."

Or perhaps this tramp at the gate of Nain has an echo in your own bereft spirit. You went out to the grave, and you felt you never could come back again. You left your heart there. The white snow of death covered all the garden. You listen for the speaking of voices that will never be heard again, and the sounding of feet that will never move in your dwelling again, and there is this morning, while I speak, a dull, heavy, leaden pressure on your heart. God has dashed out the light of your eyes, and the heavy spirit that that woman carried out of the gate of Nain is no heavier than yours. And you open the door, but he comes not in. And you enter the nursery, but she is not there. And you sit at the table, but there is a vacant chair next to you. And the sun does not shine as brightly as it used to, and the voices of affection do not strike you with so quick a thrill, and your cheek has not so healthy a hue, and your eye has not so deep a fire. Do I not know? Do we not all know? There is an unlifted woe on your heart. You have been out carrying your loved one beyond the gate of the city of Nain. But look yonder. Some one stands watching. He seems waiting for you. As you come up he stretches out his hand of help. His voice is full of tenderness, yet thrills with eternal strength. Who is it? The very one who accosted the mourner at the gate of Nain, and he says, "Weep not."

Perhaps it is a worse grief than that. It may be a *living* home trouble that you can not speak about to your best friend. It may be some domestic unhappiness. It may be an evil suspicion. It may be the disgrace following in the footsteps of a son that is wayward, or a companion who is cruel, or a father that will not do right; and for years there may have been a vulture striking its beak into the vitals of your soul, and you sit there to-day feeling it is worse than death. It is. It is worse than death. And yet there is relief. Though the night may be the blackest, though the voices of hell may tell you to curse God and die, look up and hear the voice that accosted the woman of the text as it says, "Weep not."

> "Earth hath no sorrow
> That heaven can not cure."

I learn, again, from all this that Christ is *the master of the grave*. Just outside the gate of the city, Death and Christ measured lances; and when the young man rose, Death dropped. Now we are sure of our resurrection. Oh, what a scene it was when that young man came back! The mother never expected to hear him speak again. She never thought that he would kiss her again. How the tears started, and how her heart throbbed, as she said, "Oh, my son, my son, my son!" And that scene is going to be repeated. It is going to be repeated ten thousand times. These broken family circles have got to come together.

These extinguished household lights have got to be rekindled. There will be a stir in the family lot in the cemetery, and there will be a rush into life at the command, "Young man, I say unto thee, Arise!" As the child shakes off the dust of the tomb, and comes forth fresh and fair and beautiful, and you throw your arms around it and press it to your heart, angel to angel will repeat the story of Nain, "He delivered him to his mother." Did you notice that passage in the text as I read it? "He delivered him to his mother." O ye troubled souls! O ye who have lived to see every prospect blasted, peeled, scattered, consumed! wait a little. The seed-time of tears will become the wheat harvest. In a clime cut of no wintry blast, under a sky palled by no hurtling tempest, and amidst redeemed ones that weep not, that part not, that die not, friend will come to friend, and kindred will join kindred, and the long procession that marches the avenues of gold will lift up their palms as again and again it is announced that the same one who came to the relief of this woman of the text came to the relief of many a maternal heart, and repeated the wonders of resurrection, and "delivered him to his mother." Oh, that will be the harvest of the world. That will be the coronation of princes. That will be the Sabbath of eternity.

BARTERING FOR ETERNITY.

"Buy the truth, and sell it not."—*Proverbs* xxiii., 23.

CHRIST never forgot the occupation of the people to whom he spake. His metaphors and illustrations were apt to be drawn from the every-day business of the people whom he addressed. Speaking to the fishermen, he said, "The Gospel is a net let down into the sea." Addressing himself to the farmers, he said, "A sower went forth to sow, and some of the seed fell on good ground, and some on thorny ground." That he might attract the attention of the shepherds, he tells the parable of the lost sheep, and how the shepherd went out in the wilderness to bring it home to the fold. In order that the plainest woman that ever mixed bread might not be in doubt as to what he meant, he said, "The kingdom of heaven is like leaven, or yeast, which leavens the whole lump." Indeed, there were no learned allusions, there was no profound disquisition, there was no acute analysis, in the addresses of Christ. They were merely a plain talk from a heart overflowing with love for the people, in a way that all the people understood.

There is hardly a style of mind that is not susceptible to illustration. One Sabbath I was preaching on an Indian reservation to an audience of Indians. I was trying, at that time, to impress upon them the fact that childhood generally indicated the character of manhood. They did not seem to understand until I told them that *a crooked young tree makes a crooked old tree*, and then their eyes flashed with intelligence.

When my text says, "Buy the truth, and sell it not," it employs an illustration which ought to attract the attention of all those directly or indirectly engaged in merchandise. Would to God that we were all as wise in managing the matters of the soul as we are in worldly traffic! I want, this morning, to give some of the characteristics of a wise spiritual merchant.

In the first place, I remark that the wise spiritual merchant *will not neglect to take an account of stock*. We are coming on toward the 1st of January, and all our business men will be absorbed. They who ordinarily go over at eight or nine o'clock in the morning to business will go at seven; and if you happen to be on the street some night at eleven or twelve o'clock, you will meet them; and if you ask, "Why are you coming home so late?" they will say, "We are taking an account of stock." Every wise business-man does that. Once a year all the goods must be handled, and every shelf must be ransacked, and the remnants must be unrolled, and the dusty bundles unwrapped, and every thing in the store must be upturned. Once a year the business man wants to know how things stand. He reviews the books, writes them up, and draws out on a fair balance-sheet all his worldly circumstances; so many goods, so many liabilities; so much capital that is comparatively worthless, so much that can be easily turned into cash; so many debts; so many bills out that are perfectly good, so many that are doubtful. In other words, he looks over all the affairs of the year, and knows just what position he occupies. Now, my friends, ought we not to be just as scrutinizing in the matters of the soul? The Rothschilds or the Stewarts never did a business of such infinite importance as that going on in the heart of every man and woman in this audience. There are the goods—the faculties and energies and passions of your soul. There are the liabilities—to temptation, to danger, and death. Can it be that we have never taken an account of stock? Can it be that we have been running this tremendous business for eternity, and never drawn out our affairs on a balance-sheet? I know such a review is not pleasant. Neither does any merchant find it agreeable to take an account of stock. You all put the day off as long as you can. You do not know what it may reveal to you. You say, "There may come up something in review that I don't want to know, and yet, after all, I must, as a business-man, attend to it." And though you put it off as long as you can, you after a while say, "Boys, we'll go and take an account of stock." Many a man has been surprised, at the close of that operation, to find how poorly he was off. Ah! it is just as unpleasant to review our spiritual condition. The fact is, we are insolvent. We owe debts we can never pay. We have been running this business of the soul so poorly that we have got to be wound up. We can not pay one cent on a dollar. We can not answer for one of ten thousand of our transgressions. There has never, in worldly affairs, been such a miserable failure in Wall Street or State Street as we have made in spiritual affairs. We owe God every thing. We have paid him nothing; some of us have never tried to pay him any thing.

But sometimes, when a man is thoroughly cornered in business matters, and he says, "I must stop payment," while he is sitting in his store or office thoroughly discouraged, there is a rap at the door. "Come in," he says; an old friend enters. He says, "I hear you are in great difficulty; how much money will get you out of this embarrassment?" "Well," you say, "five thousand dollars would." He says, "Here it is"—bank, pay so and so. The man is delivered from all his commercial distresses. Just so, while we are sitting down disheartened on account of our sin, and feeling that there is no hope, there is a rap at the door of the heart; it is Jesus coming in. He says, "What do you want?" We answer, "We want pardon, we want peace, we want the eternal salvation of the Gospel." Jesus says, "There it is." The debts are paid, the obligations are canceled. Now, we do business on an infinite capital. Now, all the banks of eternity are ready with their loans. Now, we have on paper the name of the King. There is no condemnation to them who are in Christ Jesus.

> "'The soul that on Jesus hath leaned for repose,
> I will not, I will not desert to its foes;
> That soul, though all hell should endeavor to shake,
> I'll never, no, never, no, never forsake.'"

I remark again, the wise spiritual merchant will be on his *guard against burglars.* How long it takes you to lock up your store at night! You put your valuables in the safe, you shove the door to, you turn the lock; you try it afterward to be sure it is fastened; you bolt and rebolt your doors. You have a watchman, perhaps, at the store. You charge the police, when they go up and down, once in a while to look in. In addition to that, perhaps, you have a burglar-alarm, so that the opening of a window or door in the night with a great rattle will wake up the watchman. Perhaps you have a watch-dog under the counter, who feels the responsibility of the store resting on his shaggy neck, his mouth down between his paws. If there be the least sound, he lifts one ear, he lifts his head, he rises up, and then lies down again with a growl, as much as to say, "I wish it had been somebody." Would to God that we were as wise in regard to spiritual burglaries! There are a thousand temptations around about our soul ready to blow it up; ready to blast it; ready to shove the bolt and steal the infinite and immortal treasure. The apostle says, "What I say unto one, I say unto all—watch!" That is, look out for burglars. Here comes a thief stealing our Christian belief, and it is very easy to lose it, but it is not so easy to get it back again. Let it once be gone, and all the detectives on earth can not fetch it back. Alas for the man who, once believing in Christianity, now rejects it! He tries to be satisfied, and he tries to make you believe he is satisfied; but the most doleful thing on earth is a religion without Jesus Christ in it. If there are any pries at the door of your heart, if any of those burglars are trying to break in the windows of your soul, you had better fly at them with infinite vehemence, and ask the Lord God to help you in the arrest.

Here is another trying to break in and steal your patience. It puts something explosive in your temper, and tries to blow it up. Here you have a casket of diamonds made of days and hours and months of precious time. Oh, how many burglars there are around trying to steal those diamonds! Temptations to pride, temptations to self-indulgence, temptations to neglect the great things of eternity, make up a gang of desperadoes that have broken out of the jail of hell, and are prowling around our soul trying to steal this treasure; and, in the name of God, I bid you, arm against them. They have taken many of the spoils already, and I cry, "Stop thief!"

> "My soul, be on thy guard,
>   Ten thousand foes arise,
> And hosts of sin are pressing hard
>   To draw thee from the skies.
>
> "Ne'er think the victory won,
>   Nor once at ease sit down,
> Thine arduous work will not be done
>   Till thou hast got thy crown."

I remark, again, that the wise spiritual merchant will *watch the state of the markets.* When the business man takes up the paper in the morning, he does not first look at the marriages and deaths or the editorials. He looks at the price-current. Before ten o'clock merchants all know whether gold has gone up or down, whether the goods they have on the shelf have increased or decreased in value. A man might say, "It is nothing to me how others do business, or what prices others get; I shall go straight on without any reference to any body else in business." You know that would be the precursor of bankruptcy. He watches the markets; he can not afford to be indifferent. Now, I say we ought to be just as alert in looking at the spiritual markets. We ought to know whether the cause of God in the earth is going up or down. No man can be independent of the general state of morals and of religion in the community. For this reason, every intelligent Christian will be examining the churches, the schools, and the benevolent organizations. The failure of a crop in Russia, or of a bank in London, or the breaking-out of a war in India affects prices in the New York market; and the conversion of one soul in Central Africa ought to leave its impression on every intelligent Christian in Brooklyn. It is my business this morning to proclaim to you the state of the spiritual markets, and I tell you the cause of God is advancing. The people are buying the truth, and are not so disposed to sell it as they used to be. The ships of Tarshish are coming into the harbor of God, and the gold and frankincense and myrrh are showering down at the feet of Jesus. The religion of the Lord Jesus Christ is rising. The nations are bidding for this Gospel, and the merchandise of it is better than the merchandise of silver.

If this religion of Christ is advancing in value, and must continue advancing, your business judgment will tell you the larger the investment you make in it, the better. Other values may have depressions. You might buy Michigan Central, perhaps, at 125, and it might drop to 120; you might buy Pittsburg, Fort Wayne, and Chicago for 85, and it might drop to 83, and you might be ruined. But these Gospel values always will be on the advance. Sometimes the Government comes on the marts of business and upsets the planning of the gold-gamblers, and vindicates justice and the rights of the people; and the Lord God Almighty is the mightiest of financiers, and he will scatter to the four winds of heaven all the plotters of iniquity, and he will vindicate his government, and make his own children the princes of eternity.

O these spiritual values! Men do not know how to estimate them. You give a dollar to a Christian object, and say, "That's gone; I'll never hear of that again." You give twenty-five dollars to worldly gratification, and you think you have made a good investment. Have you? Of the twenty-five dollars you gave to the worldly gratification you will hear nothing; but that one dollar has been an investment that will go on accumulating interest and adding compound interest until it will take the mightiest intelligence of heaven to estimate what is the value of that dollar rolling on through all eternity until the banking-houses of heaven can not hold the accumulation. We can not understand now God's way of estimating things. The woman who sells in her thread-and-needle store one thousand dollars' worth a year can not estimate the plans of a man who sells two millions of dollars' worth of goods a year. God's projects are too vast for us. We talk of one man buying a railroad, or of another buying half a city. Why, the Lord Jesus Christ bought the whole earth, and paid for it in one day—paid for it in tears and agony and blood! You talk about vast corporations and moneyed institutions and powerful companies; but the richest company in all the universe is the company of Christ's disciples, and the poorest one of them will be a millionaire to all eternity. I take one of these bonds of the company, and I tear off just one coupon, and hand it to you, and you read on that coupon these words, "All are yours." If a man wants a better dividend than that, I do not know where he will get it.

Again, I remark that the wise spiritual merchant is *careful to get a profit out of every thing that passes through his hands.* You go into the store. You see the roll of nankeen, or the barrel of sugar, or the string of bananas, or the coil of ship cable. Before the merchant lets them pass out of his hands, he will make a profit out of them. If he has paid ten cents a yard for something, he will get twelve or fifteen; if he has paid twenty-five cents for a pound, he will get thirty. Now, I say the wise spiritual merchant will get a spiritual advantage out of every thing that comes across him—from all sorrows, all perplexities, all vexations. He will take these harrows and furnaces of trouble, and from them get an everlasting profit. Affliction has failed of its object if it does not leave a soul worth more than when it came. It is very interesting to get into confidential conversation with a man who has gained a large property, and to have him tell you just how he made his money; but it is more interesting to get into the confidence of an old Christian, and have him tell you just how he accumulated his wealth of Christian character. He will say, "My property went down in 1857, but I came out of that trouble with infinite resources of spiritual comfort and strength." He will say, "I was sick for three months, and could not do a stroke of work; and when I came forth I was as weak as a child, and staggered along the street; but, oh! my soul had the strength of a giant." And he will tell you of the dark day that came in his household when a loved one was carried out, and he felt that every thing was gone with it; and on his way back from the cemetery Jesus met him and said, "Weep not, I will make up for thy loss; I will more than make up for it. Those little feet are already bounding along the corridors of heaven. That hand is already sweeping the harp-strings of glory." Jesus took that afflicted father to the verge of the grave, and bid him look down into it, and instead of a grave it became a chest of immortal brilliants. As he ran his hand up and down the gate of the sepulchre he found it hard, cold, rusty iron, but Jesus touched it and it became solid pearl —bars of pearl, bolts of pearl, hinges of pearl, and, lo! it was the gate of heaven. "All things work together for good to those who love God;" and I pray the Lord Almighty that, whatever misfortune, whatever vexation, whatever trial, whatever bereavements pass through our soul, we may reap from them a spiritual tariff that will make us richer while we live on earth, and glad through all eternity.

I remark, again, that the wise spiritual merchant will not take any *unnecessary risks*. Before the ship goes out of the harbor, application is made to the marine insurance company; the Board of Underwriters say it is all right; the insurance papers are signed and delivered. It is the only safe way to do. Twelve hours after the ship gets beyond the Hook, it might perish, and the whole thing be a total loss. A man will not take such a risk for himself. You have your store insured, you have your stock of goods insured. If the insurance runs out on Saturday, you do not wait until Monday to renew it. You say, on Sunday the whole thing may perish in a conflagration. You can not afford to take the risk. Somebody shows you an operation by which you might make, perhaps, five thousand dollars; but you say, "Perhaps I might not. Perhaps I might lose that, and ruin my credit. I can't take the risk." So you do not enter into the enterprise. Oh that we were as wise in taking spiritual risks! We will, after a while, founder on the sea of death. What is the amount of our policy? How will we come out of that disaster? Suppose a man says, "I am not ready now for eternity, but I mean to be." Let us calculate the risk; not as a minister talks to the people, but as one business man talks to another, let us calculate the risk that man runs. The lungs may congest; the brain may be fevered; the foot may slip; a brick may fall from the workman's hod; ferry-boats may collide; a frightened horse may dash over him; a pistol may go off accidentally; poisoned air may be breathed; the reason may topple; the heart may stop. The man who stays away from Jesus Christ, and makes no preparation for eternity, runs ten thousand risks, infinite risks, every day of his life. After Lord Byron died, they cut his heart out and put it in a beautiful case; and some people who were infatuated with him thought that there was in that heart in the case some wonderful charm; and the Greeks carried it out into battle, and it was lost — lost in the swamps, and never heard of. It was considered an ominous and a terrible loss. But, my friends, it was only a dead heart. What was that compared with the loss of a *living, immortal soul?* Christ saw that soul from eternity, and, traveling in the greatness of his strength across all the ages, he comes to save it, and stands this morning in its presence. Will you let him save it? Oh this soul that you have beating within your breast!—this soul of tremendous faculties; a soul that can soar higher than angel's wing ever flew, or sink deeper than devil's foot ever plunged; a soul that will soon weigh anchor for a ceaseless voyage; a soul for which all the armies of light with drawn swords, and all the battalions of the darkness with the artillery of death, are contending; and while the battle rages there are songs and curses, opening of gates of light and slamming to of prison doors. Lord God! have I such a soul? How shall I defend it? How shall I hide it? In what cave of the mountain shall I secrete it? Rather than surrender that soul, I must pass the stream; I must go through the fire; I must climb the rocks; I must station myself in some defile of the mountain, and with immortal courage and persistence fight against those influences that would capture my soul and destroy it.

Blessed be God, in Jesus Christ the soul is safe. There is no risk for that soul that is in Christ's keeping. All other banks may fail, all other securities may prove worthless; but the greater the rush upon this bank, the wider the doors will open. As other gold depreciates, this treasure will rise in value. After all earthly shares have failed, heaven will declare its largest dividend. Long after the last stock-exchange of earth has been disbanded, "the foundation of the Lord standeth sure, having this seal, the Lord knoweth them that are his." If you have made these spiritual investments, I congratulate you. They will increase in value while you live; they will be worth more in eternity than they are now. I bid you be of good cheer. Look out that none of your treasures are stolen.

Are there some here who have never bought the truth? or, after buying it, have you sold it? Let me say, you are not wise. The Indian who sells a thousand acres of land for one poor string of beads makes a better bargain than that man who wins the world but loses his soul.

"What is the thing of greatest price
The whole creation round?
That which was lost in paradise,
That which in Christ is found."

A BASKET OF SUMMER FRUIT.

"And he said, Amos, what seest thou? And I said, A basket of summer fruit."—*Amos* viii., 2.

A STOUT-CHESTED, swarthy-limbed, brave-hearted man was called out to rebuke Israel. His name was Amos. He had been brought up amidst sheep and cattle, and, in addition to his occupation of herdsman, he had the business of gathering sycamore fruit—a very difficult business, because if the fruit were not properly ripened, and just before its maturing it were not punctured with the teeth of an iron comb, then the fruit would be bitter, and thoroughly unpalatable. Having always lived in the country, when Amos comes to write or to speak, his allusions are rural—full of threshing-floors, and sheaf-laden carts, and grasshoppers, and mowings, and orchards, and vineyards, and, in my text, "a basket of summer fruit." Just what kind of fruit this was I do not know, whether sycamore fruit or pomegranates or figs; but I do know that God meant for Israel, and means to-night for us, the truth that spiritual blessing, like summer fruit, must be used immediately, or it will perish.

Last week I saw farmers out on Long Island gathering their winter apples; and if these apples are carefully put away, they will last until next spring. You know there are pears which are better two or three months after they are taken from the orchard than at the time they drop. And there were clusters of grapes yesterday that went in from the arbor that will next Christmas or Thanksgiving-day hang above the banquet. But my text compares our opportunities of repentance and return to more perishable products. Ay, it sets before you in graphic vision a basket of *summer* fruit.

Many of you remember a few years ago when the peach crop suddenly ripened, and all the rail trains and steamers coming to our city were laden with the delicious product. The fruit was dead ripe, and not able to wait until the glutted markets were cleared, and so there were hundreds of thousands of dollars' worth of the fruit thrown into the streets and into the rivers, or carted back again to enrich the soil. O the perishable nature of summer fruit! It is so much like our spiritual blessings, which must be used immediately, or never used at all. To-night, instead of having you wander around as through the stalls of an agricultural fair, I would have you, with profound and agitated feelings of soul, look upon this text as depicting your last chance for heaven as it is all-suggestively set forth. "Behold, a basket of summer fruit."

Was this statement of the text the blundering comparison of a man not used to literary composition? Do you think the analogy will hold out? Is there any similarity between the Gospel and summer fruit? Oh yes. They both, in the *first place*, mean *health*. God every summer doctors the ailments of the world by the orchards and groves. The failing of the orchards is a license to all kinds of diseases, and plenty of fruit ordinarily means improved sanitary condition. So this Gospel means health. It makes a man mighty for work and strong for contest. It cures spiritual ailments. It helps the soul that is decrepit, bound on in the road to heaven. It is juvenescence.

It is convalescence. It kindles the eye with brilliant anticipations. It thrills the soul with glories to come. It is not a weak sentimentality. It helped Paul to stand unblanched on the deck of the foundering corn-ship, and it helped Luther to nail his defiant "theses" against the door of the electoral college, the thumping of his hammer echoing through all the ages. It has helped ten thousand souls to spring through flood and fire to glories immortal. Oh, it is a swarthy Gospel! Mighty in itself, it makes men mighty. It gives one overmastering power in the day of trouble. The Church cries out to Christ, in the Canticles, "Comfort me with apples;" and so to-night I shake down upon you a whole orchard of fruit, while I read that the fruits of the Spirit are love, joy, peace, patience, brotherly kindness, charity. Gather it up from the ground—large, round, luscious. Take it home with you—"a basket of summer fruit."

I notice that the analogy, also, is found in the fact that summer fruit *is pleasant to the eye and the taste.* So the Gospel, when a man rightly sees it and tastes it, is very pleasant. Whether summer fruit be piled up in the orchard, or on the barn floor, or on the platter of the table, the commingling of green and gold and red and brown in the cheek of the fruit is very fascinating. You know that some artists deal chiefly with pictures of fruit; and while Correggio delights to sketch physical beauty, and Turner drops the sea-foam on the canvas, and Cuyp drives up his cattle at evening-tide, and Rosa Bonheur catches by the halter the rearing steeds at the "Horse Fair," and Edwin Landseer whistles up the dogs, there are many of our modern painters who are putting all their power on fruit pieces; and I do not wonder at it. There is a beauty in fruit indescribable. So it is with the Gospel of Christ. It charms the young and the old, the well and the sick, the wise and the ignorant. It has the glitter of the wave, the aroma of flowers, the fascination of music. It is the luxury of the ages. Religion is not an abbess—is not a cenobite. "Her ways are ways of pleasantness, and all her paths are peace."

In June, 1815, there was a very noble party gathered in a house in St. James's Square, London. The prince regent was present, and the occasion was made fascinating by music and banqueting and by jewels. While a quadrille was being formed, suddenly all the people rushed to the windows. What is the matter? Henry Percy had arrived with the news that Waterloo had been fought, and that England had won the day. The dance was abandoned; the party dispersed; lords, ladies, and musicians rushed into the street, and in fifteen minutes from the first announcement of the good news the house was emptied of all its guests. O ye who are seated at the banquet of this world, or whirling in its gayeties and frivolities, if to-night you could hear the sweet strains of the Gospel trumpet announcing Christ's victory over sin and death and hell, you would rush forth, glad in the eternal deliverance! The Waterloo against sin has been fought, and our Commander-in-chief hath won the day. O the joys of this salvation! I do not care what metaphor, what comparison you have; bring it to me that I may use it. Amos shall bring one simile, Isaiah another, David another, John another. Beautiful with pardon. Beautiful with peace. Beautiful with anticipations. I spread out the heaped-up, large, round, luscious "basket of summer fruit."

You have noticed that *if summer fruit is not taken imme-*

diately, it soon fails. First, the speck; then a multiplication of defects; after a while a softening that is offensive; and then it is all flung out. So I have to tell you that all religious advantages, all Gospel opportunities, all religious privileges, while they are beautiful and attractive, perish right speedily if you do not take them. I suppose you have noticed how swiftly the days and the years go by. Every day seems to me like "a basket of summer fruit;" the morning sky is vermilion, the noonday is opaline, the evening cloud is fire-dyed. Every day has its cluster of blessings and its fruity branch of opportunities. But how soon they are gone! Where is 1873? 1870? 1860? 1850? Gone as thoroughly as the fruit which dropped from the trees and rotted last August. Every year may have its characteristic. In one, the war broke out; in another, the locusts made terrible ravages; in another, the yellow fever raged; but I care not what be the characteristics—they are all gone save one. Of the six thousand years of this world's existence, only one is left. Ay, ten months of that are gone, or nearly gone, and the tongue in the clock of the months will soon strike twelve, and then this year will be as dead as all its predecessors. In your library, you put the historical volumes side by side, volume first, volume second, volume third, volume fourth; and the history of the past is made up of six thousand volumes, three hundred and sixty-five pages in each of the volumes, and in the last day, at one flash, you will read all of them. Time, how swiftly it goes! Gray hairs are here and there upon you, and some of you know it not. The "crow's-foot" is walking nearer up toward the corner of the eye. You stoop more than you used to. You have been discussing as to the propriety of wearing glasses. You are going from the thirties into the forties, and from the forties into the fifties, and from the fifties into the sixties, and from the sixties into the seventies. The color is going out of the "basket of summer fruit." The curculio of trouble hath left the mark of its sting. The work of decay has begun, and the full basket of human life will soon be emptied into the trench of the grave. When I first became anxious about my soul, there was a soliloquy I read in Mr. Pike's "Address to the Unsaved." It was a soliloquy on this very subject. It represented a man dying; and, as he was dying, the clock struck. As the clock struck, the man was startled, and he cried out, "O Time! it is fit that thou shouldst strike thy murderer to the heart. How art thou gone forever! A month! Oh for a week! I ask not for a year, though an age were too short for the work I have to do. Remorse for the past throws my thoughts on the future. Worse dread of the future throws my thoughts on the past. I turn and turn, and find no ray. If thou didst feel one-half the mountain that is on my heart, thou wouldst struggle with the martyr for his stake, and bless Heaven for the flame: that is not an unquenchable fire. O thou blasphemed yet most indulgent Lord God! hell itself is a refuge, if it hide me from thy frown!"

Still further, I remark *upon the perishable nature of all religious surroundings.* You sometimes go into a religious association, and you say, "Isn't this beautiful? How many ripe, religious experiences! Why, it is like 'a basket of summer fruit.'" But do you not know, my brother, that all these Christian associations fade away from the soul? Your Christian father and mother who have been holding beneficent influences over you, do you not realize they are going away from you? Do you not notice that they do not get over sickness as soon as they used to? Are you not aware of the fact that they do not get over a cold as quickly as once? The fact is that they have made more prayers for you than they will ever make again. They have passed the last mile-stone on the road home; and if you are going to get any benefit from that "basket of summer fruit," get it now, or get it never. Some of you do not know what it is to stand and look down upon the still and rigid features of a Christian father or a Christian mother. I do. In five minutes you will think of all the unkind words you ever said to them. You may cover up the coffin with wreaths and crosses and crowns; but you can not make any thing attractive out of it. It is trouble, and nothing but trouble, for those who sit and sigh with the consciousness that those dear lips will never pray for you again, and those lips will never sympathize with you again. When you stoop down and kiss for the last time the wrinkled brow just before the lid is screwed on, you will think of what I tell you to-night. Oh, if father and mother be still alive with their Christian influences, cherish them while you may. Take their example. Be profited by their prayers. They are ripe for heaven, and can not stay. The "basket of summer fruit" will soon be gone.

So, also, it is, my friends, with all God's offers of mercy and salvation. Are you to-night under the infatuation that those privileges are going to be continued? Oh no! Every opportunity of salvation seems to be restless until it gets away from us. Going away, the sermons; going away, the songs; going away, the strivings of God's eternal Spirit. The fruits of immortal life, fair and luscious, are no sooner set before the soul than they disappear. The Theban legion consisted of six thousand six hundred and sixty-six men. Maximian decreed that that host should be decimated—that is, every tenth man should be put to the sword. So it was done; but the soldiers did not submit to the kingly authority, and so another decimation took place, and the work went on until all of the six thousand six hundred and sixty-six men had perished. Now, I do not know how many people may be in this house to-night, but it is an army. It is going to be decimated. One out of every ten will soon be gone, and after that the work will go on; and again one out of every ten will be gone, and again the decimation will take place, until not a single person in this house to-night will be alive. Our bodies, some of them, will be in Greenwood, in Laurel Hill, in Mount Auburn, in Oaklands, in Grey Friars Churchyard, in the village cemetery; but your souls will be in one of two places, the names of which I need not mention, for they rush upon you this moment with thunderous articulation and emphasis.

Many have missed their chance. Now, there is no hiding that fact—they have missed their chance. They came in and looked at the "basket of summer fruit." They admired the gracefulness of the wicker-work, the delicacy of the rind, the greenness of the leaves. They went off. They came back and admired again. But one day they came, and they found that all the glory had faded, and that the fruit had been thrown out. They came to a certain evening. They saw the sun set. They never saw the sun rise again. The pastor pronounced upon them the benediction. It was the last benediction they ever heard. They took their last step, missed their last chance. Fortunately for us, their voice is not strong enough to ring up until we can hear it, or it would make life on earth intolerable with the wailing. The wall is so thick that we hear not one word of their pang. Perished! Perished! They talk no more about there being time enough yet. They have no time. They worry no longer about the inconsistencies of Christians; they are looking after their own condition. They no more argue that there is no such a thing as a lost soul; they have felt the pang that comes from a fall ten thousand fathoms down. O skeptical man, go out and persuade them that there is no retribution for a soul that forgets God. Break open the gate; dash through the fire; leap the intervening cliff, and cry out to them, "There is no hell!" and ten thousand voices will answer back, "There is. See you not the gate? Feel you not the sorrow? We have been here five hundred years, and yet the woe has just begun. Go back and tell all you have seen. Tell them that we once were as they are, and that they, unless they repent, shall be as we are ourselves. We had the fruits of life set before us, fair as 'a basket of summer fruit;' but we would not take them, and we everlastingly died."

My friends, the practical question is now, Will you miss *your* chance? The offer of salvation is now extended to us. It will not always be continued. The day of grace will be past. The probability is that there are some in this audience who will miss their opportunity. I put my hand on your pulse, and I find that the fever has begun. I look upon your brow, and I find the shadow of impending doom. I listen to your breath, and I find it is suggestive of the last gasp. Some of you will be lost! See! you are falling now—down from heaven, from life, from peace—

down, down. I remember reading how Leonidas, with three hundred men, stood in the pass between Œta and the sea, fighting back the Persian hosts. The Persian hosts came on. They trampled him down. Oh that God, to-night, would arm me, a poor weak man, with a supernatural courage to stand in the pass of this glorious Sabbath hour, and dispute with this army that I see before me the way to death. Halt! ye infatuated souls. I swing the two-edged sword both ways. Halt! Halt! Take not one step more on this downward path. Why will ye die, when there is no use in it? Are you so charmed with pain, and sin, and sorrow, and woe, that you will wade through the foaming billows of perdition to win them? Is there nothing in the sympathetic tears of friends, nothing in the sacrificial blood of the Son of God, nothing in the death-bed experiences of those whom you have loved, nothing in the crash of the judgment avalanche, to make you think?

I must tell you plainly that your idea that there is time enough yet is a delusion wild and terrific. If some of you knew how little time there is left to you, you would not wait until the close of this service. Your breath will stop before you are ready. Death will meet you before you have a cloak to keep out the chill, or a lantern to light the way, or a dragoman to speak out for you. You will be silenced, with ten thousand things to say; you will be speechless; and in the convulsions of this American continent, when the Alleghanies shall roll over into the Atlantic, and the Rocky Mountains shall roll over into the Pacific, amidst the rifts and crevices of disorganized nature, there will be no place where you can secrete yourself, though with blanched cheek, and flying hair, and uplifted hand, and outcrying voice, you say, "Rocks and mountains fall on me, and hide me from the face of Him that sitteth upon the throne, and from the wrath of the Lamb, for the great day of his wrath has come, and who, *who* shall be able to stand?"

I can tell from the way the country sexton rings the bell when he is about to stop ringing it. When he begins to ring, the music comes softly out on the air; the bell fills all the air with music. He lays hold with strong pull; but after a while, when the horses have been tied, and the people have gathered, then there is some distance of time between the strokes of the bell. It gets slower and slower, for he has begun to toll, and after a while it stops. O sinner! how swiftly the invitations of the Gospel came to you! Call after call. Invitation after invitation. Floods of them. How merrily the bell did ring! But it seems as if, with some of you, God's patience is exhausted; as if his mercy were almost gone. The bell rings more slowly to-night than it ever rang before, and as if about to stop. Ay, it seems to have come to the dying toll. Thrice more it will speak—perhaps only thrice. Toll! Toll! Toll!

It was to set forth this solemn truth, that religious advantages, while they last, are attractive, but very soon leave us, that God let down to Amos, the herdsman, in vision the beautiful but perishable basket of summer fruit.

THE LAST ACT OF THE TRAGEDY.

"And the people stood beholding."—*Luke* xxiii., 35.

THERE is nothing more wild and ungovernable than a mob. Some of the older people in the audience may remember the excitement in New York during the riot when the people went howling through the streets at the time Macready stood on the stage of the Astor Place Opera-house. Those of you who have read history may remember the excitement in Paris during the time of Louis XVI., and how the mob rushed up and down frantically. To this day you may see the marks of the bullets that struck the palace as the Swiss Guards stood defending it.

There is a wild mob going through the streets of Jerusalem. As it passes along, it is augmented by the multitudes that come out from the lanes and the alleys to join the shouts and the laughter and the lamentation of the rioters, who become more and more ungovernable as they get toward the gates of the city. Fishermen, vagabonds, rude women, grave officials, merchant princes, beggars, mingle in that crowd. They are passing out now through the gates of the city. They come to a hill white with the bleached skulls of victims—a hill that was itself the shape of a skull, covered with skulls, and called Golgotha, which means the place of a skull. Three men are to be put to death—two for theft, one for treason, having claimed to be King of the Jews. Each one carries his own cross, but one of them is so exhausted from previous hardship that he faints under the burden, and they compel Simon of Cyrene, who is supposed to be in sympathy with the condemned man, to take hold of one end of the cross and help him to carry it. They reach the hill. The three men are lifted in horrid crucifixion. While the mob are howling and mocking, and hurling scorn at the chief object of their hate, the darkness hovers and scowls and swoops upon the scene, and the rocks rend with terrific clang; and the choking wind, and moaning cavern, and dropping sky, and shuddering earthquake declare, in whisper, in groan, in shriek, "This is the Son of God!"

I propose to speak of the two groups of spectators around the cross—*the friendly and the unfriendly.* In the unfriendly group were the Roman soldiers. Now, it is a grand thing to serve one's country. There is not an Englishman's heart but thrills at the name of Havelock, brave for Christ and brave for the British Government. When there was a difficult point to take, the officers would say, "Bring out the saints of old Havelock." I think if Paul had gone into military service, he would have eclipsed the heroism of the Cæsars and the Alexanders and the Napoleons of the world by his bravery and enthusiasm. There is a time to be at peace, and there is a time when a Christian has to fight. I do not know of a graver or braver thing than for a young man, when it is demanded of him, to turn his back upon home and quiet and luxury, and in the service of his country go forth to camp and field, and carnage and martyrdom. It was no mean thing to be a Roman soldier; it was no idle thing. You know what revolutions dashed up against the walls of that empire. You know to what conquest she devoted herself, flinging her war-eagles against the proudest ensigns. But the noblest army has in it sneaks, and these were the men who were detailed from that army to attend to the execution of Christ. Their dastardly behavior puts out the gleam of their spears, and covers their banner with obloquy. They were cowards. They were ruffians. They were gamblers. No noble soldier would treat a fallen foe as they treated the captured Christ.

Generally there is respect paid to the garments of the departed. It may be only a hat or coat or a shoe, but it goes down in the family wardrobe from generation to generation. Now that Christ is to be disrobed, who shall have his coat? Joseph of Arimathea would have liked to have had it. Mary, the mother of Jesus, would have liked to have had it. How fondly she would have hovered over it! and when she must leave it, with what tenderness she would have bequeathed it to her best friend! It was the only covering of Christ in darkness and storm. That was the very coat that the woman touched when from it there went out virtue for her healing. That was the only wedding-garment he had in the marriage at Cana, and the storms that swept Galilee had drenched it again and again. And what did they do with it? They raffled for it. We have heard of men who gambled away their own garments, who gambled away their children's shoes, who gambled away the family Bible, who gambled away their wife's last dress; but it adds to the ghastliness of a Saviour's humiliation and the horror of the crime, when I hear Jesus in his last moments declaring, "They parted my garments among them, and for my vesture did they cast lots."

In this unfriendly group around the cross, also, were *the rulers and the scribes and the chief priests.* Lawyers and judges and ministers of religion in this day are expected to have some respect for their offices. In this land, where the honors of the judiciary sometimes come to besotted politicians and men noted for drunkenness—even in this land where we live, it is an unheard-of thing that a judge comes down from the bench and strikes a prisoner in the face. No minister of religion would scoff at or mock a condemned criminal. And yet the great men of that land seemed to be equal to any ruffianism. They were vying with each other as to how much scorn and billingsgate they could cast into the teeth of the dying Christ. Why, the worst felon, when his enemy has fallen, refuses to strike him. But these men were not ashamed to strike Jesus when he was down.

So it has been in all ages of the world, that there have been men in high positions who despised Christ and his Gospel. What popes have issued their anathemas! What judgment-seats have kindled their fires! What inquisitions have sharpened their swords! "Not this man, but Barabbas. Now Barabbas was a robber." Against the Christian religion have been brought the historical genius of Gibbon, and the polish of Shaftesbury, and the kingly authority of Frederick of Prussia, and the brilliancy of John Earl of Rochester, and the stupendous intellect of Voltaire. Innumerable pens have stabbed it, and innumerable books have cursed it, and that mob that hounded Christ from Jerusalem to "the place of a skull" has never been dispersed, but is augmenting yet, as many of the learned men of the world and great men of the world come out from their studios and their laboratories and their palaces, and cry, "Away with this man! away with him!" The most bitter hostility which many of the learned men of this day exercise in any direction they exercise against Jesus Christ, the Son of God, the Saviour of the world, without whom we will die forever.

In this group of enemies surrounding the cross, in this unfriendly group, I also find *the railing thief*. It seems that he twisted himself on the spikes; he forgot his own pain in his complete antipathy to Jesus. I do not know what kind of a thief he was. I do not know whether he had been a burglar or a pickpocket or a highwayman; but our idea of his crimes is aggravated when we hear him blaspheming the Redeemer. O shame indescribable! O ignominy unsupportable! Hissed at by a thief! In that ridicule I find the fact that there is a hostility between sin and holiness. There can not be, there never has been, any sympathy between honesty and theft, between purity and lasciviousness, between zeal and indolence, between faith and unbelief, between light and darkness, between heaven and hell. And when I see a good man going out to discharge his duty, and he is enthusiastic for Christ, and I see persecution after him, and scorn after him, and contempt after him, I say, "Hark! another hiss of the dying thief!" And when I see Holiness going forth in her white robes, and Charity, with great heart and open hand, to take care of the sick and help the needy and restore the lost, and I find her lashed with hypercriticism, and jostled of the world, and pursued from point to point, and caricatured with low witticisms, I say, "Aha! another hiss of the dying thief!"

It is a sad thing to know that this malefactor died just as he had lived. People nearly always do. Have you never remarked that? There is but one instance mentioned in all the Bible of a man repenting in the last hour. All the other men who lived lives of iniquity, as far as we can understand from the Bible, died deaths of iniquity. If you live a drunkard's life, you will die a drunkard; the defrauder dies a defrauder; the idler dies an idler; the blasphemer dies a blasphemer; the slanderer dies a slanderer; the debauchee dies a debauchee. As you live, you will die, in all probability. Do not, therefore, make your soul believe that you can go on in a course of sin, and then in the last moment repent. There is such a thing as death-bed repentance, but I never saw one—I never saw one. God in all this Bible presents us only one case of that kind, and it is not safe to risk it, lest our case should happen not to be the one amidst ten thousand.

"Repent! the voice celestial cries,
No longer dare delay;
The wretch that scorns the mandate dies,
And meets the fiery day."

But there were rays of light that streamed into the crucifixion. As Christ was on the cross and looked down on the crowd of people, he saw some very warm friends there. And that brings me to the remarking upon the friendly group that were around the cross.

The first in all that crowd was his mother. You need not point her out to me. I can see by the sorrow, the anguish, the woe, by the upthrown hands! That all means mother! "Oh," you say, "why didn't she go down to the foot of the hill, and sit with her back to the scene? It was too horrible for her to look upon." Do you not know, when a child is in anguish or trouble, it always makes a heroine of a mother? Take her away, you say, from the cross. You can not drag her away. She will keep on looking; as long as her son breathes, she will stand there looking. What a scene it is for a tender-hearted mother to look upon! How gladly she would have sprung to his relief! It was her son. Her son! How gladly she would have clambered up on the cross and hung there herself if her son could have been relieved! How strengthening she would have been to Christ if she might have come close by him and soothed him! There was a good deal in what the little sick child said, upon whom a surgical operation of a painful nature must be performed! The doctor said, "That child won't live through this operation unless you encourage him. You go in, and get his consent." The father told him all the doctor said, and added, "Now, John, will you go through with it? Will you consent to it?" He looked very pale, and he thought a minute, and said, "Yes, father, if you will hold my hand, I will!" So the father held his hand, and led him straight through the peril. O woman! in your hour of anguish, whom do you want with you? Mother. Young man, in your hour of trouble, whom do you want to console you? Mother. If the mother of Jesus could have only taken those bleeding feet into her lap! If she might have taken the dying head on her bosom! If she might have said to him, "It will soon be over, Jesus — it will soon be over, and we will meet again, and it will be all well." But no; she dared not come up so close. They would have struck her back with their hammers. They would have kicked her down the hill. There can be no alleviation at all. Jesus *must* suffer, and Mary *must* look. I suppose she thought of the birth-hour in Bethlehem. I suppose she thought of that time when, with her boy in her bosom, she hastened on in the darkness in the flight toward Egypt. I suppose she thought of his boyhood when he was the joy of her heart. I suppose she thought of the thousand kindnesses he had done her, not forsaking her, or forgetting her even in his last moments; but turning to John, and saying, "There is mother; take her with you. She is old now. She can not help herself. Do for her just as I would have done for her if I had lived. Be very tender and gentle with her. Behold thy mother!" She thought it all over, and there is no memory like a mother's memory, and there is no woe like a mother's woe.

There was another friend in that group, and that was Simon the Cyrenian. He was a stranger in the land, but had been long enough there to show his favoritism for Christ. I suppose he was one of those men who never can see any body imposed upon but he wants to help him. "Well, Simon," they cried out, "you are such a friend to Jesus, help him to carry the cross. You see him fainting under it." So he did. A scene for all the ages of time and all the cycles of eternity; a cross with Jesus at the one end of it and Simon at the other, suggesting the idea to you, O troubled soul! that no one need ever carry a whole cross. You have only half a cross to carry. If you are in poverty, Jesus was poor, and he comes and takes the other end of the cross. If you are in persecution, Jesus was persecuted, and he comes and takes the other end of the cross. If you are in any kind of trouble, you have a sympathizing Redeemer. Oh, how the truth flashed upon my soul this morning! Jesus at one end of the cross and the soul at the other end of the cross; and when I see Christ and Simon going up the hill together, I say we ought to help each other to carry our burdens. "Bear ye one another's burdens, and so fulfill the law of

Christ." If you find a man in persecution or sickness or in business trouble, go right to him, and say, "My brother, I have come to help you. You take hold of one end of the cross, and I will take hold of the other end of the cross, and Jesus Christ will come in and take hold of the middle of the cross; and after a while there will be no cross at all."

> "Shall Jesus bear the cross alone,
> And all the world go free?
> No; there is a cross for every one,
> And there is a cross for me."

But there was another marked personage in that friendly group. That was the penitent malefactor. He was a thief, or had been—no disguising that fact. What was he to do? "Oh!" he says, "what shall I do with my sins upon me?" and he looks around and sees Jesus, and sees compassion in his face, and he says, "Lord, remember me when thou comest into thy kingdom." What did Jesus do? Did he turn and say, "You thief! I have seen all your crimes, and you have jeered and scoffed at me; now die forever!"—did he say that? Oh no; Jesus could not say that. He says, "This day shalt thou be with me in paradise." I sing the song of mercy for the chief of sinners. Murderers have come and plunged their red hands in this fountain, and they have been made as white as snow. The prodigal that was off for twenty years has come back and sat at his father's table. The ship that has been tossed in a thousand storms floats into this harbor. The parched and sun-struck soul comes under the shadow of this rock. Tens of thousands who were as bad as you and I have ever been have put down their burdens and their sins at the feet of this blessed Jesus.

"The dying thief rejoiced to see
That fountain in his day;
And there may I, as vile as he,
Wash all my sins away."

But there was another friendly group. I do not know their names—we are not told; but we are simply told there were many around the cross who sympathized with the dying sufferer. Oh! the wail of woe that went through that crowd when they saw Jesus die! You know the Bible says if all the things Jesus did were recorded, the world would not contain the books that would be written. It implies that what we have in the Bible are merely specimens of the Saviour's mercy. We are told that one blind man got his eye-sight. I suppose he cured twenty that we are not told of. When he cured the one leper whose story is recorded, he might have cured twenty lepers. Where he did one act of kindness mentioned, he must have done a thousand we do not know about. I see those who received kindnesses from him standing beneath the cross, and one says, "Why, that is the Jesus that bound up my broken heart!" And another, standing beneath the cross, says, "That is the Jesus that restored my daughter to life." Another looks up, and says, "Why, that is Jesus who gave me my eye-sight!" And another looks up, and says, "That is the Jesus who lifted me up when I was sick; oh, I can't bear to see him die!" Every pelt of the hammer drove a spike through their hearts. Every groan of Christ opens a new fountain of sorrow. They had better get on with that crucifixion quickly, or it will never take place. These disciples will seize Christ and snatch him from the grasp of those bad men, and take those ringleaders of the persecution and put them up in the very place. Be quick with those nails! Be quick with that gall! Be quick with those spikes! for I see in the sorrow and the wrath of those disciples a storm brewing that will burst on the heads of those persecutors.

To-day we come and we join the friendly crowd. Who wants to be on the wrong side? I can not bear to be in the unfriendly group. There is not a man or woman in this house who wants to be in the unfriendly group. I want to join the other group. We come while they are bewailing, and join their lamentations. We see that brow bruised; we hear that dying groan; and while the priests scoff and the devils rave and the lightnings of God's wrath are twisted into a wreath for that bloody mount, you and I will join the cry, the supplication, of the penitent malefactor, "Lord, remember me when thou comest into thy kingdom." Oh! the pain, the ignominy, the ghastliness, the agony! and yet the joy, the thrilling, bounding, glorious hope! Son of Mary! Son of God!

Is there one here who will reject this atonement made for the people—not for one man here and one man there, but for all who will accept it?

There was a very touching scene among an Indian tribe in the last century. It seemed that one of the chieftains had slain a man belonging to an opposite tribe, and that tribe came up, and said, "We will exterminate you, unless you surrender the man who committed that crime." The chieftain who did the crime stepped out from the ranks, and said, "I am not afraid to die; but I have a wife and four children, and I have a father aged, and a mother aged, whom I support by hunting, and I sorrow to leave them helpless." Just as he said that, his old father from behind stepped out, and said, "He shall not die. I take his place.

I am old and well stricken in years. I can do no good. I might as well die. My days are almost over. He can not be spared. Take me." And they accepted the sacrifice. Wonderful sacrifice, you say; but not so wonderful as that found in the Gospel; for we deserved to die, ay, we were sentenced, when Christ, not worn out with years, but in the flush of his youth, said, "Save that man from going down to the pit. I am the ransom! Put his burdens on my shoulders. Let his stripes fall on my back. Take my heart for his heart. Let me die, that he may live." Shall it be told to-day in heaven that, notwithstanding all those wounds, and all that blood, and all those tears, and all that agony, you would not accept him?

> "Well might the sun in darkness hide
> And shut his glories in,
> When Christ, the mighty maker, died
> For man, the creature's sin.
>
> "Thus might I hide my blushing face
> While his dear cross appears,
> Dissolve my heart in thankfulness,
> And melt my eyes to tears.
>
> "But drops of grief can ne'er repay
> The debt of love I owe;
> Here, Lord, I give myself away,
> 'Tis all that I can do."

O Lord Jesus, we accept thee! We all accept thee now. There is no hand in all this audience lifted to smite thee on the cheek now. No one will spear thee now. No one will strike thee now. Come in, Lord Jesus! Come quickly!

DROWNED IN THE LAKE.

"The deep that coucheth beneath."—*Deuteronomy* xxxiii., 13.

SWITZERLAND has the glaciers of Mont Blanc as a crown for her brow, and Lake Geneva for an emerald on her right hand. In the Swiss railway we were told that we must look out for the bridge where, as he emerges, there suddenly dashes upon the eye of the traveler one of the most extraordinary scenes of beauty and grandeur in all Europe. In the twinkling of an eye appears Lausanne, seated on her throne of three hills, with twenty-one thousand population; her cathedral, nine hundred years old, with apsed chapels and Byzantine capitals; her museums, distinguished the world over for the finest specimens in minerals, and animals, and shell-fish; her terraces and gardens, bewitching with aroma and luxuriance; her schools, which, by the rarest opportunity for culture, invite the youth of America and of all the world; Lake Geneva, deep, yet the clearest of waters, traversed by steamers crowded with passengers from all lands, and fishing-smacks here and there hauling out trout, and pike, and perch, and salmon; and sail-boats going out from the castles on the beach occupied by gentlemen of fortune. This sheet of water, skirted by mountains, Jura and the Alps, some green with verdure, some white with snow, some cleft with streams, crystalline and arrowy, the chalices of the floods emptying into this great bowl of the mountain. On the banks of this lake Gibbon, Rousseau, and Voltaire studied, and Byron dramatized, and John Kemble, the tragedian, lies buried, and Rothschild built his mansion, and ten thousand men and women, far better than any I have mentioned, have gone up and down, adoring the God who lifted the hills and sunk this great inland sea. May you all live to behold the Alps, cloud-turbaned, looking down into the mirror of beautiful Geneva!

A few days ago, two lads of our own city, and much of the time of our own congregation, pushed out from Lausanne on those exquisite waters, on a pleasure excursion. It was in the leisure of school-hours. A sudden storm swept over the lake, capsizing that boat; or there was a defect in the vessel, and those precious lives were emptied into a watery grave. You say that they ought not to have gone where there was danger. I reply, where will you go and find no danger? You go down the street, a scaffold may fall on you. You go to the park, the horses may become unmanageable. You take the rail train, a switchman may turn the track the wrong way. You stay at home, the lightning may strike through the roof, or miasma may come in through the open window. Dangers stand round us everywhere to press us to the tomb.

There is great health for a student in rowing with the oar, and great exhilaration in the spreading of the sail; but the lake that you stroke and fondle, thinking it harmless and asleep, sometimes proves treacherous to the yacht, and springs upon it like a panther, clutching it down with wrathful, overmastering strength. So that Moses, in the text, graphically and truthfully describes the fatal slyness of river and lake and sea when he says, "*The deep that coucheth beneath.*"

The particulars of that sad event have not yet come to

us; but never, through the coral caves of the Atlantic, and amidst the gardens of sea-weed, and along by the hulks of the wrecked shipping, could a more fearful message travel the submarine cable than that which came last week announcing that John and James Crane, two American students at Lausanne, Switzerland, had ended their mortal life in Lake Geneva. Such a transition is the easiest and most painless of all modes of getting out of this life. After one minute of submergence, generally, consciousness is gone. The Navarino sponge-divers can not bear to stay under the water more than two minutes, notwithstanding all their experience; and yet persons who have been resuscitated tell us that the mind at such a time acts with wonderful velocity. And so I suppose these dear lads had time to think of home, and the sadness of the parental hearts whom they expected to join next October. God decreed otherwise, and may his omnipotent grace soothe the bereaved and the desolate.

There is in this event that I am called to speak about to-night a new illustration of a very old lesson. You tell me nothing but a stereotyped thing when you tell me of life's uncertainty. I have heard that a thousand times from ministers and prayer-meeting talkers and Sabbath-school teachers; and when you make that announcement, I open my eyes no wider, nor does my heart beat quicker; but when you tell me that a boat flung two beloved lads into a watery grave, then I am stunned by the telegram, and compelled to read the truth written by pen of lightning stretched up from under the sea. How quickly our life comes, and how soon it goes! We pass along a perilous cliff, and we almost hold our breath, and balance ourself lest we fall off, and, getting beyond the pass, we thank

God for our deliverance, but perhaps lie down and die in the smooth plain beneath. Many a man has gone through three or four battles unclipped of bullet or sabre, who has had his life at last dashed out on the icy pavement in front of his door-step, or by the snapping of a whiffletree. You go two thousand miles in an express train unharmed, to lose your life at the hands of a reckless hackman in your own village. These two lads of whom I am speaking went through three thousand miles of stormy Atlantic unharmed, to find their death on a lake that they might sail across in thirty minutes. When we picture our exit from this world, we are very apt to think of a soft couch and a shaded room and careful attendants; but many of us who are here to-night will never have any thing like that. It will be a rush, and a plunge, and a leap, and a fall, and the world flashes out, and eternity flashes in.

You tell me that this lesson of life's uncertainty is appropriate only for the old, for the emaciated, for the sick. Ah no! these lads did not come crawling down to the boat, they did not come on crutches, they were not fagged out. They came bounding into the boat, elastic, ruddy, robust. They expected to live seventy years. Their lungs sound, their hearts beating with healthful pulsation, their limbs lithe, their clear eye taking in the sheen of wave and the frown of crag and the azure of sky, they sprung to their places in the prow or stern with shout and laughter. They had no premonition that they were to go. So, my friends, it will be with many of us. You pay a certain amount of money, premium for life-insurance, that, when you are gone, your family may get relief from it; but what life-insurance company would dare to say to a man, "You will live a year," or "You will live six months," or "You will live a week," or "You will live a day," or "You will live an hour," or "You will live a second"—and warrant it? I came to this platform to-night strong and well, but that is no assurance that I shall go off alive. To-morrow morning you cross the ferry in good health; that is no assurance that you will come back without being helped. Our physical organism is such a delicate, intricate, elaborate piece of Divine mechanism, that if but the little finger of disaster touch it too roughly it crushes into ruin. God, as if to show that you can not depend upon physiological appearances, lets some invalid crawl on to eighty-five years of age, kept up by tonics and plasters, and helped by spectacles and ear-trumpets and canes, while there are thousands, muscular, roundly developed, and athletic, who drop dead under apoplectic stroke. Feel in your pockets and bring me out, if you can, a document rightly signed and sealed warranting you to get through this night alive. I saw plunging into Lake Geneva the River Rhone. It came on with swift uproar, and you could tell some distance back that it was coming on to that plunge. But who can tell at what moment, at what day, the river of our life shall empty into the deep, wide, infinite future? All the heavy shipping that goes out of New York goes through the "Narrows;" but by what different tack! to what different harbors!

One of the most fascinating excursions in Switzerland is to the Castle of Chalons, in the midst of those very Genevan waters. History and poetry tell us that Bonivard, the hero, was chained in that castle six years; and you can see the bolt and ring where he was fastened, and the circular depression in the ground where he tramped about. After a while a flotilla came down, and he was freed; but he heard them coming before his shout of deliverance mingled with their shout of victory. Yet here, my friends, we go tramping around in this earthly prison-house, chained to a body from which we can not get free, not knowing at what moment the forces of the great future may break in upon us to shatter these manacles of flesh, and disendungeon our immortal spirit, until the prisoner of Chalons shall become the victor of the skies.

Do you not feel that we walk amidst a vast uncertainty, not knowing what peril may swoop from above or what deep may be crouching beneath? Suppose you had been with those boys in that boat, would you have been ready? It was well for them that they were children of the Covenant—"I will be a God to thee and to thy seed after thee." —and that they were praying boys, in their Brooklyn home kneeling down with their mother and praying aloud, not ashamed to let the world hear any more than to let God hear. Oh, when the boat became unmanageable, and they were trying to haul in sail, they would not have had so good an opportunity for spiritual preparation as they had in their calm Brooklyn home, where they were not ashamed to acknowledge Jesus! Many of you will go out of life just as suddenly. Whether by flood, or fire, or earthquake, or lightning-flash, or colliding rail trains, or a fatal slip on an orange-peeling in the street, I know not; but you will have then no time to repent, and you will have no time to pray. If all the churches and cathedrals of the world should then go crying unto God in your behalf, it would not do you any good. All the preparation a man makes for the great future, he has to make this side the sharp line that divides the two residences.

I see in this event that hilarity and gladness can not

keep back the fatal attack. When three or four students are together, and in such a tonic and exhilarating air as that of Switzerland, there is mirth and exuberance unbounded. They did not see the soft paws of the wave reaching up around the gilded boat, nor did they imagine that the deep lay couched beneath, ready to spring upon them. I believe in mirth and in boating and in pleasure-excursions; but I want you to understand that gladness and hilarity of surrounding can not keep back our last moment. It may come treading over rose-leaves; it may come keeping step to the thrum of the harp, while hands are clapping, while feet are bounding, while all sails are set over a glassy sea. So it came when the *Arctic* and the *Vesta*, mid-Atlantic, struck. So it came when the *Austria* burned on the high seas. So it came when Richmond Court-house fell. So it came when the *Ville du Havre* sunk. "In such a day, and in such an hour as ye think not, the Son of man cometh." Oh, this bell of warning that rings to-night has not attached to it a short rope that any sexton may seize, but a twisted strand of wire three thousand miles long, and the red fingers of the lightning pull it until it rings from continent to continent, "Whatsoever thy hand findeth to do, do it with thy might, for there is no work, nor device, nor knowledge, nor wisdom, in the grave whither thou goest." What a voice for the youth of my congregation—the voice that comes from Lake Geneva to-night! Young people do not like any thing dull or stupid. Neither do I, and I do not blame them for that; but there is nothing tame in this event. It comes with a great thrill, and it seems that your body and mind and soul must feel the shock.

They had every prospect of living. Just look at their

pictures. See what broad shoulders they had, what stout chests, what ruddy cheeks, what grand foreheads. "Oh!" you say, "if they had only known how to swim, it would have been all right." They could swim; they could outswim you. They were as familiar with the water as many with the land. They were splendid swimmers. Their father had taught them how to take this exercise. But they were too far from shore, or the boom struck them, and they are gone. They had no pluck to stand up against a lake one thousand feet deep. Their father, who had often been with them on the water, was not there. He could give them no relief. But I think that He who walked Lake Gennesaret walked Lake Geneva, and that they are safe. O man! O woman! when your last moment comes, you want something more than a human arm to help you. No one but Jesus then; no one but Jesus now.

They had brilliant prospects. In Germany, in Paris, and in Switzerland they had studied, at the fountain-head, those languages through which comes so much of the culture and refinement of the world. The gates of knowledge and of success were open before them; but they died at the gates, and all the plans for earthly welfare ended then and there. My hearers, do not build too much upon this world. It is a glassy surface, with a thousand feet of graves beneath. Do you think you can sail that craft, and clew down the topsail-yards, and haul out the reef tackles? A sudden squall may come, and you will go down, unless there be a Christ sleeping in the hinder part of the ship, ready in the nick of time to rise up and hush the wind and silence the sea. I believe the Son of God was in that tossing boat, and that when these lads cried out, in their extremity, "Master, save us, we perish!" I think then and there he came to their spiritual and immortal rescue.

Let us pray God he will comfort those who are waiting for more minute tidings of this event. The tongue of the cable seems to have been palsied with the tidings, and it does not talk plainly. I wish their bodies might be found. It would be a satisfaction, though a sad satisfaction, to have them here in one of our own cemeteries. As the mother said to me a few hours ago, it would seem like tucking them away in bed safely for the night. But if God shall deny these parents this, it will make no difference to the lads, and the archangel's trumpet that wakes up the sea will wake up also the lake. And, after all, they can find no grander place to sleep than where they are sleeping now; the shadows of Jura and the Alps blanketing them in their slumbers, while vast, majestic Mont Blanc bends over them snow-white, the only fit type of the great white throne before which they and we shall be assembled.

But I am to-night oppressed almost to suffocation with the idea that there may be some here who are unprepared for that ordeal. Certainly some of you are not ready now, and you are not taking any steps toward preparation. What, O young man! O man in mid-life! O aged man! if this night thy soul should be required of thee? It is a serious question to ask. It is a serious question to answer. You are no safer on the land than you are on the wave. Oh, make one mighty struggle for heaven! Put out for the shore of eternal safety before your soul sinks. There comes to you to-night, not so much my voice as the voices of the lads John and James, sounding over the mountains, sounding across the sea, declaring with startling emphasis,

"In such a day and hour as ye think not, the Son of man cometh."

Before they went away, two years ago, on the finger of one of the lads was placed a gold ring with the inscription, "God bless you;" and on the finger of the other lad was placed a gold ring with the inscription, "Remember father and mother;" but God your Father would this night put upon your soul immortal the signet-ring of his everlasting affection. Will you wear it?

> "While life prolongs its precious light,
> Mercy is found, and peace is given;
> But soon, ah! soon, approaching night
> Will blot out every hope of heaven."

THE RED CORD IN THE WINDOW.

"And she bound the scarlet line in the window."—*Joshua* ii., 21.

IF you have any idea that I have chosen this text because it is odd, you do not know me nor the errand on which I come. Eternity is too near and life too short for men to take texts merely because they are peculiar. I take this because it is full of the old Gospel.

There is a very sick and sad house in the city of Jericho. What is the matter? Is it poverty? No. Worse than that. Is it leprosy? No. Worse than that. Is it death? No. Worse than that. A daughter has forsaken her home. By what infernal plot she was induced to leave, I know not; but they look in vain for her return. Sometimes they hear a footstep very much like hers, and they start up and say, "She comes!" but only to sink back again into disappointment. Alas! alas! The father sits by the hour, with his face in his hands, saying not one word. The mother's hair is becoming gray too fast, and she begins to stoop, so that those who saw her only a little while ago in the street know her not now as she passes. The brothers clench their fists, swearing vengeance against the despoiler of their home. Alas! will the poor soul never come back? There is a long, deep shadow over all the household. Added to this, there is an invading army six miles away, just over the river, coming on to destroy the city; and what with the loss of their child, and the coming-on of that destructive army, I think the old people wished that they could die. That is the first scene in this drama of the Bible.

In a house on the wall of the city is that daughter. That is her home now. Two spies have come from the invading army to look around through Jericho, and see how best it may be taken. Yonder is the lost child, in that dwelling on the wall of the city. The police hear of it, and soon there is the shuffling of feet all around about the door, and the city government demands the surrender of those two spies. First, Rahab—for that was the name of the lost child—first, Rahab secretes the two spies, and gets their pursuers off the track; but after a while she says to them, "I will make a bargain with you. I will save your life if you will save my life, and the life of my father, and my mother, and my brothers, and my sisters, when the victorious army comes upon the city." Oh, she had not forgotten her home yet, you see! The wanderer never forgets home. Her heart breaks now as she thinks of how she has maltreated her parents, and she wishes she were back with them again, and she wishes she could get away from her sinful inthrallment; and sometimes she looks up in the face of the midnight, bursting into agonizing tears. No sooner have these two spies promised to save her life, and the life of her father, and mother, and brothers, and sisters, than Rahab takes a scarlet cord and ties it around the body of one of the spies, brings him to the window, and, as he clambers out—nervous lest she have not strength to hold him—with muscular arms such as woman seldom has, she lets him down, hand over hand, in safety to the ground. Not being exhausted, she ties the cord around the other spy, brings him to the window, and just as successfully lets him down to the ground. No sooner have these men untied the scarlet cord from their bodies than they look up, and they say, "You had better get all your friends in this house—your father, your mother, your brothers, and your sisters; you had better get them in this house. And then, after you have them here, take this red cord which you have put around our bodies, and tie it across the window; and when our victorious army comes up, and sees that scarlet thread in the window, it will spare this house and all who are in it. Shall it be so?" cried the spies. "Ay, ay," said Rahab, from the window, "it shall be so!" That is the second scene in this Bible drama.

There is a knock at the door of the old man. He looks up, and says, "Come in;" and, lo! there is Rahab, the lost child; but she has no time to talk. They gather in excitement around her, and she says to them, "Get ready quickly, and go with me to my house. The army is coming! The trumpet! Make haste! Fly! The enemy!" That is the third scene in this Bible drama.

The hosts of Israel are all around about the doomed city of Jericho. Crash! goes the great metropolis, heaps on heaps. The air suffocating with the dust, and horrible with the screams of a dying city. All the houses flat down. All the people dead. Ah no, no. On a crag of the wall—the only piece of the wall left standing—there is a house which we must enter. There is a family there that has been spared. Who are they? Let us go in and see. Rahab, her father, her mother, her brothers, her sisters, all safe, and the only house left standing in all the city. What saved them? Was the house more firmly built? Oh no; it was built in the most perilous place, on the wall, and the wall was the first thing that fell. Was it because her character was any better than any of the other population of the city? Oh no. Why, then, was she spared, and all her household? Can you tell me why? Oh, it was the scarlet line in the window. That is the fourth scene in this Bible drama.

When the destroying angel went through Egypt it was the blood of the lamb on the door-posts that saved the Israelites; and now that vengeance has come upon Jericho, it is the same color that assures the safety of Rahab and all her household. My friends, there are foes coming upon us, more deadly and more tremendous, to overthrow our immortal interests. They will trample us down, and crush us out forever, unless there be some skillful mode of rescue open. The police of death already begin to clamor for our surrender; but, blessed be God, there is a way out. It is through the window, and by a rope so saturated with the blood of the cross that it is as red as that with which the spies were lowered; and if once our souls shall be delivered, then, the scarlet cord stretched across the window of our escape, we may defy all bombardment, earthly and Satanic.

In the first place, carrying out the idea of my text, we must stretch this scarlet cord *across the window of our rescue.* There comes a time when a man is surrounded. What is that in the front door of his soul? It is the threatenings of the future. What is that in the back door of the soul? It is the sins of the past. He can not get out of either of those door-ways. If he attempts it he will be cut to pieces. What shall he do? Escape through the window of God's mercy. That sunshine has been pouring in for many a day. God's inviting mercy. God's pardoning mercy. God's all-conquering mercy. God's everlasting mercy.

But, you say, the window is so high. Ah, there is a rope, the very one with which the cross and its Victim were lifted. That was strong enough to hold Christ, and it is strong enough to hold you. Bear all your weight upon it, all your hopes for this life, all your hopes for the life that is to come. Escape now through the window. "But," you say, "that cord is too small to save me; that salvation will never do at all for such a sinner as I have been." I suppose that the rope with which Rahab let the two spies to the ground was not thick enough; but they took that or nothing. And, my dear brother, that is your alternative. There is only one scarlet line that can save you. There have been hundreds and thousands who have been borne away in safety by that scarlet line, and it will bear you away in safety. Do you notice what a very narrow escape those spies had? I suppose they came with flustered cheek and with excited heart. They had a *very* narrow escape. They went in the broad door of sin; but how did they come out? They came out of the window. They went up by the stairs of stone; they came down on a slender thread. And so, my friends, we go easily and unabashedly into sin, and all the doors are open; but if we get out at all it will be by being let down over precipices, wriggling and helpless, the strong grip above keeping us from being dashed on the rocks beneath. It is easy to get into sin, young man. It is not so easy to get out of it.

A young man, to-night, goes to the marble counter of the bar-room of the Fifth Avenue Hotel. He asks for a brandy-smash—called so, I suppose, because it smashes the man that takes it. There is no intoxication in it. As the young man receives it, he does not seem to be at all excited. It does not give any glassiness to the eye. He walks home in beautiful apparel, and all his prospects are brilliant. That drink is not going to destroy him, but it is the first step on a bad road. Years have passed on, and I see that young man after he has gone the whole length of dissipation. It is midnight, and he is in a hotel—perhaps the very one where he took the first drink. He is in the fourth story, and the delirium is on him. He rises from the bed and comes to the window, and it is easily lifted; so he lifts it. Then he pushes back the blinds, and puts his foot on the window-sill. Then he gives one spring, and the watchman finds his disfigured body, unrecognizable, on the pavement. Oh, if he had only waited a little—if he had come down on the scarlet ladder that Jesus holds from the wall for him and for you and for me! But no, he made one jump of it, and was gone.

A minister of Christ was not long ago dismissed from his diocese for intoxication, and in a public meeting at the West he gave this account of his sorrow. He said, "I had a beautiful home once; but strong drink shattered it. I had beautiful children; but this fiend of rum took their dimpled hands in his and led them to the grave. I had a wife—to know her was to love her; but she sits in wretchedness to-night while I wander over the earth. I had a mother, and the pride of her life was I; but the thunder-bolt struck her. I now have scarcely a friend in all the world. Taste of the bitter cup I have tasted, and then answer me as to whether I have any hatred for the agency of my ruin. Hate it! I hate the whole damning traffic. I would to God to-night that every distillery were in flames, for then in the glowing sky I would write in the smoke of the ruin, 'Woe to him that putteth the bottle to his neighbor's lips!'" That minister of the Gospel went in through the broad door of temptation; he came out of the window. And when I see the temptations that are all about us, and when I know the proclivity to sin in every man's heart, I see that, if any of us escape, it will be a very narrow escape. Oh, if we have, my friends, got off from our sin, let us tie the scarlet thread by which we have been saved across the window. Let us do it in praise of Him whose blood dyed it that color. Let it be in announcement of the fact that we shall no more be fatally assaulted. "There is now no condemnation to them that are in Christ Jesus." Then let all the forces of this world come up in cavalry charge, and let spirits of darkness come on, an infernal storming party attempting to take our soul; this rope twisted from these words, "The blood of Jesus Christ cleanseth from all sin," will hurl them back defeated forever.

Still further, we must take this red cord of the text and stretch it *across the window of our households.* When the Israelitish army came up against Jericho, they said, "What is that in the window?" Some one said, "That is a scarlet line." "Oh," said some one else, "that must be the house that was to be spared. Don't touch it." That line was thick enough and long enough and conspicuous enough to save Rahab, her father, her mother, her brothers, and her sisters — the entire family. Have our households as good protection? You have bolts on the front door and on the back, and fastenings to the window, and perhaps burglar alarms, and perhaps an especial watchman blowing his whistle at midnight before your dwelling; but all that can not protect your household. Is there on our houses the sign of a Saviour's sacrifice and mercy? Is there a scarlet line in the window? Have your children been consecrated to Christ? Have you been washed in the blood of the atonement? In what room do you have family prayers? Show me where it is you are accustomed to kneel. The sky is black with the coming deluge. Is your family inside or outside the ark? It is a sad thing for a man to reject Christ; but to lie down in the night of sin, across the path to heaven, so that his family come up and trip over him into an infinity of horrors—that is the longest, the deepest, the mightiest! It is a sad thing for a mother to reject Christ; but to gather her family around her, and then take them by the hand and lead them out into paths of worldliness, away from God and heaven—oh, it will take all the dirges of earth and hell to weep out that agony.

I suppose there are in this church to-night families represented where there has not been an audible prayer offered for ten years. There may be geranium and cactus in the window, and upholstery hovering over it, and childish faces looking out of it; but there is no scarlet thread stretched across it. Although that house may seem to be on the finest street in all the city, it is really on the edge of a marsh across which sweep most poisonous malarias, and it has a sandy foundation, and its splendor will come down, and great will be the fall of it. A home without God! A prayerless father! An undevout mother! Awful! awful! Is that you? Will you keep on, my brother, on the wrong road, and take your loved ones with you? May God arrest you before you complete the ruin of those whom you ought to save. You see I talk plainly to you, just as I would have you talk plainly to me. Time is so short, that we can not waste any of it on apologies or indirections or circumlocutions. You owe to your children, O father! O mother! more than food, more than clothing, more than shelter—you owe them the example of a prayerful, consecrated, pronounced, out-and-out Christian life. You can not afford to keep it away from them.

Now, as I stand here, you do not see any hands outstretched toward me, and yet there are hands on my brow and hands on both my shoulders. They are hands of parental benediction. It is quite a good many years ago now since we folded those hands as they began the last sleep on the banks of the Raritan, in the village cemetery; but those hands are stretched out toward me to-night, and they are just as warm and they are just as gentle as when I sat at their knee at five years of age. And I shall never shake off those hands. I do not want to. They have helped me so much a thousand times already, and I do not expect to have a trouble or a trial between this and my grave where those hands will not help me. Theirs was not a very splendid home, as the world calls it; but we had a family Bible there, well worn by tender perusal; and there was a family altar there, where we knelt morning and night; and there was a holy Sabbath there; and stretched in a straight line, or hung in loops or festoons, there was a scarlet line in the window. Oh, the tender, precious, blessed memory of a Christian home! Is that the impression you are making upon your children? When you are dead—and it will not be long before you are—when you are dead, will your child say, "If there ever was a good Christian father, mine was one. If there ever was a good Christian mother, mine was one?" Will they say that after you are dead? Standing some Sabbath night in church preaching the glorious Gospel, as I am trying to do, will they tell the people in that day how there are hands of benediction on their brow and hands of parental benediction on both their shoulders?

Still further, we want this scarlet line of the text drawn *across the window of our prospects.* I see Rahab, and her father, and her mother, and her brothers, and sisters looking out over Jericho, the city of palm-trees, and across the river, and over at the army invading, and then up to the mountains and the sky. Mind you, this house was on the wall, and I suppose the prospect from the window must have been very wide. Besides that, I do not think that the scarlet line at all interfered with the view of the landscape. The assurance it gave of safety must have added to the beauty of the country. To-night, my friends, we stand or sit in the window of earthly prospect, and we look off toward the hills of heaven and the landscape of eternal beauty. God has opened the window for us, and we look out; but how if we do not get there? If we never get there, better never to have had even this faint glimpse of it. We now only get a dim outline of the inhabitants. We now only here and there catch a note of the exquisite harmony.

But blessed be God for this scarlet line in the window! That tells me that the blood of Christ bought that home for my soul, and I shall go there when my work is done here. And as I put my hand on that scarlet line every thing in the future brightens. My eye-sight gets better, and the robes of the victors are more lustrous, and our loved ones who went away some time ago—they do not stand any more with their backs to us, but their faces are this way, and their voice drops through this Sabbath air, saying, with all tenderness and sweetness, "Come! Come! Come!" And the child that you think of only as buried—

why, there she is, and it is May-day in heaven; and they
gather the amaranth, and they pluck the lilies, and they
twist them into a garland for her brow, and she is one of
the May-queens of heaven. Oh, do you think they could
see our waving to-night? It is quite a pleasant night out-
doors, pretty clear, not many clouds in the sky, quite star-
light. I wonder if they can see us from that good land?
I think they can. If from this window of earthly pros-
pect we can almost see them, then from their towers of
light I think they can fully see us. And so I wave them
the glory, and I wave them the joy, and I say, "Have you
got through with all your troubles?" and their voices an-
swer, "God hath wiped away all tears from our eyes." I
say, "Is it as grand up there as you thought it would be?"
and the voices answer, "Eye hath not seen nor ear heard,
neither have entered into the heart of man the things
which God hath prepared for them that love him." I say,
"Do you have any more struggle for bread?" and they an-
swer, "We hunger no more, we thirst no more." And I
say, "Have you been out to the cemetery of the golden
city?" and they answer, "There is no death here." And
I look out through the night heavens, and I say, "Where
do you get your light from, and what do you burn in the
temple?" and they answer, "There is no night here, and
we have no need of candle or of star." And I say, "What
book do you sing out of?" and they answer, "The Halle-
lujah Chorus." And I say, "In the splendor and magnif-
icence of the city, don't you ever get lost?" and they
answer, "The Lamb which is in the midst of the throne
leadeth us to living fountains of water." Oh, how near it
seems to-night! Their wings—do you not feel them?
Their harps—do you not hear them? And all that through

the window of our earthly prospect, across which stretcheth the scarlet line.

Be that my choice color forever. Is it too glaring for you? Do you like the blue because it reminds you of the sky, or the green because it makes you think of the foliage, or the black because it has in it the shadows of the night? I take the scarlet because it shall make me think of the price that was paid for my soul. Oh, the blood! the blood! the blood of the Lamb of God that taketh away the sin of the world! Through it we escape sin. Through it we reach heaven. Will you let it atone for you? Believe in it, and you live. Refuse it, and you die. Will you accept it, or will you pull over on you the eternal calamity of rejecting it?

I see where you are. You are at the cross-roads tonight. The next step decides every thing. Pause before you take it; but do not pause too long, lest the wind of God's justice slam to the door that has been standing open so long. I hear the thunder of God's artillery. I hear the blast of the trumpet that wakes the dead. Look out! look out! For in that day, and in our closing moment on earth, better than any other defense or barricade, however high or broad or stupendous, will be one little, thin, scarlet thread in the window.

THE LAMP.

"Thy word is a lamp."—*Psalm* cxix., 105.

FROM six o'clock last evening until six o'clock this morning darkness rested on our part of the earth, and every few hours there rolls a wave of natural night all over the nations. With lamps, and chandeliers, and torches, and lanterns, we try to drive out the night from houses, and churches, and stores, and shops. He who invents a new kind of a light invents his own fortune and the fortune of his children. But there is a night of sin and suffering and shame which needs another kind of illumination. Ancient philosophy made a lamp, but it was a dead failure, and the people kept crying out, "Give us a light! give us a light!" After a while prophet and evangelist and apostle made a lamp. A coal from heaven struck it into a blaze, and uncounted multitudes of people, with an open Bible before them, cry out in rapture and in love, "Thy word is a lamp."

When, a few years ago, there was a great accident in Hartley Colliery, in England, and two hundred persons lost their lives, the Queen telegraphed down to the scene of disaster, "Can we give you any help? Will you be able to get the men out? How many are lost? Give my sympathy to all the bereft." What consolation it was to the families who stood amidst the consternation and the terror that the throne of England throbbed in sympathy with their disaster! But I have to tell you to-day a more glorious truth, and that is, from the throne of God the King of heaven and earth telegraphs down through this Bible into the dungeons of our sin and suffering a message of pardon, of love, of sympathy, of comfort, of eternal life. Like some light-house on high promontory, blessed by ships passing through darkness and storm, so on the heights of God's love and grace there flames forth a light upon the great sea of man's wretchedness and of God's providence, so that angels on their way earthward, and ransomed spirits on their way heavenward, and devils on their way hellward, pass through its flash, crying, "Thy word is a lamp."

You have four or five Bibles in your house—perhaps ten, perhaps twenty. They are such common property you do not appreciate them. If you had only one Bible, and for that you had paid five hundred dollars (the price that was paid in olden time for a copy of the Scriptures), then you would more thoroughly appreciate it. I was once a colporteur for a few months in a vacation, and I came into a home of destitution. I saw a woman there eighty-five years of age, and I said to her, "May I give you a Bible?" "Oh," she replied, "a Bible would be of no use to me. I can't see to read. I used to read, but for twenty years I haven't been able to read a word." I pulled out of my sachel one of the copies of the Psalms of David and the New Testament in great, large, round type, and I said, "Now, put on your spectacles and see if you can't read this." She wiped her spectacles and put them on. "Oh yes," she said; "why, I can see, after all! I am very thankful to you. Why, yes, I see it: 'I love the Lord because he hath heard my voice and my—' Oh yes, I can read it, I can read it!" I wish that God to-day would make the Bible as new and fresh to us as it was to her.

I want to show you that the Bible is a lamp—a parlor-lamp, a street-lamp, a store-lamp, a church-lamp, a sepulchral lamp.

In parlors all aflash with gas-light and gleaming mirror, and blazing chandelier and candelabra, there may be Egyptian darkness; while in some plain room which a frugal hand has spread with hospitality and refinement, this one lamp may cast a glow that makes it a fit place for heavenly coronations. We invoke no shadow to fall upon the hilarities of life. We would not have every song a dirge, and every picture a martyrdom, and every step a funeral pace. God's lamp, hung in the parlor, would chill no joy, would rend no harmony, would check no innocent laughter. On the contrary, it would bring out brighter colors in the picture; it would expose new gracefulness in the curtain; it would unroll new wreaths from the carpet; it would strike new music from the harp; it would throw new polish into the manners; it would kindle with light, borrowed from the very throne of God, all the refinements of society. Oh that the Christ who was born in a barn would come to our parlor! We need his hand to sift the parlor music. We need his taste to assort the parlor literature. We need his voice to conduct the parlor conversation. We are apt to think of religion as being a rude, blundering thing, not fit to put its foot upon Axminster, or its clownish hands on beautiful adornments, or lift its voice amidst the artistic and refined; so, while we have Jesus in the nursery when we teach our children to pray, and Jesus in the dining-hall when we ask his blessing upon our food, and Jesus in the sitting-room when we have family prayers, it is a simple fact that from ten thousand Christian homes in this country Christ is from one end of the year to the other shut out of the parlor. Oh that housekeepers understood that the grace of God is the greatest accomplishment, and that no seat is too luxuriant for religion to sit in, and no arch too grand for religion to walk under, and no circle too brilliant for religion to move in! If Christianity at last is to walk up the streets of heaven with seraphim and archangel, it is good enough to go anywhere where you go or where I shall go. To purify the heart, to cleanse the life, to culture the taste, to expurgate all hypocrisy and falsehood and sham, we must have the Bible in the parlor. When Christian people come to spend an evening, they talk about the weather, and they talk about the scandal, and they talk about the crops, and they talk about the markets; but they do not talk about God and Christ and heaven. The thing we most want to-day in all our parlors is the lamp of the Bible.

Still further, the Bible is the *street-lamp*. When night comes down on the city, crime goes forth to its worst achievements. Not only to show honest citizens where to walk, but to hinder the burglar, and assassin, and highwayman, and pickpocket, we must have artificial lights all over the city. I remember what consternation there was in Philadelphia when one night the gas-works were out of order, and the whole city sat in darkness. Between eleven o'clock at night and three o'clock in the morning, in the dark and unlighted places of the town, crime has its holiday. If the lamp-lighter ceased his work for one week, the town would rot. But there is a darkness beyond all power of gas-light. What is the use of police-station and almshouse and watchman's club, if there be no moral and religious influence to sanction the law and to purify the executive, and to hang over legal enactment the fear of God and an enlightened public opinion. When in a city crime runs rampant, and virtue is at a discount, and jails are full, and churches are empty, and the nights are hideous with the howl and the whoop of drunkards, and the saloons boil over with scum, and public officials think more of a bribe than they do of their own conscience, and when great tides of wickedness set down the streets —the first want of such a city as that is the street-lamp of the Bible. Did you ever stand in a church-tower and look down upon a city at night? It is overwhelming. But you feel that beneath all that brilliancy of gas-light there is a surging sea of want and suffering and woe. History says that Dionysius had a great cave built for his prisoners. He was a cruel man, and he used to go to the top of the cave, put his ear to the opening and listen, and the groans and the sighings of the prisoners came up into his ear and made music for him. God stands at the head of our world, but for a different purpose and with a different heart. He puts his ear to the dungeon, and every sigh comes up stirring his sympathies, and every groan wounding his heart; and he listens and listens all night long. There is but one lamp that can throw light into the dungeon where the prisoner groans, into the hovel where the beggar pines, into the cellar where the drunkard wallows, into the alley where the libertine putrefies, into the madhouse where the maniac raves. Travelers in Africa tell us that they have seen serpents—a vast number of them—coiled together, and piled up in horrid fold above horrid fold; and then they would hear hundreds of them hissing at once, and the sight and the sound were appalling and unbearable. But if you should take the wickedness of our best of cities, and bring it all together in one place, and pile it up fold above fold, it would be a hissing horror and ghastliness that no human eye could look at without being blasted, and no human ear could hear without being stunned.

Now, how will all these scenes of iniquity in our cities be overcome? They will not be overcome until the church and the school and a Christian printing-press kindle all around about us God's street-lamp of the Bible. Send the Bible down that filthy alley, if you would have it cleansed. Send it against those decanters, if you would have them smashed. Send it against those chains, if you would have them broken. Send it through all the ignorance of the city, if you would have it illumined as by a flash from heaven's morning. The Bible can do it, will do it. Gather all the ignorance and the wickedness and the vice of our cities in one great pile—Alps above Alps, Pyrenees above Pyrenees, Himalaya above Himalaya—and then give one little New Testament full swing against the side of that mountain, and down it would come, Alps after Alps, Pyrenees after Pyrenees, Himalaya after Himalaya. What is the difference between New York and Pekin? What is the difference between London and Madras? What is the difference between Edinburgh and Canton? No difference, save that which the Bible makes. O city missionary! O philanthropist! O Christian! go everywhere, and kindle up these great street-lamps of the Gospel; and our city, purified and cleansed, will proclaim what the Psalmist so long ago declared, "Thy word is a lamp."

I know there are people who suppose that the vice of our cities is going to conquer the virtue of the people. I do not believe it. Let error and vice run, if you only let truth run along with them. Urged on by skeptic's shout and transcendentalist's spur, let error run! God's angels of wrath are in hot pursuit, and, quicker than eagle's beak clutcheth out a hawk's heart, God's vengeance will tear it to pieces. Let it run, if you only let God's Word run along with it.

Still further, the Bible is the best *store-lamp*. Blessed is the merchant who under its glow reads his ledger, and transacts his business, and pockets his gains, and suffers his losses. It may be well to have a fine sky-light, to have a magnificent glass show-window, by night to have bronzed brackets spouting fire in a very palace of merchandise; but if you have not this eternal lamp, you had better quit keeping store. What is the reason so many who started in merchandise, with good principles and fair prospects and honorable intentions, have become gamblers, and defrauders, and knaves, and desperadoes, and liars, and thieves? They did not have the right kind of a store-lamp. Why is it, in our day, merchandise is smitten with uncertainty, and three-fourths of the business of our great cities is only one huge species of gambling, and society is upturned by false assignments, and two-third acts, and repudiations, and imperiled trust-funds, and fraudulent certificates of stock, and wild schemes in railroads without any track, and banks without any capital, and cities without any houses, and joint-stock companies without any conscience? And why are ten thousand of our business men ridden with a nightmare enough to crush Hercules and Prometheus? It is the want of a right kind of store-lamp. What ruined the merchant princes of Tyre, that great city of fairs and bazaars and palaces; her vessels of trade, with cedar masts and embroidered sails and ivory benches, driven by fierce blasts on Northern waters, and then dropping down on glassy Indian seas; bringing wine from Helbon, and chariot cloths from Dedan, and gold and spices from Rahmah, and emerald and agate from Syria; her waters foaming with innumerable keels; her store-houses bursting with the treasures of all nations—that queen of cities, on a throne of ivory and ebony, under a crown of gold, and pearl, and diamond, and carbuncle, and chrysoprase? The want of a right kind of store-lamp. If the principles of religion had ruled in her trade, do you suppose that dry-rot would have sunk the ships, and that vermin would have eaten up her robes, and that God's mills would have ground up the agate, and that fishermen would dry their nets on the rocks which once were aquake with the roar and tread of a great metropolis? Oh, what thrones have fallen, what monuments have crumbled, what fleets have sunk, what statues have been defaced, what barbarisms have been created, what civilization retarded, what nations damned, all for the want of the right kind of a store-lamp!

Men of business! take your Bibles with you to-morrow morning. Place them in your store or shop. Do not be ashamed if any body at noon finds you reading the Scriptures. It is safe always to do business by their teachings. There was a young man in a store in Boston, standing behind the counter, selling goods. A gentleman came in, and asked for some Middlesex cloths. "Oh," said the young man, "we haven't any Middlesex cloths, but here is something just as good." "No," replied the gentleman, "I don't want them;" and he passed out. The head man of the firm came down to the young man, and said, "What did that man want?" "He wanted Middlesex cloths," replied the young man. "Why didn't you tell him they were Middlesex cloths?" "Because they were not, sir." "Then, you can take your hat and leave." The young man took his hat and left. He went into merchandise in Cincinnati, went on up till he became a merchant prince, and not more eminent for wealth than for piety. God will never let a young man suffer for doing right. Full justice may not be done him in this world; but in the last day, before an assembled universe, it will be found out whether or not they were Middlesex cloths.

Still further, the Bible is the best *church-lamp*. I care not how many chandeliers there may be in a church, how many brilliant lights there may be, the Word of God is the best church-lamp. Oh, is there any thing more beautiful than an audience gathered on the Sabbath for Christian worship? There may be no dazzle of theatric assemblage, there may be no glitter of foot-lights, there may be no allegoric images blossoming from pit to dome; but there is something in the place and in the occasion that makes it supernatural. In the light of this lamp I see your faces kindle with a great joy. Glorious church-lamp, this Bible! Luther found it in the cloister at Erfurt, and he lifted it until the monasteries and cathedrals of Germany, and Italy, and France, and England, and the world saw its illumination. It shone under the trap-doors. It looked behind the curtains. It shone under the breastplate of sacerdotal authority; and in the mosques of Turkey, and in the pagodas of India, and in the ice huts of Greenland, and in the mud hovels of Africa, and in the temples of China, God's regenerated children, in musical Tamil, and sweet Italian, and nasal Chinese, and harsh Choctaw, cried out, "Thy word is a lamp." It throws its light on the pulpit, making a bulwark of truth; on the baptismal cup, until its waters glitter like the crystals of heaven. It strikes penitence into the prayers and gladness into the thanksgiving. It changes into a church John Bunyan's prison, and Covenanter's cave, and Calvin's castle, and Huss's stake, and Hugh M'Kail's scaffold of martyrdom. Zwinglius carried it into Switzerland, and John Wickfield into England, and John Knox into Scotland, and Jehudi Ashmun into Africa.

Begone, ye scoffers! Down to the lowest pit, ye emissaries of darkness! for by the throne of an omnipotent judgment I declare it that all iniquity shall fall, and all bondage be broken, and all wounds be healed, and all darkness be dispelled, when God's truth shall go forth "as a lamp that burneth." We want no sappers or miners to level the wall; we want no axemen or engineers to prepare the way; we want no glittering steel or booming gun or howling Hotchkiss shell to get us the victory, for the mountains are full of horses and chariots of fire. Hallelujah! for the kingdoms of this world are become the kingdoms of our Lord Jesus Christ. I do not wonder that the stranger who sat the other day beside me in the rail-car reading his Bible, after he had concluded his reading, closed it, and kissed it, and put it in his pocket. There have been times when you did the same. When all else failed you, it was so bright, it was so loving, it was so sympathetic a book that you, too, kissed it.

Still further, the Bible is a *sepulchral lamp*. You know that the ancient Egyptians used to keep lights burning in the tombs of their dead. These lights were kept up for scores, even hundreds, of years. Friends would come from generation to generation and put oil in the lamps, and it was considered a disaster if those lamps went out. You and I will some day go down into the house of the dead. Some have looked upon it as an unknown land, and, when they have thought of it, their knees have knocked together and their hearts fainted. There were whole generations of men that had no comfort about death, no view of the eternal world; and whenever they brought their friends and put them away into the dust, they said, without any alleviation, "This is horrid! this is horrid!" And it was. The grave is the deepest, ghastliest pit that a man ever looks into, unless the lamp of God's word flashes into it. For whole ages men thought that the sepulchre was a den where a great monster gorged himself on human carcasses. "I will put an end to that," said Jesus of Nazareth; "I will with mine own voice go down and make darkness flee;" and as he stepped out from the gate of heaven, all the grave-yards of earth cried, "Come! come!" And he came down, bringing a great many beautiful lights; and above this babe's grave he hung a light, and over this mother's tomb he hung a light, and over this wife's grave he hung a light, and over all the sleeping-places of the Christian dead he hung a light. Then he uttered his voice, and it ran along under the ground from city to city, and along under the sea from continent to continent, until mausoleum and sarcophagus and sepulchre throbbed with the joy: "I am the resurrection and the life; he that believeth in me, though he were dead, yet shall he live." And now, if Greenwood and Laurel Hill and Mount Auburn could break their beautiful silence and should speak, their lips of bronze and granite would break forth in the strains of my text, "Thy word is a lamp."

O ye bruised souls! O ye who have been cutting yourselves among the tombs! O ye who have been sowing seed for the resurrection-day! O ye of the broken heart! I come out to-day and put into your hand this glorious Gospel lamp. It will throw a glow of consolation over your bereft spirit. "Weeping may endure for a night, but joy cometh in the morning." "They that sow in tears shall reap in joy."

Rabbi Mier went off from home to be gone a few days, and left two beautiful boys. While he was gone, the two lads died. Rabbi Mier returned, not knowing that any thing had happened. His Christian wife knew he would be overcome with grief, and she met him at the door and said to him, "My husband, I once had two beautiful jewels loaned to me. I had them for a little while. And, do you know, while you were gone the owner came for them. Ought I to have given them?" "Of course," said Rabbi Mier, "you ought to have given them up; you say they were only loaned." Then she called her husband to the side-room, and removed the cloth that covered the dead children. After Rabbi Mier had for a few moments given way to his grief, he rose up and said, "Now I know what you meant by the borrowed jewels. 'The Lord gave, and the Lord hath taken away. Blessed be the name of the Lord.'" And so Rabbi Mier was comforted.

Let this sepulchral light gild all the graves of your dead. May this lamp of the text be set in all your parlors, in all your streets, in all your stores, in all your churches, in all your sepulchres! Amen.

THE DYING NEED OF THE CHURCH.

"Behold, I will send my messenger, and he shall prepare the way before me: and the Lord, whom ye seek, shall suddenly come to his temple, even the messenger of the covenant, whom ye delight in: behold, he shall come, saith the Lord of hosts."—*Malachi* iii., 1.

SOMETIMES a minister's subject is suggested by his artistic tastes; sometimes, by the occurrences of the previous week; sometimes, by a hearer who desires some particular religious theme discussed. My subject comes in no such way. It drops straight from God into my heart. Give me your prayerful and intense listening.

I want to show this morning, so far as God may help me, that the dying need of the Church universal is a mighty awakening. The ox in the pasture-field looks around, and perhaps comes to the conclusion that all the world is a clover-field. So we, standing in the midst of luxuriant religious advantages, might think, perhaps, that the earth is covered with the knowledge of God; but so far from that, if this platform were the world, so much of it as I now cover with my right foot would represent all that is conquered for Emmanuel. Or if this whole Tabernacle were the world, then one pew would represent so much of it as the grace of God has already conquered. Oh, there is need of a radical change! Something must be done; and I shall show this morning that the great—ay, as I have already said, the dying—need of the Church is a great awakening.

I learn this need, in the first place, from the *coldness in the majority of church members*. If a religious society have a thousand members, eight hundred of them are sound asleep. If it have five hundred members, four hundred are lethargic. If the Christians can rally—that is, the professed Christians—for communion-day, and succeed in not dropping the wine-cup, how many of them are satisfied? If it be a choice between Christ and the world, the world has it. You know it as well as I do. If a religious meeting be on a certain night, and on that same night there be an extraordinary operatic entertainment, or a social gathering, or a literary club, or a political meeting, or a Freemasons' society, or an Odd-fellows' association, you know which they go to. God there fairly demonstrating that while such professed Christians pretend to be on his side, they are really on the other side; for there is a point-blank issue between Christ and the world, and the world has it. You know very well, whether you are a professed Christian or not, that the dividing line between the Church and the world to-day is—like the equator, or the arctic or antarctic circle—an imaginary line; and that there are men and women sworn of God who sit discussing infinitesimal questions, "Shall we dance? Shall we play cards? Shall we go to the theatre? Shall we attend the opera?" while there are five hundred millions of the race going down to darkness unwarned. These sham Christians will go on, occasionally taking a little religion with the tip-end of their fingers, sauntering on lazily toward the bar of Christ, until they come in front of God's swift revolving mill, and find themselves to be "the chaff which the wind driveth away."

Oh, how much dead wood we have in all our churches!

The day of judgment will make a fearful thinning-out among professed Christians. I suppose it will be found on that day that there are hundreds of thousands of men who have their names on the church books who really made religion a second-rate or third-rate thing; living for themselves, unmindful of God and the salvation of the race, and then tumbling over the embankment where Judas went, and Achan went, and where all those shall go who do not make religion the primordial thing—the first and the last matter of the soul. O worldly professor of religion, vacillating professor, idle professor, tremble before God to-day! Do you not know that if you die as you are, all the communion-tables at which you have ever sat will lift up hands of blood, crying for your condemnation? And your neglected Bible, and your prayerless pillow, will cry, "Go down! go down! You pretended to have religion, but you had none. Out of the seven days of the week, you gave not five hours to Christ. You broke your sacramental oath. Go down! go down!" And the fieriest and mightiest thunder-bolt of God's indignation that is ever forged will smite you into darkness. I would rather be the man, in the last day, who has never seen a church, than you who professed to be so much, and to do so much, and yet did nothing! You shall perish in the way when God's wrath is kindled but a little. O worldly professor of religion!—and there are hundreds of them here to-day, I am aiming at the mark—if you could now realize your true condition and your true position before God, you would bite your lip until the blood came; you would wring your hands until the bones cracked; you would utter a cry that would send this whole audience to their feet with a horror. May God wake you up, worldly professor of religion, before you wake up in the barred and flaming dungeons of a destroyed eternity! When you look abroad and see lethargy among the professors of religion almost all the world over, do you not see that there is a need that the bugles, and the cymbals, and the drums, and the trumpets of all earth and heaven call upon the Church to wake up the dormant professors of religion? "Awake, thou that sleepest; awake, and Christ shall give thee light."

Still further, I see a need for a great awakening in the fact that *those of us who preach the Gospel have so little enthusiasm and zeal compared with what we ought to have.* Now, you see, the gun kicks. It is a tremendous thing to stand before an audience on Sabbath-days, realizing the fact that the majority of them will believe what you say about God and the soul and the great future! Suppose a man asked of you the road to a certain place, and you carelessly and falsely told him, and afterward you heard that through lack of right direction that man wandered on the mountains, fell over the rocks, and lost his life. You could not forgive yourself. You would say, "I wish I had taken more time with that man. I wish I had given him specific directions so he would not have been lost. How sorry I feel about it!" But, oh, to misdirect the eternal interests of a large congregation! How cold and stolid we stand in our pulpits, actually sometimes priding ourselves on our deliberation, when we have no right to be cold, and ought to be almost frantic with the perils that threaten our hearers; so much so that some of us give no warning at all, and we stand Sabbath after Sabbath talking about "human development," and we pat men on the back and we please them, and we hide eternal retribution, and we sing them all down through the rapids to the last plunge. Or, as the poet has it,

> "Smooth down the stubborn text to ears polite,
> And snugly keep damnation out of sight!"

Oh, my brethren in the ministry—for I see them always in the audience—my brethren in the ministry, we can not afford to do that way. If you prophesy good things, smooth things, to your people, without regard to their character, what chance will there be for you in the day when you meet them at the bar of God? You had better stand clear of them then. They will tear you to pieces. They will say, "I heard you preach five hundred times, and I admired your philosophic disquisition, and your graceful gestures, and your nicely molded sentences, curvilinear and stelliform, and I thought you were the prince of proprieties; but you didn't help me to prepare for this day. Cursed be your rhetoric, cursed be your art! I am going down, and I'll take you with me. It is your fault; witness all the hosts of heaven and all the hosts of darkness, it is your fault, sir;" and the chorus will come up from all worlds, "His fault! his fault!" All of us who preach this Gospel need to speak as though the pulpit quaked with the tramp of eternal realities; as though beneath us were the bursting graves of the resurrection morn; as though rising above us, tier above tier, were the myriads of heaven looking down, ready to applaud our fidelity, or hiss at our stolidity, while coming through the Sabbath air were the long, deep, harrowing groans of the dying nations that are never dead. May God with a torch from heaven set all the pulpits of England, and Scotland, and Ireland, and the United States on fire! As for myself, standing here in this presence this morning, I feel as if I had never begun to preach. If God will forgive me for the past, I will do better for the future.

> "'Tis not a cause of small import
> The pastor's care demands;
> But what might fill an angel's heart,
> It filled a Saviour's hand.

> "They watch for souls for which the Lord
> Did heavenly bliss forego;
> For souls that must forever live
> In raptures or in woe."

Still further, I see a need for a great awakening in the fact that *the kingdom of God is making so slow progress.* I simply state a fact when I say that in many places the Church is surrendering, and the world is conquering. Where there is one man brought into the kingdom of God through Christian instrumentality, there are ten men dragged down by dissipations. Fifty grog-shops built to one church established. Literary journals in different parts of the country filled with scum and dandruff and slag, controlled by the very scullions of society, depraving every thing they put their hands on. Three hundred and ten newspapers, journals, and magazines in New York, and more than two hundred of them depraving to the public taste, if not positively inimical to our holy Christianity. Look abroad and see the surrender, even on the part of what pretend to be Christian churches, to spiritualism and humanitarianism and all the forms of devilism. If a man stand in his pulpit and say that unless you be born again you will be lost, do not the tight kid-gloves of the Christian, diamonds bursting through, go up to their foreheads in humiliation and shame? It is not elegant. A mighty host in the Christian Church, positively professing Christianity, who do not believe in the Bible out and out, in and in, from the first word of the first verse of the first chapter of the book of Genesis down to the last word of the last verse of the last chapter of the book of Revelation. And when, a few Sabbaths ago, I stood in this pulpit, and said, "I fear that some of this audience will be lost for the rejection of Christ," there were four or five of the daily papers that threw up their hands in surprise at it.

Oh, we have magnificent church machinery in this country! We have sixty thousand American ministers; we have costly music; we have great Sunday-schools; and yet I give you the appalling statistic that in the last twenty-five years, laying aside last year, the statistics of which I have not yet seen—within the last twenty-five years the churches of God in this country have averaged less than two conversions a year each. There has been an average of four or five deaths in the churches. How soon, at that rate, will this world be brought to God? We gain two; we lose four. Eternal God, what will this come to? I tell you plainly that while here and there a regiment of the Christian soldiery is advancing, the Church is falling back for the most part, and falling back, and falling back; and if you do not come to complete rout—ay, to ghastly Bull Run defeat — it will be because some individual churches hurl themselves to the front, and ministers of Christ, trampling on the favor of this world and sacrificing every thing, shall snatch up the torn and shattered banner of Emmanuel, and rush ahead, crying, "On! on! This is no time to run; this is the time to advance."

I see, still further, the need of a great awakening in *the multitudinous going-down of unforgiven souls.* Since many of you came on the stage of action, a whole generation has gone into the gates of eternity. Your opportunity to act upon them is gone. They have disappeared from the churches, from the stores, the shops, the streets, from the homes. Many of them are now—what is the use of my hiding the fact and being the coward in regard to it? no, I will tell you just as it is—many of them are going out of this world without one item of preparation. Their soul dropped flat into the lost world. That is, if the Bible is true; and I am supposing it is. You, O Christian man! had an opportunity of meeting them. You did meet them. You talked with them on other subjects. You had an opportunity of saying the saving word, and you did not say that saving word. Just think of that! Oh, where is the fountain where, with sleeves rolled up, we may wash our hands from the blood of souls? There is no need, perhaps, of mourning over that just now. We can not change it. They are dead, and they are destroyed—those who believed not in Christ—they are destroyed.

The only question is, whether, as Christian men and women, we can now interrupt the other procession that is marching down, and will, after a while, if unarrested by God's grace, fall off. There are going out from our stores hundreds of thousands of clerks; going out from our factories hundreds of thousands of operatives; there are going out of our colleges hundreds of thousands of students; there are going out of our fields hundreds of thousands of husbandmen, to join the ranks of death. They are fighting their way down. They storm and take every impediment put in their way; and who will throw himself in the way of this stampede of dying men and women—who?—crying, "Halt! halt!" If there be eight hundred millions of the race unblessed, and the churches average two souls saved in a year, will you let this generation go down, and the next, and the next?

Is it not time for something desperate? Inanimate solicitation will not do. They will not stop for that. You need a momentum gathered by a whole night's wrestle with the omnipotent God. Oh, these dying souls! these dying souls! What shall we say to them? What shall we do for them? Catch them before they make the last spring. Put down every thing else, and run for their rescue. To-morrow may be too late. To-night may be too late. Three o'clock this afternoon may be too late. *Now* reach over the pew and seize that soul before it flashes out of your sight forever. Their house is on fire, and no ladder to the window. Their ship is going down, and no lifeboat. O men and women of God, awake! awake! Fly! fly! Death! death! Judgment! judgment! Heaven! heaven! Hell! hell! Oh that all rewards and punishments, all joys and sorrows, and the agonizing and rapturous vociferation of three worlds would arouse you to-day! The death-knell of a great multitude of souls is tolling now, and your hand is on the rope. O God! flame upon us these overwhelming realities! Kill our stolidity. Knock from under us our couches of ease. Consume our indifference, and throw us into the battle. An eternity of work —an eternity of work to do in ten years. Ay, perhaps in one year, perhaps in one month, perhaps in one day, perhaps in one hour, perhaps in one minute, perhaps in one second, and this the last. But no one drops down, and so I think God is going to spare us to wake up out of our indolence and realize the truth that the dying need of the Church to-day is a great awakening.

I need not rehearse in this presence what God has done for us as an individual church. You have heard with your own ears the cries for mercy, and you have seen the raining tears of repentance, for the last eighteen months. I do not believe that there is any church in this land that owes God more of gratitude than this church owes him to-day. But who can count the number of our permanent congregation who are not Christians? And what about the eighty or one hundred thousand souls of strangers that, during the last year, floated in and out our assemblages? and what about the eternity of those who are now, and will be this year, in our permanent congregation, and the eighty or one hundred thousand souls that during this coming twelve months will float in and out our services, and the vaster audience to whom this church preaches week by week on both sides of the sea through the Christian printing-press? Oh, I feel as if I should sink down, sometimes. I feel almost wild with the sense of responsibility. Shall I meet them at the last, and I know I have not half done my duty? Shall you meet them at the last, and I know that you have not done yours? O fathers and mothers, brothers and sisters in Jesus Christ, we must get on faster than this! We want not so much a shower of blessings as a deluge; not so much a regiment as a phalanx, as a battalion. Can you get it? Yes. Nothing conjectural about it; nothing adventitious about it. Yes, if you will pray for it, and toil for it, and be sure it is coming. If John Livingston, in a small church, in one service had five hundred souls brought to God, why may you not, in a larger church, have three thousand souls as easily as he had five hundred? It is the same Gospel. John Livingston did not save them. It is the same Holy Ghost. It is the same great Jehovah. If John Knox could put the lever of prayer under Scotland until he moved it from end to end, shall you not by the lever of importunate petition move this whole city of Brooklyn, from the East River to New Utrecht, and from New Utrecht to Hunter's Point? God can do, and he will do, it, if you mightily and relentlessly ask him to do it. Oh, fling body, mind, and soul, and eternal destiny into this one thing. Swing out and enlarge in your prayerful expectations. You asked God for hundreds of souls, and he gave them to you; and I sometimes heard you ask for thousands; and I am very certain that if you asked for thousands with the same faith that you had asked for hundreds, God would have given you thousands. There is no need, in this presence, of bringing the old stereotyped illustrations of the fact that God hears prayer, nor telling you about Hezekiah's restored health, and about Elijah and the great rain, and about the post-mortem examination of the apostle James, which found that his knees had become callous by much praying; nor of Richard Baxter, who stained the walls of his study with the breath of prayer; nor of John Welch and the midnight plaid; nor of George Whitefield flat on his face before God. No need of my telling you these things. I turn in on your own consciousness, and I review the memory of that time when your own soul was sinking, and God heard your cry; and of that time when your child was dying, and God heard your petition; and of that time when your fortune failed, and God set in your empty pantry the cruse of oil and the measure of meal. I want no illustration at all. I just take a ladder with three rungs, and set it down at your feet. Oh that you would mount it, and, if you will look off, see the salvation of ten thousand of your fellow-citizens.

"Ask, and it shall be given you; seek, and ye shall find; knock, and it shall be opened unto you." Put your right foot on the lower rung of that ladder, and your left on the second rung of it, and that will bring your right foot on the top rung. Then hold fast, and look out and see the wave of the Divine blessing dashing higher than the topgallants of your shipping. Oh yes, God is ready to hear.

I think the Lord puts on us, as a Church, a great responsibility. We set our hands to the work of evangelization. We are doing nothing else here. We do not want to do any thing else here but this work of evangelization; that is, we want to bring men and women to Christ, and bring them now.

I do not know how you feel, my brethren, but my heart is breaking with a longing that I have for the redemption of this people. If God does not give me my prayer, I can not endure it. I offer myself, I offer my life, to this work. Take it, O Lord Jesus! and slay me if that be best. Whether by my life or by my death, may a great multitude of souls here be born to God. If from the mound of my grave more can step into the kingdom of God than through my life, let me now lie down to the last sleep. But only let the people be saved. Lord Jesus, it is sweet to live for thee; methinks it would be sweet to die for thee. If in the Napoleonic wars six millions fell; if in the wars of the Roman empire one hundred and eighty millions fell, shall there not be a great many in our day who are willing to sacrifice, not only worldly ambition, but sacrifice all for Christ? I wish we knew how to pray. I do not. I mean the prayer that always brings the blessing. I wish we might be so overborne with anxiety for the salvation of men that from ten o'clock at night until six o'clock in the morning sleep would fly from our eyelids. Oh for a whole night of prayer! I have a notion to try it. I will try it. Will you? Shall it be to-night, or to-morrow night, or the next night? If there come to your soul such a night as that—a sleepless night, because full of prayer to God for his blessing on your own soul and on the souls of others—then, let there be mourning that night. Break forth into weeping that night over your sins. O Church of God, cry aloud for mercy on your own souls and on the souls of others. Let there be wailing, wailing, wailing. Let there be shouting, shouting, shouting. But, lest God may not leave us a night for prayer; lest, before the setting of this day's sun, our account be made up, let us now go down so low before God that there shall be no lower depth of humiliation. Oh for a blood-red prayer that will bow the heavens, and make all the unforgiven souls in this house surrender just now to the bleeding, groaning, dying Jesus—a blessing that shall shake this house as by tempest and earthquake! To your knees, to your knees, ye who know how to pray. But I can not lead you in such a prayer as that. Let every one pray for himself. Let the prayer be in silence, God only hearing. Every one praying for himself and praying for others, that even now the cloud of mercy may drop. Hush! all the voices. Let it be silent prayer!

VIEW FROM THE PALACE WINDOW.

"Vanity of vanities, saith the Preacher; all is vanity."—*Ecclesiastes* xii., 8.

WHEN a book is placed in your hands, the first question you ask is, "Who wrote it?" Not all the political astuteness and classic grace and unparalleled satire of "Junius's Letters" can satisfy you, because you do not know who Junius was—whether John Horne Tooke, or Bishop Butler, or Edmund Burke. Mightier than a book always is the man who wrote the book.

Now, who is the author of this text? King Solomon. It seemed as if the world exhausted itself on that man. It wove its brightest flowers into his garland. It set its richest gems in his coronet. It pressed the rarest wine to his lip. It robed him in the purest purple and embroidery. It cheered him with the sweetest music in that land of harps. It greeted him with the gladdest laughter that ever leaped from mirth's lip. It sprinkled his cheek with spray from the brightest fountains. Royalty had no dominion, wealth no luxury, gold no glitter, flowers no sweetness, song no melody, light no radiance, upholstery no gorgeousness, waters no gleam, birds no plumage, prancing coursers no mettle, architecture no grandeur, but it was all his. Across the thick grass of the lawn, fragrant with tufts of camphire from En-gedi, fell the long shadows of trees brought from distant forests. Fish-pools, fed by artificial channels that brought the streams from hills far away, were perpetually ruffled with fins, and golden scales shot from water-cave to water-cave with endless dive and swirl, attracting the gaze of foreign potentates. Birds that had been brought from foreign aviary glanced and fluttered among the foliage, and called to their mates far beyond the sea. From the royal stables there came up the neighing of twelve thousand horses, standing in blankets of Tyrian purple, chewing their bits over troughs of gold, waiting for the king's order to be brought out in front of the palace, when the official dignitaries would leap into the saddle for some grand parade, or, harnessed to some of the fourteen hundred chariots of the king, the fiery chargers, with flaunting mane and throbbing nostril, would make the earth jar with the tramp of hoofs and the thunder of wheels. While within and without the palace you could not think of a single luxury that could be added or of a single splendor that could be kindled, down on the banks of the sea the dry-docks of Ezion-geber rang with the hammers of the shipwrights who were constructing larger vessels for a still wider commerce; for all lands and climes were to be robbed to make up Solomon's glory. No rest till his keels shall cut every sea, his axemen hew every forest, his archers strike every rare wing, his fishermen whip every stream, his merchants trade in every bazaar, his name be honored by every tribe; and royalty shall have no dominion, wealth no luxury, gold no glitter, song no melody, light no radiance, waters no gleam, birds no plumage, prancing coursers no mettle, upholstery no gorgeousness, architecture no grandeur, but it was all his.

"Well," you say, "if there is any man happy, he ought to be." But I hear him coming out through the palace, and see his robes actually incrusted with jewels, as he stands in the front and looks out upon the vast domain. What does he say? King Solomon, great is your dominion, great is your honor, great is your joy? No. While standing there amidst all that splendor, the tears start, and his heart breaks, and he exclaims, "Vanity of vanities; all is vanity." What! Solomon not happy yet? No, not happy.

I learn from this subject, in the first place, that *official position will never give solace to a man's soul.* I know there have been very happy men in high positions, such as Wilberforce, as Theodore Frelinghuysen, as Governor Briggs, as Prince Albert. But the joy came not from their elevated position; it came from the Lord God, whom they had tried to serve. This man Solomon was king thirty-five years. All the pleasure that comes from palatial residence, from the flattery of foreign diplomates, from universal sycophancy, gathered around him. For a long while his throne stood firm and the people were loyal; and yet hear his awful sigh of disheartenment in the words of my text. How many people in all ages have made the same experiment with the same failure! How often you see people who think, "If I could only get in this or that position—if I could be a mayor, or a governor, or a senator, or a president, I should be perfectly happy!" And they have gone on, climbing from one position to another, never finding the solace they anticipated.

Ask the men who have gone through the political life of the last forty years, in their old days, what they think of the honors of this world, and they will tell you, "Ashes! ashes!" An old man told me some time ago that he called at the White House just before the expiration of the second term of President Jackson. He sent a message in; the

President came not. He sent a second time, and a third
time. After a while the President came out in great in-
dignation, and said, "Gentlemen, people envy me in this
White House, and they long to get here; but I tell you, at
the end of the second term, I am glad to get out of it, for
it is a perfect hell." The honors and the emoluments of
this world bring so many cares with them, that they bring
also torture and disquietude. Pharaoh sits on one of the
highest earthly eminences, yet he is miserable because
there are some people in his realm that do not want any
longer to make bricks. The head of Edward I. aches un-
der his crown because the people will not pay the taxes,
and Llewellyn, Prince of Wales, will not do him homage,
and Wallace will be a hero. Frederick William III. of
Prussia is miserable because France wants to take the
Prussian provinces. The world is not large enough for
Louis XIV. and William III. The ghastliest suffering,
the most shriveling fear, the most rending jealousies, the
most gigantic disquietude, have walked amidst obsequious
courtiers, and been clothed in royal apparel, and sat on
judgment-seats of power.

Honor and truth and justice can not go so high up in
authority as to be beyond the range of human assault.
The pure and the good in all ages have been execrated by
the mob who cry out, "Not this man, but Barabbas. Now,
Barabbas was a robber." By patriotic devotion, by hon-
esty, by Christian principle, I would have you, my hearers,
seek for the favor and the confidence of your fellow-men;
but do not look upon some high position in society as
though that were always sunshine. The mountains of
earthly honor are like the mountains of Switzerland, cov-
ered with perpetual ice and snow. Having obtained the

confidence and the love of your associates, be content with such things as you have. You brought nothing into the world, and it is very certain you can carry nothing out. "Cease ye from man, whose breath is in his nostrils." There is an honor that is worth possessing, but it is an honor that comes from God. This day rise up and take it. "Behold what manner of love the Father hath bestowed upon us, that we should be called the sons of God." Who aspires not for that royalty? Come now, and be kings and priests unto God and the Lamb forever.

Still further, I learn from my subject that *worldly wealth can not satisfy the soul's longing.* The more money a man has, the better, if he gets it honestly and uses it lawfully. The whole teaching of the Word of God has a tendency to create those kinds of habits and that kind of mental acumen which lead on to riches. A man who talks against wealth as though it were a bad thing is either a knave or a fool, not meaning what he says, or ignorant of the glorious uses to which money can be put. But the man who builds his soul's happiness on earthly accumulation is not at all wise, to put it in the faintest shape. To say that Solomon was a millionaire gives but a very imperfect idea of the property he inherited from David, his father. He had at his command gold to the value of six hundred and eighty million pounds, and he had silver to the value of one billion twenty-nine million three hundred and seventy-seven pounds sterling. The Queen of Sheba made him a nice little present of seven hundred and twenty thousand pounds, and Hiram made him a present of the same amount. If he had lost the value of a whole realm out of his pocket, it would have hardly been worth his while to stoop down and pick it up; and yet, with all that affluence, he writes the words of my text, "Vanity of vanities; all is vanity." Alas! if that man could not find in all his worldly possessions enough to satisfy his immortal soul, no amount that you and I will ever gather by the sweat of our brow, or by the strength of our arm, will make us happy.

I have been amused to hear people, when they start in life, say at what point in life they will be contented with worldly possessions. One man says, "I want to get twenty thousand dollars, and I will be satisfied." Another, "I want to get fifty or a hundred thousand, or a million, and then I will be satisfied. Then I will say to my soul, 'Now, just look at that block of store-houses. Just look at those Government securities. Just look at those bonds and mortgages. Just look what lucrative investments you have. Now, my soul, take thine case; eat, drink, and be merry!'" Thou fool! If you are not happy now with the smaller possessions, you will never be with the larger possessions. If with decent and comely apparel you are not grateful to God, you would be ungrateful if you had a prince's wardrobe crowded till the hinges burst. If you sat this morning at your table, and the fare was so poor that you complained, you would not be satisfied though you sat down to partridge and pine-apple. If you are not contented with an income to support comfortably your household, you would not be contented though your income rolled in on you fifty or a hundred thousand dollars a year.

It is not what we get, it is what we *are*, that makes us happy or miserable. If that is not so, how do you account for the fact that many of those who fare sumptuously every day are waspish, and dissatisfied, and overbearing, and foreboding, and cranky, and uncompromising; with a countenance in which wrath always lowers, and a lip which scorn curls; while many a time in the summer even-tide you see a laboring man going home in his shirt-sleeves, with a pail on his arm and a pick-axe over his shoulder, his face bright with smiles, and his heart with hope, and the night of his toil bright with flaming auroras? It is an illustration and proof of the fact that it is not outward condition that makes a man happy.

Oh, I wish this morning I could, by the power of the Lord Almighty, break the infatuation of those men who are neglecting the present sources of satisfaction, hoping that there is to be something in the future for them of a worldly nature that will satisfy their souls. The heart right, all is right. The heart wrong, all is wrong. But I ask you to higher riches; to crowns that never fade; to investments that always declare dividends. Come up this day and get it—the riches of God's pardon, the riches of God's mercy, the riches of God's peace. Blessed are all they who put their trust in him.

I go still further, and learn from this subject that *learning and science can not satisfy the soul.* You know that Solomon was one of the largest contributors to the literature of his day. He wrote one thousand and five songs. He wrote three thousand proverbs. He wrote about almost every thing. The Bible says distinctly he wrote about plants, from the cedar of Lebanon to the hyssop that groweth out of the wall, and about birds and beasts and fishes. No doubt he put off his royal robes, and put on hunter's trapping, and went out with his arrows to bring down the rarest specimens of birds; and then with his fishing apparatus he went down to the stream to bring up the denizens of the deep, and plunged into the forest and found the rarest specimens of flowers; and then he came back to his study and wrote books about zoology, the science of animals; about ichthyology, the science of fishes; about ornithology, the science of birds; about botany, the science of plants. Yet, notwithstanding all his achievements, he cries out in my text, "Vanity of vanities; all is vanity."

Have you ever seen a man try to make learning and science his God? Did you ever know such a fearful autobiography as that of John Stuart Mill, a man who prided himself on his philosophy, and had a wonderful strength of intellect; yet now, after his death, his autobiography goes forth to the world, showing that his whole life was a gigantic wretchedness. We have seen men go out with mineralogist's hammer, and geologist's pry, and botanist's knife, and ornithologist's gun, and storm the kingdom of nature in her barred castles of cave and grove and forest; and if there is any heaven on earth, it is that. With your eyes prepared for all beautiful sights, and your ears for all sweet sounds, and your soul for all great thoughts, if you go forth in the place where God breathes in the aroma of flowers, and talks in the wind's rustling, and sings in the roar of forest and mountain cataract, then you know why Linnæus spent his life amidst plants, and Cuvier found intelligent converse among beasts, and Werner grew exhilarant among minerals, and Audubon reveled among birds, and Agassiz found untraveled worlds of thought in a fish. But every man who has testified, after trying the learning and science of the world for a solace, testified that it is an insufficient portion. The philosopher has often wept in astronomer's observatory and chemist's laboratory and botanist's herbarium. There are times when the soul dives deeper than the fish, and soars higher than the bird, and, though it may be enraptured with the beauties of the natural world, it will long after trees of life that never wither, and fountains that never dry up, and stars that shall shine after the glories of our earthly nights have gone out forever.

Oh, what discontents, what jealousies, what uncontrollable hate have sprung up among those who depended upon their literary success! How often have writers, with their pens plunged into the hearts of their rivals—pens sharper than cimeters, striking deeper than bayonets! Voltaire hated Rousseau. Charles Lamb could not endure Coleridge. Waller warred against Cowley. The hatred of Plato and Xenophon is as immortal as their works. Corneille had an utter contempt for Racine. Have you ever been in Westminster Abbey? In the "Poet's Corner," in Westminster Abbey, sleep Drayton the poet; and a little way off, Goldie, who said the former was not a poet. There sleep Dryden; and a little way off, poor Shadwell, who pursued him with fiend's fury. There is Pope; and a little way off is John Dennis, his implacable enemy. They never before came so near together without quarreling! Byron had all that genius could give a man, and that sympathy with nature could give a man, and that literary applause could give a man, and yet died in wretchedness.

I come to learn one more lesson from my subject, and that is *that there is no comfort in the life of a voluptuary.* I dare not draw aside the curtain that hides the excesses into which Solomon's dissoluteness plunged him. Though he waved a sceptre over others, there arose in his own soul a tyrant that mastered him. With a mandate that none dared disobey, he laid the whole land under tribute to his iniquity. Delilah sheared the locks of that Samson. From that princely seraglio there went forth a ruinous blight on the whole nation's chastity; but after a while remorse, with feet of fire, leaped upon his soul, and with body exhausted and loathsome and dropping apart with putrefaction, he staggers out from the hell of his own iniquity to give warning to others. Oh, how many have ventured out on that wild sea of sensuality, driven by fierce winds of passion, hurled against rocks, swallowed in the whirl of hell's maelstrom! That was the last of them. No! that was not the last of them. Everlastingly ruined, with their passions unsubdued, and burning on the soul more fiercely than unquenchable fire, they shall writhe in a torture that shall make the cheek of darkness pale, and utter a blasphemy that shall shock devils damned. Oh, how many young men have gone on that path of sin because it seemed blooming with tropical splendor, and the sky was bright, and the air was balm, and from the castles that stood on the shore of glittering seas there came ringing up laughter as merry as the waves that dashed on the crags beneath! By some infernal spell their eye was blinded and their ear was stopped, or they would have heard the clank of chains and the howl of woe, and across their vision would have passed spectres of the dead, with shrouds gathered up about faces blistered with pain, and eyes starting from their sockets in agony. But, alas! they saw it not, they heard it not, until from the slippery places the long, lean, skeleton hands of despair reached up and snatched them down, destroyed without remedy! Has this sorcerer cast its eye on you? O young man! have you been once and again to the places where the pure never go? Have you turned your back upon a mother's prayer and a sister's love? and, while I speak, does your conscience begin to toll dismally the burial of your purity and honor?

Put back now or never. Put back! That shadow that falls upon your soul is from no passing cloud, but from a night deep, starless, eternal. God's eye watcheth thy footsteps. A little farther on, and no tears can wash out thy sin, and no prayer will bring a pardon. Put back now or never! I tear off the garlands which hide this death's head, and hold before you to-day the reeking skull of sinful pleasure. Nations have gone down under this sin. Exhumed cities on broken pillars and on temple walls have preserved in infamous sculpture the memory of scenes before which the antiquarian turns his head, and asks if there be a God where so long has slept his vengeance. The world still trembles under the weight of this behemoth of iniquity, and, from the myriad graves in which it holds the scarred carcasses of the slain, lifts up its hands, crying, "How long, O Lord, how long?" From Christian circles, from the very altars of God, the ranks of ruin are made up. They march on with scorched feet over a pathway of fire, the ground trembling with earthquake, and the air hot with the breath of woe, and sulphurous with the fleet lightnings of God's wrath. Scorpions strike out at every step, and the "worm that never dies" lifts its awful crest, with horrid folds to crush the debauched. Oh, there is no peace in the life of a voluptuary! Solomon answers, "None! none!"

But, my friends, if there is no complete satisfaction in worldly office, in worldly wealth, in worldly learning, in sinful indulgence—where is there any? Has God turned us out on a desert to die? Ah no; look at this One that comes this morning—this fair one. Immortal garlands on her brow. The song of heaven bursting from her lips! "Her ways are ways of pleasantness, and all her paths are peace." In Christ is peace. In Christ is pardon. In Christ is everlasting joy, and nowhere else.

> "Substantial comfort will not grow
> In nature's barren soil;
> All we can boast, till Christ we know,
> Is vanity and toil.
>
> "But where the Lord has planted grace,
> And made his glories known,
> There fruits of heavenly joy and peace
> Are found, and there alone."

PAUL'S VALEDICTORY.

"The time of my departure is at hand."—2 *Timothy* iv., 6.

THE way out of this world is so blocked up with coffin and hearse, and undertaker's spade and screw-driver, that the Christian can hardly think as he ought of the most cheerful passage in all his history. We hang black instead of white over the place where the good man gets his last victory. We stand weeping over a heap of chains which the freed soul has shaken off, and we say, "Poor man! What a pity it was he had to come to this!" Come to what? By the time the people have assembled at the obsequies, that man has been three days so happy that all the joy of earth accumulated would be wretchedness beside it, and he might better weep over you because you have to stay, than you weep over him because he has to go. It is a fortunate thing that a good man does not have to wait to see his own obsequies, they would be so discordant with his own experience. If the Israelites should go back to Egypt and mourn over the brick-kilns they once left, they would not be any more silly than that Christian who should forsake heaven and come down and mourn because he had to leave this world. Our ideas of the Christian's death are morbid and sickly. We look upon it as a dark hole in which a man stumbles when his breath gives out. This whole subject is odorous with varnish and disinfectants, instead of being sweet with mignonnette. Paul, in my text, takes that great clod of a word "death," and throws it away, and speaks of his "departure"—a beautiful, bright, suggestive word, descriptive of every Christian's release.

Now, departure implies a starting-place and a place of destination. When Paul left this world, what was the starting-point? It was a scene of great physical distress. It was the Tullianum, the lower dungeon of the Mamertine prison. The top dungeon was bad enough, it having no means of ingress or egress but through an opening in the top. Through that the prisoner was lowered, and through that came all the food and air and light received. It was a terrible place, that upper dungeon; but the Tullianum was the lower dungeon, and that was still more wretched, the only light and the only air coming through the roof, and that roof the floor of the upper dungeon. That was Paul's last earthly residence. It was a dungeon just six feet and a half high. It was a doleful place. It had the chill of long centuries of dampness. It was filthy with the long incarcerations of miserable wretches. It was there that Paul spent his last days on earth, and it is there that I see him to-day, in the fearful dungeon, shivering, blue with the cold, waiting for that old overcoat which he had sent for up to Troas, and which they had not yet sent down, notwithstanding he had written for it.

If some skillful surgeon should go into that dungeon where Paul is incarcerated, we might find out what are the prospects of Paul's living through the rough imprisonment. In the first place, he is an old man, only two years short of seventy. At that very time when he most needs the warmth and the sunlight and the fresh air, he is shut out from the sun. What are those scars on his ankles? Why, those were gotten when he was fast, his feet in the stocks. Every time he turned, the flesh on his ankles

started. What are those scars on his back? You know
he was whipped five times, each time getting thirty-nine
strokes—one hundred and ninety-five bruises on the back
(count them!) made by the Jews with rods of elm-wood,
each one of the one hundred and ninety-five strokes bring-
ing the blood. Look at Paul's face and look at his arms.
Where did he get those bruises? I think it was when he
was struggling ashore amidst the shivered timbers of the
shipwreck. I see a gash in Paul's side. Where did he
get that? I think he got that in the tussle with highway-
men, for he had been in peril of robbers, and he had mon-
ey of his own. He was a mechanic as well as an apostle,
and I think the tents he made were as good as his sermons.

There is a wanness about Paul's looks. What makes
that? I think a part of that came from the fact that he
was for twenty-four hours on a plank in the Mediterranean
Sea, suffering terribly, before he was rescued; for he says
positively, "I was a night and a day in the deep." Oh,
worn-out, emaciated old man! surely you must be melan-
choly: no constitution could endure this and be cheerful.
But I press my way through the prison until I come up
close to where he is, and by the faint light that streams
through the opening I see on his face a supernatural joy,
and I bow before him, and I say, "Aged man, how can
you keep cheerful amidst all this gloom?" His voice star-
tles the darkness of the place as he cries out, "I am now
ready to be offered, and the time of my departure is at
hand." Hark! what is that shuffling of feet in the upper
dungeon? Why, Paul has an invitation to a banquet, and
he is going to dine to-day with the king. Those shuffling
feet are the feet of the executioners. They come, and they
cry down through the hole of the dungeon, "Hurry up,

old man. Come now; get yourself ready." Why, Paul was ready. He had nothing to pack up. He had no baggage to take. He had been ready a good while. I see him rising up, and straightening out his stiffened limbs, and pushing back his white hair from his creviced forehead, and see him looking up through the hole in the roof of the dungeon into the face of his executioner, and hear him say, "I am now ready to be offered, and the time of my departure is at hand." Then they lift him out of the dungeon, and they start with him to the place of execution. They say, "Hurry along, old man, or you will feel the weight of our spear. Hurry along." "How far is it," says Paul, "we have to travel?" "Three miles." Three miles is a good way for an old man to travel after he has been whipped and crippled with maltreatment. But they soon get to the place of execution—Acquæ Salvia—and he is fastened to the pillar of martyrdom. It does not take any strength to tie him fast. He makes no resistance. O Paul! why not now strike for your life? You have a great many friends here. With that withered hand just launch the thunder-bolt of the people upon those infamous soldiers. No! Paul was not going to interfere with his own coronation. He was too glad to go. I see him looking up in the face of his executioner, and, as the grim official draws the sword, Paul calmly says, "I am now ready to be offered, and the time of my departure is at hand." But I put my hand over my eyes. I want not to see that last struggle. One sharp, keen stroke, and Paul *does* go to the banquet, and Paul *does* dine with the King.

What a transition it was! From the malaria of Rome to the finest climate in all the universe—the zone of eternal beauty and health. His ashes were put in the catacombs of Rome, but in one moment the air of heaven bathed from his soul the last ache. From shipwreck, from dungeon, from the biting pain of the elm-wood rods, from the sharp sword of the headsman, he goes into the most brilliant assemblage of heaven, a king among kings, multitudes of the sainthood rushing out and stretching forth hands of welcome; for I do really think that as on the right hand of God is Christ, so on the right hand of Christ is Paul, the second great in heaven.

He changed kings likewise. Before the hour of death, and up to the last moment, he was under Nero, the thick-necked, the cruel-eyed, the filthy-lipped; the sculptured features of that man bringing down to us to this very day the horrible possibilities of his nature—seated as he was amidst pictured marbles of Egypt, under a roof adorned with mother-of-pearl, in a dining-room which by machinery was kept whirling day and night with most bewitching magnificence; his horses standing in stalls of solid gold, and the grounds around his palace lighted at night by its victims, who had been bedaubed with tar and pitch and then set on fire to illumine the darkness. That was Paul's king. But the next moment he goes into the realm of Him whose reign is love, and whose courts are paved with love, and whose throne is set on pillars of love, and whose sceptre is adorned with jewels of love, and whose palace is lighted with love, and whose lifetime is an eternity of love. When Paul was leaving so much on this side the pillar of martyrdom to gain so much on the other side, do you wonder at the cheerful valedictory of the text, "The time of my departure is at hand?"

Now, why can not all the old people of my congregation

have the same holy glee as that aged man had? Charles I., when he was combing his head, found a gray hair, and he sent it to the queen as a great joke; but old age is really no joke at all. For the last forty years you have been dreading that which ought to have been an exhilaration. You say you most fear the struggle at the moment the soul and body part. But millions have endured that moment, and why may not we as well? They got through with it, and so can we. Besides this, all medical men agree in saying that there is probably no struggle at all at the last moment —not so much pain as the prick of a pin, the seeming signs of distress being altogether involuntary. But you say, "It is the uncertainty of the future." Now, child of God, do not play the infidel. After God has filled the Bible till it can hold no more with stories of the good things ahead, better not talk about uncertainties.

But you say, "I can not bear to think of parting from friends here." If you are old, you have more friends in heaven than here. Just take the census. Take some large sheet of paper and begin to record the names of those who have emigrated to the other shore; the companions of your school-days, your early business associates, the friends of mid-life, and those who more recently went away. Can it be that they have been gone so long you do not care any more about them, and you do not want their society? Oh no. There have been days when you have felt that you could not endure it another moment away from their blessed companionship. They have gone. You say you would not like to bring them back to this world of trouble, even if you had the power. It would not do to trust you. God would not give you resurrection power. Before to-morrow morning you would be rattling at the gates of the cemetery, crying to the departed, "Come back to the cradle where you slept! come back to the hall where you used to play! come back to the table where you used to sit!" and there would be a great burglary in heaven. No, no. God will not trust you with resurrection power; but he compromises the matter, and says, "You can not bring them where you are, but you can go where they are." They are more lovely now than ever. Were they beautiful here, they are more beautiful there.

Besides that, it is more healthy there for you than here, aged man; better climate there than these hot summers and cold winters and late springs; better hearing; better eye-sight; more tonic in the air; more perfume in the bloom; more sweetness in the song. Do you not feel, aged man, sometimes as though you would like to get your arm and foot free? Do you not feel as though you would like to throw away spectacles and canes and crutches? Would you not like to feel the spring and elasticity and mirth of an eternal boyhood? When the point at which you start from this world is old age, and the point to which you go is eternal juvenescence, aged man, clap your hands at the anticipation, and say, in perfect rapture of soul, "The time of my departure is at hand."

I remark, again, all those ought to feel this joy of the text who have a *holy curiosity to know what is beyond this earthly terminus*. And who has not any curiosity about it? Paul, I suppose, had the most satisfactory view of heaven, and he says, "It doth not yet appear what we shall be." It is like looking through a broken telescope: "Now we see through a glass darkly." Can you tell me any thing about that heavenly place? You ask me a thousand questions about it that I can not answer. I ask you a thousand questions about it that you can not answer. And do you wonder that Paul was so glad when martyrdom gave him a chance to go over and make discoveries in that blessed country?

I hope some day, by the grace of God, to go over and see for myself; but not now. No well man, no prospered man, I think, wants to go now. But the time will come, I think, when I shall go over. I want to see what they do there, and I want to see how they do it. I do not want to be looking through the gates ajar forever. I want them to swing wide open. There are ten thousand things I want explained—about you, about myself, about the government of this world, about God, about every thing. We start in a plain path of what we know, and in a minute come up against a high wall of what we do not know. I wonder how it looks over there. Somebody tells me it is like a paved city—paved with gold; and another man tells me it is like a fountain, and it is like a tree, and it is like a triumphal procession; and the next man I meet tells me it is all figurative. I really want to know, after the body is resurrected, what they wear and what they eat; and I have an immeasurable curiosity to know what it is, and how it is, and where it is. Columbus risked his life to find this continent, and shall we shudder to go out on a voyage of discovery which shall reveal a vaster and more brilliant country? John Franklin risked his life to find a passage between icebergs, and shall we dread to find a passage to eternal summer? Men in Switzerland travel up the heights of the Matterhorn with alpenstock, and guides, and rockets, and ropes, and, getting half-way up, stumble and fall down in a horrible massacre. They just wanted to say they had been on the tops of those high peaks. And shall we fear to go out for the ascent of the eternal hills which start a thousand miles beyond where stop the highest peaks of the Alps, and when in that ascent there is no peril? A man doomed to die stepped on the scaffold, and said in joy, " Now, in ten minutes I will know the great secret." One minute after the vital functions ceased, the little child that died last night in Montague Street knew more than Jonathan Edwards, or St. Paul himself, before he died. Friends, the exit from this world, or death, if you please to call it, to the Christian is glorious explanation. It is demonstration. It is illumination. It is sunburst. It is the opening of all the windows. It is shutting up the catechism of doubt, and the unrolling of all the scrolls of positive and accurate information. Instead of standing at the foot of the ladder and looking up, it is standing at the top of the ladder and looking down. It is the last mystery taken out of botany, and geology, and astronomy, and theology. Oh, will it not be grand to have all questions answered? The perpetually recurring interrogation-point changed for the mark of exclamation. All riddles solved. Who will fear to go out on that discovery, when all the questions are to be decided which we have been discussing all our lives? Who shall not clap his hands in the anticipation of that blessed country, if it be no better than through holy curiosity? crying, " The time of my departure is at hand."

I remark, again, we ought to have the joy of the text, because, leaving this world, *we move into the best society of the universe.* You see a great crowd of people in some street, and you say, " Who is passing there? What general, what prince is going up there?" Well, I see a great throng in heaven. I say, " Who is the focus of all that admiration? Who is the centre of that glittering company?" It is Jesus, the champion of all worlds, the favorite of all ages. Do you know what is the first question the soul will ask when it comes through the gate of heaven? I think the first question will be, "Where is Jesus, the Saviour that pardoned my sin; that carried my sorrows; that fought my battles; that won my victories?" O radiant one! how I would like to see thee! thou of the manger, but without its humiliations; thou of the cross, but without its pangs; thou of the grave, but without its darkness.

The Bible intimates that we will talk with Jesus in heaven just as a brother talks with a brother. Now, what will you ask him first? I do not know. I can think what I would ask Paul first if I saw him in heaven. I think I would like to hear him describe the storm that came upon the ship when there were two hundred and seventy-five souls on the vessel, Paul being the only man on board cool enough to describe the storm. There is a fascination about a ship and the sea that I never shall get over, and I think I would like to hear him talk about that first. But when I meet my Lord Jesus Christ, of what shall I first delight to hear him speak? Now I think what it is. I shall first want to hear the tragedy of his last hours; and then Luke's account of the crucifixion, and Mark's account of the crucifixion, and John's account of the crucifixion will be nothing, while from the living lips of Christ the story shall be told of the gloom that fell, and the devils that arose, and the fact that upon his endurance depended the rescue of a race; and there was darkness in the sky, and there was darkness in the soul, and the pain became more sharp, and the burdens became more heavy, until the mob began to swim away from the dying vision of Christ, and the cursing of the mob came to his ear more faintly, and his hands were fastened to the horizontal piece of the cross, and his feet were fastened to the perpendicular piece of the cross, and his head fell forward in a swoon as he uttered the last moan and cried, "It is finished!" All heaven will stop to listen until the story is done, and every harp will be put down, and every lip closed, and all eyes fixed upon the divine narrator, until the story is done; and then, at the tap of the baton, the eternal orchestra will rouse up; finger on string of harp, and lips to the mouth of trumpet, there shall roll forth the oratorio of the Messiah, "Worthy is the Lamb that was slain to receive blessing, and riches, and honor, and glory, and power, world without end!"

> "What He endured, oh, who can tell,
> To save our souls from death and hell!"

When there was between Paul and that magnificent personage only the thinness of the sharp edge of the sword of the executioner, do you wonder that he wanted to go? O, my Lord Jesus, let one wave of that glory roll over this auditory to-night! Hark! I hear the wedding-bells of heaven ringing now. The marriage of the Lamb has come, and the bride hath made herself ready. I wish I could take that word "death" and grind it to pieces, and substitute in its place "departure"—"departure." The word is just as appropriate for the sinner as it is for the Christian. O sinner! when you do go, for what will you depart? It can not be up the way Paul went, unless you have Paul's Saviour. How long will your journey be? At what house will you stop? In what society will you mingle? What will be your destiny? Listen! Listen! Again I hear the bells ringing; but it is a fire-bell tolling for the conflagration that never goes out. I hear the drums beating; but it is the funeral march of a soul. "And there shall be weeping and wailing and gnashing of teeth."

A man on the street was fatally injured, and was carried into the nearest house. He says, "I have often heard of people who died unprepared, but I never thought I would be one of them. What must I do to be saved?" But before the answer came life was extinct. Death was departure for him; but, oh! for what place?

HONEY FROM A STRANGE HIVE.

"And, behold, there was a swarm of bees and honey in the carcass of the lion."—*Judges* xiv., 8.

A GIANT, unarmed, is on his way to Timnath. Turning aside from the road and sauntering in the jungles, suddenly a lion, with terrific roar, springs upon him. Seizing the uprearing monster by the jaws, with iron grip he twists and wrenches them apart, leaving the lion dead by the roadside. What the ordinary hunter does with trap, and trained elephants, and armed band, and fire-arms skillfully aimed at the prey, this giant did with his two hands. About a year after, going along by that place, he very naturally turned aside to see the carcass of the lion he had slain. A strange sight! There were the bones, and honey in the hollow of the skeleton. What a strange hive in which to gather honey! You might think it peculiar that bees, which are the most cleanly of all insects, should select such a place as that. Not strange at all. In that hot climate, and where there are so many other insects, in a few days all marks of death and pollution have gone from the carcass, and the skeleton is as pure and clean as the boxes in which bees in our day gather the wealth of gardens and meadows and orchards. It was a whole year after when the giant came along, and out of the bleached skeleton got that honey for himself and for his comrades.

Well, my friends, a lion has met you in the way—a lion fiercer than that which, putting its mouth to the ground, makes the Numidian jungle quake with its bellowing. Some monster bereavement has come upon you, and with merciless paw struck down your loved one, dragging him off into the dark jungles of death. All unarmed, you felt unable to cope with the grizzly, gaping, all-devouring monster; but after you had prayed a while you rose in the strength of God, and destroyed that monster trouble. You snapped it in twain. You trampled it under your foot. You left it by the roadside. And, coming along that way to-day, you see that all the promises of God have swarmed there, and the bleached skeleton of the slain monster is filled with honey from all the gardens of heaven. The jaws of the monster that gaped upon you have become the hive of sweetest Christian consolation. To bring a platter of that honey to all bereaved souls who may be in this house to-day is my work, first bringing it in general, and then to one specific trouble, the service this morning being in memoriam.

I think there is no sweeter or more potent consolation than the fact that we are to be re-associated in the future world with our Christian friends. I shall bring no passages to prove such a fact. That I have done in other sermons. I shall take it all for granted, supposing you believe it, only trying to show you what are the uses of such a warm-hearted, Christian theory. I would to God, while we are thinking about it, the church on earth might seem to respond to the church in heaven! During the last war I was down for a little while in the army, and I noticed in the night-time that one division of the army would signal to the other division, and there were times in the night when the sky seemed written all over with letters and words of fire, one division signaling to another division.

And so I would have it now, the church on earth signaling its joy to heaven, and heaven signaling back its joy to earth; for we are different divisions of one great host:

> "One army of the living God,
> To his command we bow;
> Part of the host have crossed the flood,
> And part are crossing now."

This idea of future association with our departed friends is honey out of the slain lion. In the first place, this consideration *exalts and gives stability to Christian friendship.* If our association is only a matter of five or ten or thirty years, it is not worth much. Can it be that our attachment to each other has such short arms that it can not reach across the grave? We go into a rail-train, and we sit down for a few hours beside a stranger, and talk with him. Then he leaves at one station, and we leave at another. He never thinks of us again; we never think of him again. Is that a type of our Christian attachments? Oh no. We are, in heaven, to rise up amidst infinite congratulations to renew our association. The only difference between our acquaintanceship here and our acquaintanceship there will be that there we shall know each other better and love each other more. Death will not strike any thing out of our association but its imperfections. Wading down into the river of death, it will only bathe off our impurities. If you now count me to be your friend, when I shall have quit all my sins and follies and imperfections, and my entire nature is uplifted before the throne of God, you will have for me a millionfold greater attachment. If my friendship to you is merely because you invite me to grand entertainments, or because you allow me to have your name on the back of my notes, such a mercenary and half-hearted attachment as that can not stride across the grave. But this communing of heart with heart, this mingling of sympathy with sympathy, this feeling which leads us to carry each other's burdens, and weep each other's sorrows, and laugh in each other's joy—all these are prophecies of eternal intimacy. You and I may soon part; we may pitch our tents in different zones, our graves may be cleft in opposite sides of the earth; but the scenes in which we now mingle will be renewed under milder skies. And so I strike hands with you to-day in a friendship which shall bloom immortal after the mountains have crumbled, and the stars that flower in celestial gardens shall have wilted in the hot breath of a judgment-day.

Again, this idea of future association *ought to assuage our bereavements.* There is not a family in this house to-day that has not heard the tramp of the pall-bearers. There is hardly a house on all these streets that has not had its craped door-bell. I look into your upturned faces to-day, and see the marks of many griefs. They have wrinkled your brow. They have dropped a shadow under your eye. They have taken the color out of your cheek. There have been awful agonies of separation that have gone crashing down through the heart-strings. This world is not so bright as it used to be before such and such a light was put out. You walk with listless step along places where once you danced with delight. The spring grass of this April day would have been above your grave but for the consolation of the thought that you would be reunited with the departed in the better world. The dying one spake of that heavenly greeting, and for that hour you are waiting — waiting while the home is desolate;

waiting while the years go tediously by; waiting while the heart continues to break—and you shall not be disappointed. Your lives shall join again. Hand to hand. Heart to heart. Jubilee to jubilee. Throne to throne. Hallelujah to hallelujah.

The most frequent trial that comes across the families of the earth is the loss of children. The vast majority of the race may not reach manhood and womanhood. Infantile diseases are the gauntlet they can not run. It seems as if this world were too chill and cold and drear for the flowers of childhood, so the heavenly gardener takes them in. You look down as you think of the little one that God took out of your cradle. At the moment when he was the most promising—at that moment the blast came. Oh! that was a grief—the closing of the lids over the blue eyes that shall never sparkle again at your coming. That was a heart-rending—the putting of the burial flowers that some playmate had brought into the hand that used to pluck its own wild flowers from the field, and gather them in bunches and wear them in her flaxen hair. And sometimes you sit down and look at the floor by the hour, until within the small pattern of the carpet at which you stare there come bounding in with mirth and gladness the feet that have long been still; and you wake up in the midnight as though you had heard the call of a loved one, as though it were a cry of distress, "Mother! mother!" But you fall back, for it is all a dream. I wish I could to-day hang one picture in your nursery, hang it over the place where your little ones used to play; hang it right between the windows up against which they used to press their sunny faces—a picture of the heavenly greeting. You know how it was after you had been absent a long while, and, coming home, they saw you before you got up to the front of the house, and they shouted, "They have come! they have come!" and they held to your dress, and told you a hundred things at once, and almost blocked up your entrance to the house with their gladness. So, methinks, it will be when you at last enter heaven's gate; the shout will be, "She's come! She's come!" And they will put garlands on your brow and palms in your hands, and clap and sing, waking up heaven to brighter gladness with their sweet voices and their bounding feet and their jubilant hosannas.

> "How shall we know them, the infant race?
> How will the mother her loved one trace?
> By the thrill which, when first he smiled,
> Came o'er her soul, will she know her child!"

Oh glorious anticipation, that with all our Christian dead, whether young or old, we shall meet again! Be patient, therefore. No trouble, no comfort. No cross, no crown. No battle, no victory. No slain lion of assault, no hived honey of Christian consolation.

Again, this consideration *gives great peace to the dying.* The step out of this world into the next is a very mysterious step; and though we are promised brilliant escort, some very good people shudder about dying. But how different that passage seems in one's history if he realizes that he is going from a home circle here to a home circle there; that one moment after he has said "Good-night" to friends on earth he says "Good-morning" to friends in heaven. Oh, this irradiates the pallid cheek of the dying. This rekindles the lustre of the closing eye. This lifts the hand as though to join in the heavenly hand-shaking. It is the thought that he is surrounded by friends now and will be surrounded by friends there. It is the thought that he is only going from one room to another in "the house of many mansions." Just as when you get into a boat, and some one on the shore steadies you while you get in, and some one in the boat helps you, so it will be when you come to die: there will be friends here to help you off, and friends there to help you in. You know very well that if you are to cross a swift stream, you need to take sight by some bluff or tree or fixed object; and so, when we come down to cross the swift currents of death, we had just better put our eye upon the highlands crowned with the castles of our own loved ones, and then pull and pull for the beach.

> "Steer this way, brother,
> Steer straight for me;
> Here, safe in heaven,
> I am waiting for thee."

Under this anticipation, Death, no more a lion, bears to us chalices of honey.

I bring the consolation of this subject especially to the friends of Gasherie De Witt, on this and the other side of the Atlantic. I parted with him three years ago at Victoria Station, England. Many of you parted with him at the Cunard wharf in Jersey City. Others of you parted with him at the door of the village church in Belleville. Others of you parted with him in the last moment at the foot of Mont Blanc. But we shall meet again. He was a man worth meeting. Eighteen years ago he first dawned upon me in the parsonage at Belleville, where he had come to welcome me to my new home. Since then I have been with him in a great variety of circumstances, and, beginning by thinking well of him, I have loved him more and more as the years rolled by. He was born to be a leader, and by common consent men fell into line. He was aglow with enthusiasm, and flamed when advocating the right or denouncing the wrong. He did not take things by slow besiegement, but by storm. While others planned, he both planned and executed. With his own hand he made his fortune; but though the money came rapidly, the more rapidly did his heart enlarge. He had done the work of an octogenarian at mid-life. He was one of the few men who can do many things well. Whether advocating the building of a railroad, or inventing a new machine, or hunting in a Southern forest, or speaking in a legislative hall, or advocating a temperance reform, or wielding a painter's pencil, or arousing a church meeting, he was an expert, a marksman, a connoisseur, an agitator, a commander. He was always right, and never afraid; well-balanced, yet quick; conservative where things ought to be preserved, radical where they ought to be destroyed. He was impatient of time-serving people; explosive with red-faced indignation at any thing like meanness; tearfully tender with suffering; a bubbling well of sympathy; a many-keyed soul, on which you might play anthem or dirge, battle march or lullaby. But I think the master-passion of his soul was Christian generosity. He gave to his elder son counsel that I have never heard of being given in a dying hour, and that was, "Be generous." He went everywhere, searching for sick ministers and feeble churches and struggling young men. It was his life to help somebody. At the dedication of our first Tabernacle he arose six times in the audience to make contribution, his tongue thick with that paralysis which helped after a while to end his life. I went to him, and laid before him the policy of a Lay College, the object of which should be the education of laymen for practical Christian work in all denominations. He slapped his hand on his knee, and said, "That's just what we want. I have been waiting for something of that kind for twenty years. The ministers can not do this work all alone. You must get the troops massed, and the private Christians of all denominations drilled for work. Go ahead, Talmage, and I'll back you." And he did back me with his money, and with his prayers, and with his counsel, from his dying pillow sending me stirring word of encouragement. The tide of influence through that institution set in motion will roll on forever. Many souls have already been brought to God through the instrumentality of the men who have been trained there. That institution would not have been formed but for the financial encouragement of Mr. De Witt. A colony of Chinese came near his residence, and at his own expense he opened a school to educate them for God and heaven; and in the long procession that followed him on the funeral day there was nothing more impressive than the saddened faces of those Chinese as they marched on after the dead body of their benefactor.

That man turned his back on his elegant mansion, and went out for the most dismal work that a man ever does— the hunting-up of his lost health. He sought for it in England, in Germany, in Italy, in Switzerland, staying long enough in the Christian chapels of foreign countries to help them with his money and with his prayers; staying long enough in the picture-galleries of Dresden to copy with his own hands some of the works of the great masters, astonishing the native artists with his skill; then coming to Geneva, Switzerland, to lie down and die in awful physical excruciation. It seemed as if God said to him, "Your search for health amidst the mountains of this world is a failure. Now, come up higher; breathe a better air. In the deep fountains of the rock bathe off all your physical tortures. There is no sorrow that heaven can not cure." Some of his last utterances have been preserved. You would like to hear them. They are more jubilant than sad; some of them exquisitely poetic, others have the call of a clarion: " 'This is evidently the end. My Saviour is coming for me. God will bless you, and raise you up protectors.' There had been for three days one of the high mountain winds which we had feared would annoy him, but dared not allude to it, for fear of drawing his attention to it. He did not seem to notice it. Sunday morning broke clear, beautiful, and still, with a light fall of snow covering the whole landscape. He kissed me, and said, 'I have no pain this morning, and my whole soul is in perfect peace. Thank God for this blessed peace. He giveth his beloved sleep. Oh, my dear wife! it is only the parting that I dread. We have been together so many years, so many happy years; but my Saviour is close to me now, my blessed, precious Saviour.' And he put out his arms as though he would clasp him, while his whole face lighted up with love. 'I welcome thee, I embrace thee. He will keep you, give you friends, keep our children always. Tell my dear mother I would have come to her if I could, but God ordered it otherwise. It will be only a short time before we shall meet again, and I will watch over her till then, if I can. Praise God for his mercy in raising up to me friends on both sides the ocean from among his children. This is the happiest day of my life. Notwithstanding the anguish of body, there is perfect happiness within. The storms among the mountains are all over. There is perfect quiet. So it is with my life. Not that I have had particular storms, but the storms of my life are over now, and there is only perfect peace.' He lay still for a few minutes, and commenced again, 'There is a new, pure covering over Mont Blanc. Down over all the mountains and valleys, it covers every thing—all. That is an emblem of the new, pure covering over my life—the covering Jesus has given me. God grant it may cover every thing—all.' He wanted the girls to sing 'Rock of Ages,' and 'Just as I am.' They did so, and at the end of every verse he seemed to pour his whole soul out in uttering the words, 'O Lamb of God! I come.'

"He was just expressing his regret, Monday morning, that he had done so little for Jesus, when a letter came from the Lay College, telling him of its prosperity, and containing a resolution offered by the professors and students at a special meeting, expressing their gratitude for his sympathy and co-operation. This letter was very comforting, recalling to his mind that he had done some very efficient work for the Master, after all. Wednesday evening, at eight or nine o'clock, he dropped out of his suffering into a quiet slumber, which ended with three long-drawn breaths at half-past twelve."

So Gasherie De Witt was emancipated. So he woke up. So he began to live. So he ascended. He came along where Death was, and "behold, there was a swarm of bees and honey in the carcass of the lion." If I had ten thousand tears, I would not weep one of them for our departed friend. He might better weep over our bondage than we over his liberation. I save my tears for myself and for the friends whom he has left behind. Alas for the home, beautiful but devastated! The pictures are there and the books are there and all the familiar surroundings are there; but he who made the pictures, and he who bought the books, and he who planned the house, and he who laid out the grounds comes not up the hill, nor is his quick, strong footstep heard in the door-way. May the Lord Almighty comfort you to-day. He who helped your husband and your father to die will help you in this sore bereavement. O widowed soul! O orphaned children! O mourning kindred! in God is thy refuge, and beneath thee are the everlasting arms.

I see in the audience a goodly number of his village neighbors and business associates. They have come in this morning from Belleville. You must have started early to join in this service. You are my acquaintances as well. Some of you the first parishioners I ever had. How do you do to-day, my old Belleville friends? Your presence rolls in upon me the memories of the past. I baptized in infancy some of those maidens. I united some of you in holy marriage. I buried some of your dead. I welcomed some of you into the kingdom of Christ. Good old days we used to have together, did we not? And now, after so long a separation, we meet to-day to bend over the same sorrow, and to learn the lessons of the same providence. You knew and loved Gasherie De Witt. You will never hear his voice again in the village councils, nor will you greet him again to your firesides. But you know that if there is any such place as heaven, he is there; if there is any such being as God, Gasherie De Witt is with him. Oh, my friends! aspire after the same high residence. When you quit your abode on the banks of the beautiful Passaic, may you go up to walk on the margin of the river of life with your old friends and companions, and have explained to your everlasting satisfaction why Gasherie De Witt was put to so much pain; and why he must die so far away from home; and why he must go away from his family and the Church and the world at a time when they could so poorly afford to spare him.

To all this throng to-day there comes a lesson. Among the last words of this man were these: "There is no hope to live by or die by but the Christian hope." Do you believe it? If so, to-day seek your eternal salvation. If you should this moment be hurled out of life, would you be ready? Not all ready. In proportion to the brightness of a Christian's death-bed is the darkness of a sinner's death-bed. He sings no song. He sees no light. He leaves behind him no consolation. Death to him is a wild catastrophe. He goes from the world stumbling out of it, feeling his way into the blackness of darkness forever. O dying soul! try something better. Standing to-day, as I do, in the brilliant halo that surrounds a Christian's death-bed, the cry of desolated hearts overpowered by the chanting of angelic cohorts come to fetch a good man home, I commend to you Gasherie De Witt's Redeemer. May God this moment overshadow you with his saving presence! May the Holy Ghost this moment overwhelm you with his striving!

So shall the swarms of trouble that come to buzz and sting and poison your soul leave for you the saccharine of immortal flowers. For while the honey of this world's consolation often nauseates and sickens, like that of Trebizond, because the bees make it out of the rhododendron, the honey of Christ's Gospel gives life and health, like that which drips from the delicious combs of Mount Ida and Chamouni.

THE KNELL OF NINEVEH.

"Yet forty days, and Nineveh shall be overthrown."—*Jonah* iii., 4.

ON the banks of the Tigris there is a great capital, sixty miles in circumference, surrounded by a wall broad enough to allow three chariots to go abreast; fifteen hundred turrets, each two hundred feet high, carrying aloft the grandeur of the city. There are six hundred thousand inhabitants. The metropolis is not like our crowded cities; but gardens wreathe the homes of private citizens with tropical blaze of color, wet with the spray of falling waters, and there are pasture-fields, on which cattle browse, in the very midst of the city. It is a delicious climate, even in midsummer never rising to more than seventy degrees. Through the gates of that city roll the commerce of Eastern and Western Asia. On its throne sits Sardanapalus, his every meal a banquet, his every day a coronation. There are polished walls of jasper and chalcedony, bewildering with arrow-head inscriptions, and scenes of exciting chase and victorious battle. There are mansions adorned with bronze, and vases and carved statues of ivory, and ceilings with mother-of-pearl, and mantel enameling, and floors with slabs of alabaster. There are other walls with sculptured flowers and paneling of Lebanon cedar and burnished copper, and door-ways guarded by winged lions. The city roars with chariot wheels and clatters with swift hoofs, and is all arush and ablaze with pomp and fashion and power. The river Tigris bounds the city on one side, and moat and turreted wall bound it on the other sides, and there it stands defiant of earth and heaven. Fraud in her store-houses. Uncleanness in her dwellings. Obscene display in her theatres. Iniquity everywhere. Nineveh the magnificent. Nineveh the vile. Nineveh the doomed.

One day, a plain-looking man comes through the gate into that city. He is sun-burned as though he had been under the browning process of a sea-voyage. Indeed, he had been wrecked, and picked up by such a life-boat as no other man ever rode in, a whale's fins and flukes being to him both oars and rudder. The man had been trying to escape his duty of preaching a disagreeable sermon; but now, at last, his feet strike the street of that city. No sooner has he passed under the shadow of the wall and entered it, than, clearing his throat for loud and distinct utterance, he begins; and the water-carrier sets down his jug, and the charioteer reins in the steeds, and the soldiers on the top of the wall break ranks to look and listen, while his voice shivers through the avenues, and reverberates amidst the dwellings of potentate and peasant, as he cries out, "Yet forty days, and Nineveh shall be overthrown!" The people rush out of the market-places and to the gates to listen to the strange sound. The king invites the man to tell the story amidst the corridors of the palace. The courtiers throng in and out amidst the statues and pictures and fountains, listening to the startling message, "Yet forty days, and Nineveh shall be overthrown."

"What is that fellow about?" say some of the people. "Is he a madman escaped from his keepers? He must be an alarmist, who is announcing his morbid fears. He ought to be arrested, and put in the prison of the city." But still the man moves on, and still the cry goes up,

"Yet forty days, and Nineveh shall be overthrown." There is no madness in his eye, there is no fanaticism in his manner, but only a Divine authority, and a terrible earnestness which finally seizes the whole city. People rush from place to place, and say, "Have you seen that prophet? What does he mean? Is it to be earthquake, or storm, or plague, or besiegement of foreign enemy?" Sardanapalus puts off his jeweled array and puts on mourning, and the whole city goes down on its knees, and street cries to street, and temple to temple, and the fifteen hundred turrets join the dirge, "Yet forty days, and Nineveh shall be overthrown." A black covering is thrown over the horses and the sheep and the cattle. Forage and water are kept from the dumb brutes, so that their distressed bellowing may make a dolorous accompaniment to the lamentation of six hundred thousand souls who wring their hands, and beat their temples, and throw themselves into the dust, and deplore their sin, crying out, "Yet forty days, and Nineveh shall be overthrown."

God heard that cry. He turned aside from the affairs of eternal state, and listened. He said, "Stop! I must go down and save that city. It is repenting, and cries for help, and it shall have it, and Nineveh shall live." Then the people took down the timbrels, and loosened the foot of the dance, and flung new light on the panels of alabaster, and started the suppressed fountains, and the children clapped their hands; and from Sardanapalus on the throne, clear down to the keeper of the city gate, where brown-faced Jonah first went in with his thrilling message, there were song, and laughter, and congratulation, and festivity, and jubilee. "And God saw their works, that they turned from their evil way; and God repented of the evil that he had said that he would do unto them: and he did it not."

I learn, in the first place, from this subject *the precision and punctuality of the Divine arrangement*. You will see that God decided exactly the day when Nineveh's lease of mercy should end. If Jonah preached that sermon on the first day of the month, then the doom was to fall upon Nineveh on the tenth day of the next month. So God decides what shall be the amount of our rebellion. Though there may be no sound in the heavens, he has determined the length of his endurance of our sin. It may be forty days, it may be forty hours, it may be forty minutes, it may be forty seconds. The fact that the affairs of God's government are infinite and multifarious is no reason why he should not attend to the minutiæ. God no more certainly decided that on June 15th, 1215, England should have her Magna Charta; nor that on the 4th of July, 1776, the Declaration of Independence should go forth; nor that at half-past eleven o'clock at night on the 14th of December, 1799, George Washington should die; nor that forty days after Jonah preached that sermon Nineveh's chance for mercy should end unless she repented, than he has decided the point beyond which you and I can not pass, and still obtain the Divine clemency. What careful walking this ought to make for those who are unsaved, lest the hour-glass of their opportunity be almost empty! Men and women do not lose their souls by putting off repentance forever, but only by putting it off one second after the time is up. They propose to become Christians in mid-life, but they die in youth; or they propose in old age to be Christians, but they die in mid-life; or on the forty-first day they will attend to the matter, but on the fortieth Nineveh is overthrown.

Standing on a ship's deck amidst a coil of chains, sailors roughly tell you to stand back if you do not want your limbs broken, or, by the chains, be hurled overboard, for they are going to let go the anchor; and when the anchor does go, the chains make the deck smoke with their speed. As swiftly our time runs away from us. Now it seems coiled all around us in a pyramid of years and days and minutes; but they are going, and they will take us off with their lightning velocity. If I should by some supernatural revelation to-night tell you just how long or how brief will be your opportunity for repentance and salvation, you would not believe me. You would say, "I shall have tenfold that time; I shall have a hundredfold that time." But you will not have more; you will have less. You have put off repentance so long that you are going to be very much crowded in this matter of the soul's salvation. The corner of time that is left you is so small that you will hardly have room to turn around in it. You are like an accountant who has to have a certain number of figures added up by four o'clock in the afternoon. It is two full, round hours' work, and it is a quarter-past three o'clock, and yet he has not begun. You are like a man in a case of life and death five miles from the dépôt, and the train starts in thirty minutes, and you have not harnessed the horse. You are like a man who comes to the bridge across the Naugatuck River in time of a freshet. The circumstances are such that he must go across. The bridge quivers, the abutment begins to give way; but he stands and halts and waits, until the bridge cracks in twain and goes down, hoping then that on the floating timbers he may get over to the other shore.

God is not looking inertly and unconcernedly upon the

position you occupy. Just as certainly as there is a bank
to the East River, just so certainly there is a bank to the
river of your opportunity. The margin is fixed. There
will be a limit to God's forbearance. "Yet forty days, and
Nineveh shall be overthrown."

Still further, I learn from this subject that *religious warning may seem preposterous.* Now, we think that our city is
safe from all foreign invasion. We have Fort Hamilton,
the Battery, Fort Lafayette, and a half-dozen strongholds;
but the city of Nineveh had fifteen hundred turrets, and
they were all strongholds. Then it had for a natural defense the Tigris, and it was not an easy thing for an army
to swim across that river under the shadow of a wall on
which stood a defending army; and yet it was through that
impregnable city that Jonah went, uttering the warning
words of my text. It must at first have seemed preposterous to a great many of the people. So it is now that religious warning seems to many an absurdity. It is more to
them a joke than any thing else. "Repent? Prepare?
Was there ever a man with stronger health than I have?
Vision clear, hearing alert, lungs stout, heart steady. Insurance companies tell me I shall have seventy years of
life. My father and mother were both long-lived. Feel
the muscle in my arm." Ah, my brother, it is not preposterous when I come out to tell you that you need to make
preparation for the future. I have noticed that it is the
invalids who live on. They take more care of their health,
and so they outlive the robust and athletic. I have noticed in my circle of acquaintances, for the last few years,
that five robust and athletic men go out of life to one invalid. Death prides himself on the strength of the castle
he takes. "Boast not thyself of the morrow, for thou

knowest not what a day may bring forth." Dr. Eddy, the eloquent missionary secretary, died the other day from swallowing a small flake of an oyster-shell. Emilius Lepidus lost his life by having his toe wounded. A splinter may be lancet sharp enough to bleed our life away. Look out! The slip of a railroad train from the track, the rush of a runaway horse through the street, any one of ten thousand perils may be upon you. "In such a day and hour as you think not, the Son of man cometh." Your opportunity for repentance is almost over. "Yet forty days, and Nineveh shall be overthrown."

Still further, I learn from my subject that *God gives every man a fair chance for his life*. The iniquity of Nineveh was accumulating. It had been rolling up and rolling up. There the city lay—blotched, seething, festering under the sun. Why did not God put an end to its iniquity? Why did not God unsheathe some sword of lightning from the scabbard of a storm-cloud, and slay it? Why did he not with some pry of an earthquake throw it into the tomb where Caraccas and Lisbon now lay? Why did he not submerge it with the scorn of his indignation, as he did Herculaneum and Pompeii? It was because he wanted to give the city a fair chance. You would have thought that thirty days would have been enough to repent in, or twenty days, or ten days. Ay, you would have said, "If that city don't quit its sin in five days, it never will." But see the wide margin. Listen to the generosity of time. "Yet forty days!"

Be frank, my brother, and confess to-night that God is giving you a fair chance for safety, a better chance than he gave to Nineveh. They had one prophet. You have heard the voices of fifty. They had one warning. You have had a thousand. They had forty days. Some of you have had forty years. Sometimes the warnings of God have come upon your soul soft as the breath of lilies and frankincense, and then again as though hurled from a catapult of terrific providence. God has sometimes led you to see your unsaved condition while you were walking amidst perils, and your hair stood on end, and you stopped breathing; you thought your last moment had come. Or, through protracted illness, he allowed you in many a midnight to think over this subject, when all was still save the ticking of the clock in the hall and the beating of your own anxious heart. Warned that you were a sinner. Warned that you needed a divine Saviour. Warned of coming retribution. Warned of an eternity crowded with splendor or catastrophe. Warned by the death of those with whom you were familiar. Warned day after day, and month after month, and year after year—warned, warned, warned. Oh, my dear brother! if your soul is lost, in the day of judgment you will have to acknowledge "no man in Brooklyn ever had a better chance for heaven than I had. I was preached to, and prayed for, and divinely solicited. I was shown the right, and fully persuaded of it; but I did not act and I did not believe, and now, in the presence of a burning earth and a flying heaven, I take the whole responsibility. Hear me, men! angels! devils!—I took the life of my own soul; and I did it so thoroughly that it is done forever. And now I trudge off over the hot desert and under the burning sky—a suicide! a suicide!"

Yes, I think you have all been warned; and if up until this very hour you have happened to escape such intimation, to-night I ring it in your ears: "Yet forty days, and Nineveh shall be overthrown!"

Still further, I learn from this subject that *when the people repent, the Lord lets them off.* While yet Nineveh was on its knees, and Sardanapalus sat in the ashes, and the unfed cattle were yet moaning in the air, and the people were yet deploring their sin, God reversed the judgment, and said, "Those people have repented. Let them live!" And the news flew. The gardens saved. The palaces saved. Six hundred thousand people saved. A belt of sixty miles of city saved. Let the news be flung from one wall to the other; from the east wall, clear over to the west wall. Let the bells ring! Let the cymbals clap! Let flags be flung out from all the fifteen hundred turrets! Let the king's lamp-lighters kindle up the throne-room! "And God saw their works, that they turned from their evil way; and God repented of the evil that he had said that he would do unto them: and he did it not." In other words, when a sinner repents, God repents. The one gives up his sins; the other gives up his judgments. The moment that a man turns to God, the relation of the whole universe toward him is changed, and the storms, and the lightnings, and the thunders, and the earthquakes, and the grandeurs of the judgment-day, and the realities of the eternal world, all become his coadjutors. God and the angels come over on his side. Repent, give up your sin and turn to God, and you will be saved. "Ah," says some one, "that's a tough thing to do." "I have been drinking," says some one; or, "I have been unchaste," says some one; or, "I have been blasphemous," says another; or, "I have been a Sabbath-breaker," says another; or, "I have a hard heart," says another, "and now you ask me to give up my sin. I can not do it—and I won't do it." Then you will die. That is settled. But somebody else says, "I will give up my sin, and I will now take the Lord for my portion." You will live. That is just as certainly settled. You will to-night either have to fling away sin or fling away heaven. The one is a husk—the other is a coronet. The one is a groan—the other is an anthem. The one is a sting—the other is an illumination. Christ's fair complexion, of which his contemporaries wrote, is gone, and his face is red and his hands are red and his feet are red with the rushing blood of his own suffering, endured to get you out of sin and death and hell. Oh, will you to-night implore him to let his suffering take the place of your ill desert? If you will, all is well, and you may now begin to twist garlands for your brow, for you are already a victor. All heaven comes surging upon your soul in the announcement, "There is no condemnation to them which are in Christ Jesus." Now, will you do it? I care nothing for a sermon unless it has an application, and this is the application: will you do it? "Ah," says some one, "I believe that is right. I mean some day to surrender the entirety of my nature to God. It is reasonable. I mean to be a Christian, but not now." That is what thousands of you are saying.

I am afraid if you do not give your heart to God to-night, you never will. You may have heard of the ship *Rebecca Goddard* that came near one of our ports this last winter. They were all scoured up and ready for the landing, when, coming almost into the harbor, an ice-floe took the ship and pushed it out to sea, and it drifted about two or three days, and there was great suffering, and one was frozen dead at his post. How near they got into the harbor, and yet they did not get in! How many there are here to-night who feel they are almost in the harbor of

God's mercy! Why do you not come ashore, lest some ice-floe of sin and worldliness drive you out again to the sea, and you die in the rigging? I throw you this rope to-night. I hurl you this warning. Make fast to heaven now. This moment is vanishing, and with it may go every thing; and so I run up and down through this audience with the banner of the cross—Rally, immortal men, rally!

"But," says some one in the house, "I won't take your advice. I'll risk it. I defy God. Here I take my stand, and I ask no odds either of earth or heaven." Let me tell such that they are in a battle where they will be worsted. "Yet forty days!" Perhaps thirty days. Perhaps ten days. Perhaps three days. Perhaps one day. The horses that drag on that chariot of doom are lathered with the foam of a great speed, and their hoofs clip fire from the flinty road, and their nostrils throb with the hot haste as they dash on. Get out of the way, or the wheels will roll over you. You can not endure the ire of an incensed God. Throw yourselves down on your knees now, and pelt the heavens with blood-red cries for mercy. The terminal chance is going, the last chance is going, going. Oh, wake up before you wake up among the lost! May God Almighty, by his eternal Spirit, wake you up!

There is a story running indistinctly through my mind of a maiden whose lover was doomed to be put to death when the curfew bell struck nine o'clock at night, and she thought that if she could keep that bell from ringing for a little while, her lover and friend would be spared. And so, under the shadow of the night, she crept up into the tower, and laid hold of the tongue of the bell. After a while the sexton came up to the tower, and he put his hand on the rope, and waited for the right moment to come; and then by the light of his lantern and his watch he found it was nine o'clock, and he seized the rope, and he pulled, and the bell turned, but in silence, and the maiden still held on to the tongue of the bell swinging back and forth wildly through the belfry, and the curfew bell rang not, and so time was gained, and pardon arrived, and a precious life was saved. Oh, it seems to me as if there were those here doomed to death. You have condemned yourselves. It seems to me as if the death-knell of your immortal soul were about to strike. The angel of God's justice has his hand on the rope, and yet I seize the tongue of that bell, and I hold on, hoping to gain a little time, and I cry out, "O God! not yet! not yet!" hoping that time may be gained, and pardon may fly from the throne, and your soul may live. May the God who saved Nineveh save you! But some of you have put it off so long that I fear your time is up.

16

PILLOWS UNDER THE ARMS.

"Woe to them that sew pillows to all armholes."—*Ezekiel* xiii., 18.

THE Chaldeans were to capture Jerusalem. God said so. False prophetesses denied it, and, to quell the anxieties of the people, employed a significant symbol by sewing little pillows under the arms, as much as to say, "Whenever you feel these soft pads at the arm-sleeves, bethink yourselves all shall be easy and well." But alas for the delusion! Notwithstanding all the smoothness of the prophecy, Jerusalem went down in darkness and fire and blood.

It is not more certain that you are here this morning, not more certain that that is a window, not more certain that that is a ceiling, not more certain that that is a chair, not more certain that that is a carpet, than it is certain that God has declared destruction to the finally impenitent. Universalism comes out, and tries to quell this fear, and wants to sew two pillows under my arm-sleeves, and wants to sew two pillows under your arm-sleeves. It shall not do it. God helping me, I shall, this morning, put before my own soul and yours the absorbing facts, and I shall try to snatch their pillow of false peace from under the arms of my auditors, and show you what the perils are, that you may, one and all, escape them. Suppose there is some real danger ahead, and a man comes into your house, and says, "There is no peril; be at peace!" and another neighbor comes in, and says, "There is a peril, and I know how you can escape it, and I come to tell you;"

which is the best friend and the best neighbor? Why, the latter, of course, and I want to act his part to-day.

There are two branches of Universalism: one made up of the Restorationists, who, while they admit there may be some punishment in the future world, say it will come to an end, and the soul, through a process of reformation, will come up at last into light, and joy, and peace, and victory; but the vast majority of the Universalists that I have met in the world believe that there is no future punishment at all, and that, whatever may have been our character in this world, the moment we step across the line into the future world we are completely happy! People need not tell me that is not Universalism. I take it not from books; I take it from my own observation, and my frequent converse with men who have adopted such theories. However, all Universalists agree in saying that the human race will all eventually be happy.

I shall, this morning, show you that Universalism, under any shape, is unscriptural, unreasonable, destructive of good morals, withering to all earnestness in soul-saving, and the means of eternal catastrophe to a great many. You say, "Do you think to impose upon us, this morning, by bringing out that old obsolete book, the Bible—a book fit only for grandmothers in their second childhood—and propose to prove any thing by that?" I respond by saying it is most reasonable to expect that God would give this race some kind of a revelation. Well, if God has given a revelation, which is it? I can now think of only five books that pretend to be Divine revelations: the Koran, the Shaster, the Zendavesta, the Confucius writings, and the Bible. Which of those five books do you prefer to believe a Divine revelation? The vast majority of the people in the audience say, "Give us the Bible. We take that." Will you stand by it through all this argument of the morning? "Yes," you say. So will I stand by it. Having made up our minds that this is the binding statute in the case, now I solemnly impanel all this audience as a jury for the trial, and I shall proceed to open the cause and to call the witnesses.

To prove that there is such a thing as future punishment, I first call up Dives the lost. Let him be sworn. He was a man of great influence in the world. There is no reason why he should falsify. *Question:* "Dives, is there a perdition?" *Answer:* "Yes, I have just come from it. It is torment. I can't get any thing there to cool my tongue. I want a drop of water, but I can't get it. Do send word to my five brothers, that they come not into that suffering." Universalism tries to impeach this witness by saying it is all allegory. Lazarus the saved is the Gentile converted; and Dives, who lifted up his eyes in hell, being in torment, is the Jew whose spiritual privileges were cut off in this world! If the Lord Jesus Christ were going to make an allegory, he would not make one so imbecile as that. I do not wonder that Universalists have wrenched that passage until they got red in the face, to make it mean something else; but in all ages of the past, and in all ages of the future, the common-sense reading of that Scripture is that Lazarus went to heaven, and Dives went to hell, and there was a gulf fixed between them they could never cross over.

The next witness I call in the case is an old bent-over man. It is Paul the apostle. *Question:* "Paul, is there a perdition?" *Answer:* "In flaming fire taking vengeance upon those who know not God."

The next witness is a gray-bearded man, clothed in rough hair-cloth. It is Isaiah the prophet. *Question:* "Isaiah, is there such a place as perdition?" *Answer:* "Their worm dieth not, and their fire is not quenched."

The next witness looks as though he may have been very ruddy and beautiful once, but he has lost his beauty and ruddiness, through much family trouble. It is David —David the psalmist. *Question:* "David, is there any perdition?" *Answer:* "The wicked shall be turned into hell, and all the nations that forget God."

The next witness is a very mild and lovable man. It is John the inspired. *Question:* "John, is there any such place as perdition?" *Answer:* "They shall drink of the wine of the wrath of Almighty God, poured without mixture into the cup of his indignation." And he stops a moment to take breath, and then he says, "They shall be tormented in fire and brimstone in the presence of the angels." And he stops again to take breath, and then says, "The smoke of their torment ascendeth up for ever and ever."

But the most important witness is to come. He comes with feet blistered by the long way, with sickly looks from sleeplessness and exposure. It is the Son of God; He before whom we bow ourselves down, not worthy even to kiss his feet, and we say in all reverence, "O Jesus, is there a perdition?" And he answers, "At the end of the world the Son of man shall send forth his angels, and they shall gather out of his kingdom all things that offend, and shall cast them into a furnace of fire; there shall be wailing and gnashing of teeth." And, after stopping a moment, he says, "The children of the kingdom shall be cast out into outer darkness. There shall be weeping and gnashing of teeth." Then he stops a moment, and he resumes, "Depart from me, ye cursed, into everlasting fire, prepared for the devil and his angels."

"Enough!" you say. Isaiah, and David, and Paul, and John, and Christ are enough." But I will not stop here. I bring you documentary evidence in the parable of the tares, already referred to in Christ's testimony. You remember, in the parable of the tares, that some people were thrown into a furnace of fire, while it says the righteous shine forth as the sun in the kingdom of their Father. Do you know how the Universalists have squeezed and distorted that passage? They have done so until they have made the furnace to be Jerusalem, and those who are to shine forth as the sun in their Father's kingdom are the Jews who did not happen to get killed in the earthly wars—an interpretation that would throw any audience into convulsions of laughter if the awfulness of the theme did not forbid merriment.

You said you would take the Bible for the standard of this trial. Gentlemen of the jury, now I hold you to your word, and I demand that you admit the awful truth that there is a future punishment. "But," say the Restorationists, "we admit there is a future punishment, but it comes to an end." My good friends, when will it come to an end? I think we shall have to call back some of the witnesses we have sworn in this case. "John the inspired, what is the duration of that punishment?" He answers: "The smoke of their torment ascendeth up *for ever and ever.*" How long is that? I call up Isaiah again. "Isaiah, how long does this punishment last?" "Their worm *dieth not,* their fire is *not quenched.*" I call up Paul again. He says, "They shall be punished with *everlasting* destruction in the presence of the Lord." I ask reverently again the Lord Jesus Christ how long this punishment lasts, and he replies, "These shall go away into *everlasting* punishment." And he says again, "Depart, ye cursed, into *everlasting* fire." I leave it to your common sense what that means, what it must mean.

"But," say a great many, "you ought to go back to the Greek, and find out that that word everlasting doesn't mean what you have been representing it to mean." So there are persons who could not parse a Greek sentence to save themselves from being hanged, and who do not know the difference between Kappa and Epsilon, who talk about Greek. I reply, if there had been a great difference between the original and our translation, God would before this have given it to us in plain English, so that we who do not know Greek could understand it. You can not make me believe that God would keep the truth as to our eternal destiny covered up in a heap of Greek roots. Do you want to be learned? Come, now, and let us all be learned together, and go back and read that passage: "These shall go away into *everlasting* punishment, but the righteous into life *eternal.*" The same Greek word in one place is translated "everlasting," and in the other "eternal;" and if you bedwarf the word "everlasting," you must bedwarf the word "eternal." If you dwindle up the sufferings of the lost, then you must dwindle up the rejoicings of the saved. The same effort which would break a chain would snap a harp-string. The same effort that would uptear a dungeon would pull down a mansion. The same effort that would stop a groan would choke a hallelujah. "These shall go away into *everlasting* punishment, but the righteous into life *eternal.*" If in the one case the sufferings are not to be eternal, in the other case the rejoicings are not to be eternal. But there is nothing that makes me so tired as being learned, and so I come back from the Greek to the plain English translation, good enough for you and good enough for me. This Bible says that a man who commits the unpardonable sin shall be forgiven neither in this world nor in the world to come. What does that mean? Where is your restoration after the grave? "He shall be forgiven neither in this world nor in the world to come." You Restorationists, put your hand-screw on that. Try to twist that around, so it shall not mean what God here makes it to mean. Shall neither be forgiven in this world nor in the world that is to come!

Oh, my friends, either throw overboard your Bible, or throw overboard Universalism. I press you to that choice to-day, and you must make it. The whole Bible is against Universalism. Ezekiel is against it. Jeremiah is against it. Isaiah is against it. David is against it. Matthew is against it. Mark is against it. Luke is against it. John is against it. Romans is against it. Corinthians is against it. Thessalonians is against it. Revelation is against it. Now, I do not at this moment say that the Bible is inspired, or even a virtuous book; but I do say, if the Bible is right, then Universalism is wrong—awfully wrong, outrageously wrong, infinitely wrong, everlastingly wrong.

Still further, *Universalism is unreasonable.* Here is a railroad map. There is a long line of railroads reaching from New York to California. There is a line of railroads reaching from New York to Boston. There is a line of railroads reaching from New York to Philadelphia. They will come out at the same place. "No," you say, "they do not." You tell me that one ends in Boston, and the other in Philadelphia, and the other in San Francisco. I deny it. If you want me to believe that, prove it. "Well," you say, "I can very easily prove it. One railroad goes north, and the other south, and the other goes west." "Oh," I say, "you are right. I admit you are right. I yield the position." In other words, you argue that railroads that go in opposite directions can not come out at the same place. Now, here are two roads for the soul's travel. The one is faith in Christ, helpful services to others, a struggle for consecration, and doing better all the way up. That is one road. Howard went that road. Wilberforce went that road. Paul went that road. Ten thousand times ten thousand went that road. Here is the other road. It starts with the rejection of Jesus Christ. It keeps on in sin, and in rebellion against God, all the way through. Robespierre went on that road. Nero went on that road. All the bad people that have ever lived and died have gone on that road; and the two roads being in opposite directions, they must come out at opposite termini. Nothing but moral insanity can make you think any differently. By inexorable geometry, by common sense, by a calculation plainer than that twice three are six, you come to the conclusion that opposite directions of travel must bring opposite eternal destinies.

"But," say the Restorationists, "the punishment in the lost world, which we admit, is reformatory, and the souls that go there will gradually struggle up into thorough felicity." Absurdity infinite! Two Sabbaths ago, while I stood in this place, talking, among other things, about the outrages of the Raymond Street Jail—outrages which, I have been informed by prominent official authority in this city, I did not more than half state—at that very moment there was a girl of fifteen years in that Raymond Street Jail, imploring that she might be in a cell alone. She said, "These wretches around here are telling me filthy stories all the time. I can't stand it here. I want to be alone." She knew, what every one knows, that bad associations are not reformatory. And yet you try to make me believe that in that world where all the desperadoes and abandoned have gone, the soul is going to get better. Will the thieves make it honest? Will the libertines make it pure? Will the blasphemers make it holy?

The perdition of ungodly men is a very poor reform school. By inevitable law you know that bad society makes people worse, and that Herod on earth was mild and beautiful compared with what he is now, and that the men who died on the scaffold for their crimes were benefactors and philanthropists compared with their present character. Worse, and getting worse. But if from that world they really struggle out—have any of them got out yet? Will Robespierre be in heaven in time to welcome the grandchildren of the men he butchered? Will James Fisk be in heaven in time to welcome the widows and orphans whose property he swamped in a Wall Street panic? Oh, what a delicious, savory place heaven would be if the wretches who went down into their graves unwashed got there! You have a child in heaven, you have a sister in heaven—do you think of them as being in that kind of society?

If, as the great majority of the Universalists argue, there is no hell, tell me, then, where the people of Sodom and Gomorrah went? If all is fair beyond the line of this world, irrespective of our character here, then the men who stole Charley Ross, and who were shot for their crimes, are better off to-day than the parents who sit frenzied with grief, waiting for the pattering of the feet of the little captive; then Ananias was better off than Sapphira, for he lied first, and so beat his wife three or four minutes into glory. *There is a hell.* Your common sense declares it.

Still further, Universalism is, willingly or unwillingly, the *abettor of bad morals.* It is the high-priest of suicide. How many people there have been who have got tired of their troubles, and said, "Here, we must get out of these troubles. We will just take our own lives, then we will be free. There is nothing between us and glory but a phial of laudanum or a revolver;" and so they swallowed the laudanum or cracked the revolver, and that has been the end of it. They step right over into glory. They have been taught so. You know that all those who in their right mind commit suicide—for I speak not of those who are deranged, and take their own lives; they are not responsible for any thing they do—but I say that the majority of those who in their seeming right mind take their own lives, leave a letter on the table, saying, "Meet me in heaven." They are going right over. Oh, if that doctrine be true, why do not some of you who have been struggling with overwhelming troubles put an end to them, and buy an overdose of belladonna on your way home, or this afternoon leap from the top of your house, and get straight into glory?

> "For who would bear the whips and scorns of time,
> The oppressor's wrong, the proud man's contumely,
> *   *   *   *   *   *
> When he himself might his quietus make
> With a bare bodkin?"

Why does he not do it? It is because the man knows that

if, in his sane moments, he takes his own life, he drops into ruin.

A man near Utica, New York, sent for his pastor, a Universalist minister, and said to him, "If I should die now, would I go to heaven?" "Most certainly," the minister replied. "You think there is no possible doubt about it?" "None at all, sir." "Well," said the man, "I have had trouble enough, now I am going away from it. I am going to leave the world, and I am going now;" and he drew a pistol, and put it to his own temple, when the minister clutched his arm, and said, "Stop! stop! there may be a hell!" Then the man turned to the minister, and said, "You preach what you don't believe. You are a deceiver." If there be a man in this house to-day who has at any time had the idea of taking his own life, let me persuade you not to sit down and write, "Meet me in heaven;" you will not go there. The fact that there is a perdition is the mightiest moral restraint that the world has ever felt. When you try to upset this doctrine of a future place of punishment, you are abetting crime.

Universalist churches in our cities are surrounded by so many churches of other kinds that you can not see their full influence; but in the New England villages, or the villages at the Far West, where there is only one church, and that a Universalist church, or where the Universalist church is dominant over all others—in such villages, inevitably and always, you find profane swearing, drunkenness, Sabbath-breaking, lust, and every form of abomination, rampant. Give the doctrine of Universalism full swing in any village, or in any city, and it consumes it— financially, morally, and spiritually. I have seen its effects again and again in the villages at the West, where it left not one green thing. I tell you that that doctrine is the foe of God and man; and, come fair or foul, I hold it up in the presence of this audience for your denunciation. "Thou shalt not surely die," was the first plaster that the devil ever spread; but he spread it so large, there is enough to salve the consciences of ages.

Still further, Universalism is *withering to all earnestness in soul-saving.* What is the matter with a great many of the Protestant churches to-day? They have this disease of Universalism in a milder form. They adopt the Heidelberg Catechism or the Westminster Assembly, or they sit in Methodist conferences or in Baptist associations; but there is so much Universalism in the air, they are cowed down. They dare not preach a rugged Gospel. They say "heaven" with a shout, but they say "hell" with a whisper; so that the people do not know exactly what they did say; and the Calvinists think they said "hell," and the Restorationists think they said "bell," and the merchants think they said "sell," and so they are all satisfied. Oh, I abhor this namby-pambyism in religion! What is the reason we do not have any more conversions in our churches? It is because we do not sufficiently preach rewards and punishments. We tell the righteous it shall be well with them; but not in the same emphasis do we tell the wicked it shall be ill with them.

Why did Samuel Davies, and Nettleton, and Baxter, and the Wesleys, and Whitefield, and Osborne, and Daniel Baker count the conversions under their ministry by tens and tens of thousands? It was because their sermons rang with the doxologies of the saved, and crackled with the fires of the lost.

Did you ever hear of a great awakening in a Universalist church? Never. What would they get awakened about? They are all safe, always have been safe, always will be. What is the use of the jailer's rushing through between the falling walls of the prison, crying, "What must I do to be saved?" He was safe before the prison began to rock. What is the use of the sinking man's crying, "Lord, save; I perish?" Stop your noise. The water is not up to your chin! What is the use of making such a fuss about three thousand souls saved on the Day of Pentecost? They were as saved before as they were after. What did Paul mean when he feared becoming a castaway? Cast away on what coast? The coast of everlasting love? Why are the wicked in the last day represented as crying out, "Rocks and mountains, fall on us, and hide us from the face of the Lamb?" No danger! Oh, if we want to bring souls to Jesus Christ, men and women of God, we must tell the whole truth, and hide none of it!

What means that picture, in some of the old books, representing Martin Luther almost bent double by a paroxysm of earnestness while he is preaching about men's souls? What meant Thomas Chalmers, standing in his Edinburgh pulpit, warning people to flee from the wrath to come until he actually foamed at the mouth? Why did John Summerfield and Robert M'Cheyne preach themselves so early into the grave? Why was it that when Mr. Venn described the perils of an immortal soul, history tells us the audience "dropped like slacked lime?" Why was Edward Payson so anxious for the salvation of men that his doctors said his body was in a continuous fever? Oh, my brethren, what we in the ministry most want is to be aroused, convicted, melted, rebaptized, surcharged with the power of the Lord God Almighty. Swinnoch said a thing that made me quake, body, mind, and soul, when I first read it. He said, "It is an awful thing to fall into hell from under a pulpit; but what an awful thing to fall into hell *out* of a pulpit." Oh, that God would give us grace to see the infinite sham of modern Universalism, and give us wisdom to stop sewing pillows under the arm-sleeves! O my soul, wake up! Ministers of Jesus Christ, in the United States and Great Britain, wake up! There *is* a hell, and it is our place to keep people out of it.

Still further, *Universalism has ruined for eternity a great many souls.* East-south-east of Boston there is a light-house called Minot's Ledge Light-house. It was with great difficulty that the Government, in 1857, put down but four stones, and in 1858 they put down but six layers of stone; but after a while the work was accomplished. It is very important that there should be a light-house there. When the wind is blowing from the north-east, and ships are coming on toward Boston harbor, if they happen to miss the harbor they go on that rock but for the light-house. I see one of the freight line of the Cunarders coming on toward Boston harbor. The wind is north-east. There are a hundred passengers on board the vessel. I slyly get into Minot's Ledge Light-house. I go up the winding stairs until I come to the top, and with a hammer I break the glass, and I blow out the light. The captain of the Cunarder is pacing the deck, not knowing exactly what to do. "The wind is from the north-east," he says. "It is getting pretty late to go in to-night, but we are not anywhere near Minot's Ledge Light-house. I am a little confused about the lights along the coast, but I think I will try it." Hark! There is a grating on the bottom of the steamer. There is a quiver from stem to stern. Then there is a keeling over, and *a crash!* All lost! All lost! Whose fault was it? The captain's? No. Never a braver man walked the deck. Was it the crew's? No. They were faithful fellows. Whose fault? *Mine,* for I blew out the light.

Now, let me say that every minister of the Gospel and every Christian man is a light-house-keeper. Upon him is a greater responsibility than ever rested upon the man who keeps the Bell Rock Light-house, off Scotland, or the Barnegat or Hatteras Light-house. God has kindled a great illumination on all the rocks of danger, saying, "Stand off! Yonder is your harbor. Yonder is your wharf. Yonder are your friends, waiting to greet you. Rocks here—nothing but rocks. Stand off!" What does Universalism do? It comes up, and blows out the light. It says, "Sail on. There are no rocks for immortal shipwreck. Sail on. All is well. All is well." Oh, what a responsibility! I would rather be the engineer of a rail train with four or five hundred passengers coming on when the drawbridge is off, and know it, and yet not stop, than a Universalist minister taking a whole church with him off the brink, giving them no warning, blowing no trumpet, never crying out, "The rocks! The rocks!" Universalism is a deception high as heaven and deep as hell; and if it be let alone, it will ruin half the race. But it is not going to be let alone. The Church of God, as it rises up to its mission, will cry the alarm to the people, and there will go up prayer to God, so that he will flash upon the nations these tremendous realities.

If I live forty years to preach—and I expect to preach forty years longer—I want to spend the whole time in setting before men the two destinies of eternal life and eternal darkness. But if I should not live as long as that, and if this should be the last sermon I shall ever preach, as it may be, then I want you to take this as my dying testimony: there is a heaven—there is a hell. Accept of Christ, and you reach the one; reject him, and you drop headlong into the other.

But it is time for this jury to render their verdict. I have shown you that Universalism is unscriptural, unreasonable; that it is destructive to good morals; that it is withering to all earnestness in saving souls; that it is the eternal discomfiture of a great many people. In courts of law, when the jury come in, they stand and render their verdict: the foreman giving the verdict and the clerk of the court writing it down; but in this religious assemblage you must render the verdict in silence, seated, so far as you have room to be seated, God listening, and angels recording.

If what I have said this morning is true, what are you going to do about it? What step will you take? My soul has been wrung with the awfulness of this theme. If God had not helped me, I should have fallen down between my chair and your pew; but I did not dare to hold back the theme. As I expect to meet my Maker and my Judge, I did not dare to hide any of the truth; but I was all the time sustained with the idea that I could, before I got through, tell you how to get off from your peril; and that if I pointed you to the flaming sword, it was only to show you a refuge; and if I showed you a chasm, it was only to show you a bridge over it. The Lord Jesus to-day breaks through all obstacles, and runs against the opposing spears, and tramples on the sharpened spikes, and springs into the midst of this assembly, and throws his arms around you, and begs you to be saved. Will you shake him off? Will you hurl him on his back? Will you trample on him, putting one foot on his holy heart, and the other on his mangled brow, and from the corpse of a murdered Christ will you leap into woe? Stop! Stop! Stop! Jesus came to save you. By the tears that ran down his scarred cheek—by the blood that oozed from his whipped back—by the sweat of agony that stood out in beads upon his brow—by the dying groan which broke the heart of the rocks, and made the sun faint dead away in the heavens—I beg you to accept of the Lord Jesus Christ and be saved. Oh, fling not away your immortal soul, when so much has been done to ransom it! When you may be saved, why will you be lost? Some one suggested to me yesterday that there were some persons who consoled themselves by saying, "If I am to be lost, there will be a great many others with me, so I won't care so much." Oh, what poor philosophy!

When the Lake Shore Railroad cars went off the track a year or two ago, and a hundred and fifty people were crushed, was it any mitigation of the sorrow that there were a hundred and fifty instead of one man? When, three years ago, five hundred miles off Newfoundland, we thought our ship was making the last plunge, did the screams of seven hundred frenzied passengers mitigate the horror of that night? Oh no. If there is any man determined to be lost, better be lost alone than in a crowd; their sorrow added to your sorrow, their disaster added to your disaster. I can not believe that there are any in this house who will be such fools as to reject the only salvation offered them this day in the name of the Lord Jesus Christ, the infinite Redeemer. I do not know whether my cheek turns pale at the thought; but I do know that my heart quakes as I cry out with Isaiah, "Who among us can dwell in devouring fire? Who of us can lie down in eternal burnings?"

Men and women! there is only one name given under heaven among men whereby you may be saved, and that is Jesus. "God so loved the world, that he gave his only begotten Son, that whosoever believeth in him should not perish, but have everlasting life." Depend upon it, if you are lost it will not be God's fault. He has done every thing to save you. It will not be Christ's fault. He has pleaded with blood-red earnestness for your salvation. It will not be the Holy Spirit's fault. He has this day stirred and entreated you mightily. If you are lost, it will be your own fault. You will forge your own chains. You will write your own death-warrant. You will bolt and bar the door of heaven, and doubly bolt it and doubly bar it against your own soul; and you might as well this day, if that is your determination, make your valedictory, saying: "Farewell, O Church of God! I don't want the comfort of your sacraments. Farewell, O Holy Bible! I don't want your illumination. Farewell, O Holy Ghost! bother me no more about the great future. Farewell, O heaven! I don't want to hear thy clapping cymbals, nor to mingle in thy hallelujahs. Farewell, O my glorified kindred! father, mother, sister, brother, and my dear children who broke my heart when they went away from me. Farewell! Keep no longer a seat for me by your side at the heavenly banquet. I am not coming. I take another road. I make another choice. Across these spaces I fling this kiss of everlasting separation. Good-bye, good-bye. This is my eternal valedictory!"

WHAT KILLS MINISTERS.*

"Thou wilt surely wear away, both thou, and this people that is with thee: for this thing is too heavy for thee; thou art not able to perform it thyself alone."—*Exodus* xviii., 18.

JETHRO was paying a visit to his son-in-law, Moses. The tent is lighted, and swarming with a glad levee. Until very late at night I see the swinging of the lanterns, and the glancing in and out of the guests. Good cheer, recital of stirring experiences, accounts of what they have done and what God has done, and innocent conviviality characterize the occasion. In the morning Moses sits down to listen to all the people have to say by way of complaint or appeal. He stands between them and God. It is talk, talk, talk all day long. From morning till night Moses is listening, planning, counseling, praying, preaching. Jethro gets alarmed about his son-in-law's health. "Why," he says, "this thing will wear you out. These people and this work will exhaust you. Why don't you divide up the labors and the burdens among other people? Thou wilt surely wear away, both thou, and this people that is with thee: for this thing is too heavy for thee." Moses takes the advice of his father-in-law, and calls around him some of the best men he can find as assistants, and, instead of being worn out with his labors, lives one hundred and twenty years—as long as any man ought to want to live

---

* Sixth anniversary sermon.

in this world, which was intended only as a stepping-stone to something brighter.

Jethro's warning to his son-in-law is just as appropriate now for all religious pastors, teachers, and Christian workers. You know very well that all Christendom is strewed with worn-out ministers of the Gospel. Some of them went down under brain-softening, others under throat disease, others under paralysis, others under nervous derangement and disorganization.

What is killing so many ministers? Sometimes they are destroyed through excessive use of tobacco, sometimes through culpable neglect of physical exercise, sometimes through reckless exposure; but I think that, in the vast majority of cases, it is through lack of sympathy and help on the part of their congregations. Thousands of these pastors are worried to death by insufficient salary, and pulled apart by unreasonable demands, and rung out of life by the tintinnabulation of their door-bell, and exhausted with perpetual interruptions. Now, my text suggests that no man can do every thing. If a minister of the Gospel has on one shoulder the spiritual affairs of a church, and on the other shoulder the financial affairs of a church, his feet are on the margin of an open grave, clear to the bottom of which he can look without moving. Let all ministers of the Gospel, so far as possible, gather around them sympathetic men and women upon whom they can throw much of the care and responsibility and trouble. "Thou wilt surely wear away, both thou, and this people that is with thee: for this thing is too heavy for thee; thou art not able to perform it thyself alone."

Standing before you this morning, preaching my sixth anniversary sermon as your pastor—a style of sermon in which the preacher is generally expected to be more than usually personal—I have to tell you that the burdens of life are getting to me less and less, and that as the years pass on I have fewer and still fewer anxieties. In beautiful Belleville, on the banks of the Passaic, where I began my Christian ministry, it seemed as if all the work came down on my young shoulders. Going to the West, the field was larger and the care less. Going to Philadelphia, the field was still larger and the care still less. And standing to-day, as I do, among hundreds of warm personal friends, whose hands and feet and hearts are all willing to help, I have less anxiety than I ever had. I have taken the advice of Jethro in the text, and have gathered around me a great many with whom I expect to divide all the care and the responsibility; and though sometimes, what with the conduct of this church, where we have a perpetual religious awakening, and the conduct of a religious weekly newspaper, and the conduct of the Lay College, people have often addressed me in words similar to those of my text, saying, "Thou wilt surely wear away: this thing is too heavy for thee," I am glad to know that this morning I am in perfect health, and ready to recount to you what the Lord has been doing in all these days of our sojourn together, between 1869 and 1875.

It is now six years since I preached to you my opening sermon, on the text, "God is love." I wish I could pour out my soul this morning in a doxology of praise to God, and of gratitude to this people. The difference between these years has been that the second was to me happier than the first, and the third than the second, and the fourth than the third, and the fifth than the fourth, and the sixth than the fifth. God has led us through many vicissitudes.

We are in the third church in six years. Crowded out of the first, burned out of the second, by the mercy of God led into the third.

We look back to the solitary service six years ago in the old chapel, with a congregation that almost could be accommodated on this platform. For many years the church had been in strife, until the three or four parties had exterminated each other, leaving an expanse of empty pews, a wheezy organ, a cramped-up pulpit, and a steeple the laughing-stock of the town. My personal friends applied to me an emphatic word of four letters, and two letters alike, in expressing my folly in undertaking this enterprise. Indeed, it seemed heavier than to start entirely new, for there were wide-spread prejudices in regard to the church. Still we went on. By the blessing of God, in three or four weeks our church was full; and it is astonishing how well an old building looks when it is all occupied, for there is no power in graceful arch, or in carved pillar, or in exquisite fresco to adorn a place like an audience of beaming countenances. I had rather preach in a full barn than in a sparsely attended cathedral. Empty pews are non-conductors of Gospel electricity. People came in from all ranks and conditions; and, looking over the audience to-day, I can not see more than four or five families who were with us six years ago. Some of them have been advanced into the better society of heaven, while some of them dropped off because they thought we were going too fast, and they could not keep up. We went on gathering the people in from all directions, until we have here to-day the rich and the poor, the wise and the ignorant; those who toil with pen, with printing-press, with yard-stick, and with hammer. Enough physicians—

allopathic, homeopathic, hydropathic, and eclectic—to treat us in all our disorders. Enough lawyers to defend us in all our legal contests. Enough artists to cover our walls with pictures. Enough merchants to give us the necessary fabrics, whether foreign or domestic. Enough mechanics to build and polish and make comfortable for us our residences. And I will say that never did there come together in one church a crowd of more genial, intelligent, sympathetic, enthusiastic, and warm-hearted Christian people than those which assemble here. We are all of one mind and heart. We cordially greet all who come, and give a godspeed to those who go. When any body does not like the music, or the preaching, or the plan on which our church is conducted, we say "Good-bye" as cheerfully as when he came we said "How do you do?" This church is now so large that, if a man wants to make trouble, such a small proportion hear of it that he soon gives up the undertaking as a dead failure.

We are all new together. We tarried long enough in the old Tabernacle to learn how to conduct a larger church. Then, when it was time for us to graduate from that, we got our diploma in red scroll of flame, signed, sealed, and delivered on one cold December day in 1872. When that conflagration took place, through inadequate insurance consequent upon the style of material of which the old building was constructed, we lost every thing save our faith in God and our determination to go ahead. We tarried in the Academy of Music long enough to gather up hundreds of the best families of our congregation who are worshiping with us to-day, and to get a baptism of the Holy Ghost such as never descended on any church on this continent. We came into this building with the blessing of God, and with the blessing of all denominations of Christians in this land and in Great Britain; and since we have been here the Lord has mightily blessed us, pouring out his Spirit from Sabbath to Sabbath, so that I can ask you, well knowing what your answer will be, whether you have made any too great sacrifices for Christ and his kingdom?

During these six years the Lord has sorely tried us; in the first place, by calling us to build a church with a new congregation that had not at all been consolidated; then by the demolition of that building; then by taking us a mile off from the centre of our congregation, to worship in another building; then by the almost superhuman effort of putting up this building during a financial depression such as never before afflicted this century. If God had not helped the architect, and helped the trustees, and helped the people, we should have perished in the undertaking. And while I wish to-day to recognize the indomitable perseverance and sacrifices of the congregation, I must say, to God belongs the glory. He planned this structure, making it perfect in acoustics; raising money for the building out of the very jaws of a national panic; filling the house with worshipers. Oh, let us praise him now, and let us praise him forever. I say you are not sorry for any of the sacrifices or toils through which you have gone. We have had so perpetually the blessing of God in this church, that it excites no remark when from a single service hundreds of souls step out into the kingdom of Jesus. There are in almost all the towns and cities of this country those residents who in this building first woke up to their spiritual necessities. Letters come from North and South, and East and West, from the Canadas and from both sides the sea, telling me of this fact. Oh that to-day we might make some fitting expression to the Lord! Shall it be in carved words upon the pillars? Shall it be in wreaths upon the wall? Shall it be in the organ's open diapason? All that is well; but rather let it be that our hearts shall rise to God in an intense and all-conquering acclamation of thanksgiving.

We are trying here to maintain *a well-balanced church*, and for that reason we have in all departments of Christian service the old and the young. It is a bad thing for a church when the old people have all the management, or when the young people have all the management. In the one case the church will go too slow, in the other it will go too fast. We want the fast men to keep the slow men from going too slow, and the slow men to keep the fast people from going too fast. Here are many of the aged. They have come down to us from another day. Not on their brow the snows of many winters, as people often say, but the white crocuses of an everlasting spring-time into which they are about to blossom. And how many of the young coming to us Sabbath by Sabbath! We want them all equipped for God. We want them for flying artillery in a double-quick march. When there is a storming-party to be made up, we want to wheel them into line—old men for counsel, young men for action.

We are also trying to maintain a musical church. We have an inborn antipathy to any thing like stilted and precise song in the house of God. We like oratorios, orchestras, concerts, and prima-donnas in their places; but we want vociferous singing in the house of the Lord. David cries out, "Sing aloud unto God." In other words, do not hum it or mumble it. Oh for an anthem strong enough to surge this whole audience on the beach of heaven! Persuaded that we could not do the work so well by the use of a choir, we have called into the service of the church two Bible instruments—the organ and the cornet, and so the music of the church has been sustained and led and developed. Oh, what grand and glorious singing we have had during the past years; even people who had bronchitis forgetting their infirmity, and lifting aloud their voice before God; people who could not sing a note opening their mouth reckless as to what kind of a sound came out of it. But the little discord is overwhelmed in the great symphony—a chip drowned in the rush of great waters. And yet we feel this morning that we have not done what we might, or ought, or will do, in this department of Christian service. We want more heart under it, more soul flung into it. We want the whole audience roused up to the sound of jubilee. We want the people to come from their homes on the Sabbath with hymn-books, and after the preacher shall announce the hymn, we want them to find the right page, and clear their throats, and at the first throb of the cornet on the air stretch themselves up to the magnificence and glory of this exercise. History tells us of a shout that the Persian host lifted so loud that the eagles that were flying through the air were stunned, and dropped to the earth. Oh that there might go up such a congregational anthem from this house of the Lord as shall make all heaven drop in blessing on our souls. I take partly the words of the Bible, and partly my own words, and say, "Why are ye so slack to go up and possess the orchards and the vineyards and the mountains of sacred song?" Oh that the music of heaven and earth might join midway the arches. Rise, O song of earth! Descend, O song of heaven!

Still further, *we are trying to maintain in this place a church aggressive and revolutionary.* Why build or maintain any other church in this City of Churches, where there are enough to accommodate all the people who are disposed to go to the house of God on the Sabbath, and perhaps more than enough? If you have nothing particular, nothing unique, nothing different, then what a waste of bricks and brawn and brain. But we have an idea of a church. We have built this house of God as a place where we mean to bombard iniquity. We want to smash sin, without any apology for smashing it. We have started in this line, and we mean to keep on, and study to be as well pleased with curses as blessings from the people. If there are any of you who do not like to go to a church which is assaulted of many newspapers and of the outside world, who can not understand its policies and its principles, stand clear of this church! We mean until the day of our death, and for a few days after, to keep society stirred up by the discussion of themes vital to its interests, and vital to the interests of the immortal soul. During the past six months theatrical people have been after us, and the Spiritualists have been after us, and the Unitarians have been after us, and the Universalists have been after us—one of their prominent men recently saying that he did not think there would be any hell except for one man, and that the pastor of the Brooklyn Tabernacle! But still we shall go on, as God gives us strength and health and spirit to do his will. We have only taken, as it were, the outside casement of this great rampart of iniquity. On! on! "If God be for us, *who* can be against us?"

Still further, *we are trying here to maintain a generous church.* We have as a church been able to do but little for outside charities, for the reason that we have been all the time building churches or enlarging them. But we are trying to maintain an organism on the voluntary principle. We believe that a church can be educated up to the duty and the joy of giving. We put no premium on financial meanness. We believe that people ought to give to the cause of God every farthing they can possibly give. Moreover, we believe that all can give something, and that the vast majority of the people could give more in our churches than they do, and be better off. We believe that the grandest investment a man ever makes, for this world or the world to come, is what he gives to the Church of God, since Christ pays him back fivefold, tenfold, twentyfold, fiftyfold, a hundredfold. In other words, we believe that a man is better off in this world if he is generous, and well off just in proportion as he is generous; and we believe that those people who give the most in proportion to their means will after a while have the finest houses on earth, and the grandest mansions in heaven. The stingy people keep poor, the generous get rich, as a general rule. It is the old principle of the Bible: "Cast thy bread upon the waters, for thou shalt find it after many days."

So I believe if a man takes the old Bible principle, and gives one-tenth of all his income to the cause of God, he has an insurance of prosperity such as the signature of the Bank of England can not give him. I believe our congregation will yet rise up to the positive rapture of giving. We believe that men can be so built on a large scale of heart, that they will look over their property and then say, "I will give so much toward my spiritual culture. I will give so much toward the spiritual culture of my wife. I will give so much toward the spiritual culture of my children. I will give so much toward the spiritual culture of the men who have little or no means. How small it seems, this that I am giving to Christ, who gave every thing to me! I wish it were five hundred thousand times more." Yes, we believe that the time will come when people will be so educated in this matter of Christian generosity, that instead of deciding by what other people give, or what people give in other churches, they shall give according to their own appreciation of the height, and depth, and length, and breadth, and infinity of their spiritual advantages. Do you not wish you had given that three thousand dollars to the cause of Christ that went down in Northern Pacific bonds?

I believe the time will come in the Church when the passing of a contribution plate or a subscription paper will kindle up the faces of the people as by the illumination of a great satisfaction. But now how many of us begrudge the few dollars we give to the Lord, and only give when we seem to be compelled to give, and so keep ourselves poor at the store, and rob ourselves of eternal dividends! Under the old dispensation, as I intimated, the people gave one-tenth of their property to the Lord, but that was a far inferior dispensation to the one we have. And yet how few in this day who receive a thousand dollars a year give a hundred to God! how few who receive five thousand give five hundred to God! how few who receive a hundred thousand give ten thousand to God! Those Jews, under their dark dispensation, gave one-tenth for a mere taper of spiritual life and light, while we do not give as much as that, though we have noonday radiating the hemisphere. I really think that if those old Jews gave one-tenth for their half-and-half advantages, we ought to give one-fifth for the glorious privileges which God in this day has bestowed upon us.

We talk a great deal about the evangelization of this world and the salvation of men; but there is more talk than contribution; and I do not believe that the prayer of a man for the salvation of this world ever amounts to any thing unless he, by his own generosity, shows that he is in earnest in the matter. I like the style of Elias Van Benschoten, the old man who came into a meeting of the General Synod of the Reformed Church in 1814, and, after there had been a great many long and brilliant speeches made about the education of young men to the ministry, got up, and said he would like to speak. The people looked chagrined. They thought to themselves, "He can't speak." He said, "Mr. President, I will give eight hundred and forty dollars in cash toward that object, and thirteen thousand dollars in bonds," and then sat down.

While the theory is abroad in many of the churches that men give only as they are compelled to give, I believe that the people can be educated up to a grand and glorious voluntary contribution for the support of the Gospel of Jesus; but I can not make the people believe this without your help. Remember the words of Jethro to his son-in-law. Come, let us all rally in this one respect, and try partly to pay God for our Bibles, for our churches, for our families, for our hopes of heaven. If we do not carry out this principle, there will come up, after a while, a stronger generation to execute this commission of Christ, and then they will look back and say, "Ah, what a shriveled-up minister and people that must have been in the Brooklyn Tabernacle in 1875! When the Lord opened before them an opportunity of carrying out a Gospel principle, they had not the courage to carry it out." I do not expect to bother this world much after I go out of it, but I must start the suspicion that if ever the auctioneer's hammer cracks on the back of one of these pews, it will wake me up quicker than the prophet Samuel was awakened by the Witch of En-dor.

Still further, *we are here trying to build, and organize, and keep up a soul-saving church.* I mention this last because it is first. "And the first shall be last." I have by argument, and illustration, and caricature, in these last six years tried to create in your soul an unutterable disgust for much of the religion of this day, and to lead you back, so far as God gave me strength to do it, to the old religion of Jesus Christ and his apostles. I have tried to show you that the meanest cant in all the world is the cant of skepticism, and that you ought to stop apologizing for Christianity, since it is the duty of those who do not believe in Christianity to apologize to you; and that the biggest villains in the universe are those who want to rob us of that grand old Bible; and that there is one idea in a church that ought to swallow up all other ideas, and that is the soul-saving idea. "But," you say, "are you not going to pay any attention to those who have entered into the kingdom of God, and have really become Christians?" My theory is, the way to develop a man for this world and for the world to come is to throw him chin-deep in Christian work; and if, after a man has been drawn out of the mire of his sin on to the "Rock of Ages," he wants to jump back, then he will have to jump; I am not going to stand and watch him. I believe the great work of the Christian Church is to bring men out of their sin into the hope and the joys of Christ's salvation; and then if, with all the advantages of this century, with open Bible, and the constant plying of the Holy Ghost, a man can not grow in grace, he is not worth a great deal of culture.

We want this a church set apart for the one grand object of bringing men out of their sin into hope of the Gospel. There will, in this coming year, be two hundred thousand strangers who will be seated within these gates. How many of them will you bring to Christ by your prayers and your personal solicitations? Will you bring a score, or will it be a hundred or a thousand? I must tell you that, compared with this work of saving immortal souls, all other work is cold and stale and insipid. To this one work, God helping me, I consecrate the remaining days and years of my life, and I ask you to join with me in this crusade for the redemption of immortal souls.

Now, can it be possible that six years of my pastorate have passed away never to return? How many squandered days and years—squandered by you and by me! God forgive us for the past, and help us to be more faithful for the future. Through what a variety of scenes we have gone! I have stood by you in times of sickness, and by the graves of your dead. When you came back from exhausting sickness that we feared would be fatal, I praised God that the color came to your cheek and the spring to your step. And some of you in the past six years have passed through dire bereavements. How few of the families of my congregation have not been invaded! How many of the old people have gone, in the last two or three years! They went away so gently that they had ended the second or third stanza in eternal glory before you knew they were gone. And, oh, how many of the bright, dear children have gone—the very darlings of your heart!

17*

You tried to hold on to them with your stout arms, and you said, "O Lord, spare them. I can't give them up; I can't give them up. Let me keep them a little longer." But they broke away from your arms into the light of heaven. It seemed as if Jesus and the angels were determined to have them there and then.

But we have tried to make this church a comforting place for all the broken-hearted. Oh, how many of them there are! We have tried to fill the song and the sermon and the prayer with the solace of God's promises, and so it shall be hereafter. It is no mere theory with me. I have had enough trouble of my own to know how to comfort those who are desolate, and it is my ambition to be to you a son of consolation. Standing as we do at the open portals of another pastoral year, let us to-day make a new vow of consecration. Let us be faithful to God and faithful to each other; for soon we must part, and all these pleasant scenes in which we have mingled will vanish forever. By the throne of God, our work all done, our sorrows all ended, may we be permitted to talk over the solemn, delightful, and disciplinary occurrences of this my sixth pastoral year in Brooklyn.

THE SUPERHUMAN JESUS.

"Christ came, who is over all, God blessed forever. Amen."—*Romans* ix., 5.

PAUL was a reckless man in always telling the whole truth. It mattered not who it hit, or what theological system it upset. In this one sentence he makes a world of trouble for all Arians and Socinians, and gives a cud for skepticism to chew on for the next thousand years. We must proceed skillfully to twist this passage of Scripture, or we shall have to admit the Deity of Jesus Christ. I roll up my sleeves for the work, and begin by saying, perhaps this is a wrong version. No; all the versions agree —Syriac, Ethiopic, Latin, Arabic. Perhaps this word God means a being of great power, but not the Deity. It is "God over all." But perhaps this word God refers to the first person of the Trinity—God the Father. No; it is "*Christ* came, who is over all, God blessed forever. Amen." Whichever way I take it, and when I turn it upside-down, and when I try to read it in every possible shape, I am compelled to leave it as all have been compelled to leave it who have gone before me, an incontrovertible proof of the eternal and magnificent Godhead of the Lord Jesus Christ. "Christ came, who is over all, God blessed forever. Amen."

About the differences between the evangelical denominations of Christians I have no concern. If I could by the turning-over of my hand decide whether finally all the world shall be Methodists, or Baptists, or Episcopalians, or Congregationalists, or Presbyterians, I would not turn over my hand; but between Unitarianism, which believes the Deity of Christ, and Trinitarianism, which argues his divine nature, there is a difference as wide as eternity. If Christ be not a God, then we are base idolaters. If Christ be God, then those who deny it are blasphemers. To that Christological question we come this morning, and may God help us to do right in a question where mistake is infinite!

I suppose we are all willing to take the Bible as our standard. It requires as much faith to be an infidel as to be a Christian; but it is faith in a different direction. The Christian believes in the statements of Moses, and Isaiah, and David, and Matthew, and Mark, and Luke, and Paul. The infidel believes in the statement of the freethinkers. We have faith in one class of men; they have faith in another class of men. But as I suppose the vast majority of the people in the audience this morning are willing to take the Bible as their guide in morals and religion, I shall make this book my starting-point.

You may be aware that the two great generals who have marshaled the largest army of Unitarian troops are Strauss and Renan. The multitudes of the slain under them will never be counted until the day when the archangel sounds the roll-call of the resurrection. These men, and all men who have sympathy with them, begin by attacking the fortress of the miracles. They know that when once they have captured that fortress Christianity must surrender. The great German exegete says that all the miracles are myths. The great French exegete says that all the miracles are legends. They must somehow or other explain away every thing supernatural in the Bible—every thing supernatural in the life of Christ—though to accomplish that they must go up the greatest absurdity. They prefer the miracles of human nonsense rather than the grand miracles of Jesus Christ. They say, for instance, that the miraculous birth of Christ was a myth, just as it is a fanciful idea that Romulus was born of Rhea Silvia and the god Mars. They say that Christ did not feed five thousand with a few loaves of bread; that is only a myth which got mixed up with the distribution of twenty loaves among a hundred people by Elisha. They say Christ did not turn the water into wine; that was only an improvement on the old Egyptian plague by which water was turned into blood. They say no star pointed down to the manger where Jesus lay; that was only the flash of a passing lantern. They say that Christ's sweating great drops of blood in Gethsemane was not very astonishing, for he had been exposed to the night, and had been taken suddenly physically ill. They say no tongues of fire sat on the heads of the disciples at the Pentecost; it was only a great thunderstorm, and the air was full of electricity, and it snapped and flew all around about the heads of the disciples. They say that Mary, and Martha, and Lazarus, and Christ made up their minds it was necessary to get up an excitement in order to forward their religion, and so they resolved to play funeral, and Lazarus consented to be the corpse, and Mary and Martha consented to be mourners, and Christ consented to be chief operator. I, of course, put it in my own words, but state accurately their meaning. They say that the four Gospels are spurious, written by superstitious or lying men, and that they were backed up by people who were to die, and actually did die, for a thing they did not believe. Now, I take back the limited remark I made a moment ago, and say that it requires a thousandfold more credulity and faith to be an infidel than to be a Christian, and that if Christianity demands that the whale swallow Jonah, then skepticism demands that Jonah swallow the whale.

I propose this morning to show you, so far as the Lord may help me, that Jesus Christ is God. I shall prove it, first, from what inspired men say of him; then, from what he said of himself; then, from his wonderful achievements. "Get a good fat text to start with," said Dr. Ludlow, our grand old theological professor. If I never had such a text before, I have one this morning: "Christ came, who is over all, God blessed forever. Amen." Not over Solomon's throne; not higher than David's throne; not higher than Cæsar's; not higher than the Henrys', than the Fredericks', than the Louis', than Napoleon's, than Victoria's? Oh yes. Gather all those thrones and pile them up, and my text overspans them as easily as a rainbow spans the mountain-top. "Christ came, who is over all, God blessed forever. Amen."

The Bible says, "All things were made by him." Stop! Does not that prove too much? He did not make the Mediterranean, did he? not Mount Lebanon? not the Alps? not Mount Washington? not the earth? not the stars? not the universe? Yes, all things were made by him. And, lest we should be so stupid as not to understand it, the apostle concludes by saying, "Without him, was not any thing made that was made." Why, then, he must have been a God.

The Bible says, "At the name of Jesus Christ every knee shall bow, of things on earth and things in heaven." See all heaven coming down on their knees—martyrs' on their knees, apostles on their knees, confessors on their knees, the archangel on his knees. Before whom? A man? No, a God.

The Bible goes on to say that "every tongue shall confess that Jesus Christ is Lord." Malayan, Bornesian, Mexican, Persian, Italian, German, Spanish, French, English— every tongue shall confess that Jesus Christ is Lord. He must be a God. The Bible says, "Jesus Christ, the same yesterday, to-day, and forever." Men change; the body changes entirely in seven years, the mind changes, the heart changes; but "Christ the same yesterday, to-day, and forever." He must be a God.

Philosophers say that it is gravitation, the centripetal and centrifugal forces, which keep the worlds from clashing and from demolition; but Paul says that Christ's arm is the axle on which every thing turns, and that his hand is the socket in which every thing is set; "*upholding* all things by the word of his power." He must be a God.

But I go on, in the next place, and see what Christ said of himself. Every person ought to know more about himself than any body else does. If I ask you where you were born, and you say, "I was born in Chester, England, or Dublin, or New Orleans," I would believe you. Why? Because you ought to know; it is a matter that pertains to yourself. If I asked you whether you can lift three or four hundred pounds, and you said yes, I would believe you. You ought to know. If I ask you how much money you have, a hundred or a hundred thousand dollars, and you tell me, I believe you, because you, being an honest man, will tell me truth. Now, I ask if Christ ought not to know whether or not he is God? I ask his age. He says, in so many words, "Before Abraham was, I am."

Abraham had been dead two thousand and twenty-eight years. Was Christ two thousand and twenty-eight years old? He says so. In Revelation he says, "I am Alpha;" Alpha being the first letter of the Greek alphabet, it was as much as to say, "I am the A of the great alphabet of all the centuries." Ought not he to know?

Could Christ be in a thousand places at the same time? He said so. He intimates that he can be in Madras, in Stockholm, in Pekin, in San Francisco, in Constantinople, at the same time. "Where two or three are gathered together in my name, there am I in the midst of them." This faculty of everywhereativeness, is it a human or a Divine attribute? Lest we should think that this power of everywhereativeness should give out, Christ intimates that he is going to keep on, and that on the day before the world is-burned up, he will be in all the prayer-meetings in Europe and Africa, North and South America; for he declares, in so many words, "Lo! I am with you alway, even *unto the end of the world!*" He is a God! He is a God!

He takes divine honors. He calls himself the Lord of men, the Lord of angels, the Lord of devils. Is he not? If he is not, then he is the greatest fraud that was ever enacted. To-morrow morning a man comes into your store in New York, and he says, "I am Mr. Laird, the great ship-builder of Liverpool. I built the *Alabama*. I have built a great many fine ships." You treat him with a great deal of consideration; but you find out after a while that he is not Mr. Laird, and that he never built any thing. What is that man? An impostor. Now, Christ said that he built the earth—built all things. Did he build the earth, or did he not? If he did, he was a God; if he did not, he was an impostor. A man with a Jewish countenance and German accent comes into your store. He says, "I am Rothschild, the banker, of London. I hold the wealth of nations in my vest-pocket. I loaned that money to Italy and to Austria." You treat him with a great deal of consideration for a while; but suppose you find out that he is not a banker, that he does not own a single dollar in all the world? What is that man? An impostor. Now, Christ comes, and he says he owns this world, he owns the next, he owns all the glories of land and sea; he professes to be vast in his possessions. Is he in possession of all these things? Does he own them all? If he does not, what is he? An impostor. A man with venerable aspect and gray beard comes into the White House at Washington. He says to the President, "I am King William of Germany. I have come over *incognito* for the purpose of recreation and amusement. I gained the victory at Sedan. I have castles in Berlin and Dresden." Suppose after a while the President finds that he has no castles, and that he is not the king; what is he, then? An impostor. Now, the Lord Jesus Christ professed to be king, eternal, immortal, invisible, the only wise God. If he was not, what was he? I appeal to your common sense. He was either God, or he was a villain. Strauss saw that alternative, and he says that Christ was sinful in taking homage that did not belong to him. Renan saw that alternative, and says that Christ, not through his own fault, but through the fault of others, lost some of the purity of his conscience, and slyly intimates that dishonorable women may have damaged his soul. Any thing but admit that Christ is God.

I have shown you that Christ was God, from what inspired men have said of him, and from what he said of himself; now I want to show you that he was God from his wonderful achievements. I suppose that all believe the Bible. If you do not, what do you do in the Brooklyn Tabernacle? Why do you not go over to-day and join the infidel club on Broadway? Why do you not go and kiss the foot of the new statue of Tom Paine they are rearing in Boston? Why do you not take your hat, and, not stealing the hymn-book, go out and find associates among men who do not believe in the Word of God, the only foundation for good government and for common honesty? We in this church are among the deluded souls and the narrow heads who believe the whole Bible, and take it down in one swallow as easily as you take down a ripe strawberry. Supposing that you admit the Bible to be true, let us go out, and see the Saviour's achievements—surgical, alimentary, marine, mortuary.

Surgical achievements? Did you ever in all the scientific journals of the world see such wonderful operations as he performed? He used no knife. He carried no splints. He employed no compress. He never made a patient squirm under cauterization. He never tied an artery, and yet, behold him. With one word he stuck fast Malchus's amputated ear. He stirred dust and spittle into a salve, with which he made the man who was born blind, without optic nerve, cornea, or crystalline lens, open his eyes on the glorious sunlight. He beat music on the drum of the deaf ear. He straightened a woman who, through contraction of muscles, had been bent almost double for nigh two decades. He made a man who had not used his limbs for thirty-eight years shoulder his mattress and walk off. Sir Astley Cooper, Abernethy, and Valentine Mott stood powerless before a withered arm. This doctor of omnipotent surgery comes up to the man with the lifeless, useless, shriveled arm, and he says to him, "Stretch forth thy hand." The man stretched it forth just as good as the other. This was a God! This was a God!

Alimentary achievements? A lad comes with five loaves, with which he expected to make a speculation; perhaps having bought them for five pennies and expecting to sell them for ten pennies, and thus double his money. Lo! Christ takes those loaves, and from them performs a miracle with which he satisfies seven thousand famishing people. When the Saviour's mother went into a neighbor's house to help get up a wedding party, and by a calculation she saw that they had made a mistake in the amount of beverage that was requisite, she calls Christ for help; and Christ, to relieve the awkward embarrassment, not through slow decay of fermentation, but by one word, makes a hundred and thirty gallons of pure wine.

Marine achievements? Do you not remember how he brought around a whole school of fish into the net of the men who were mourning over their poor luck, and how they had to halloo to the people in the other boat, and then both ships were loaded down to the water's edge with game, so that the sailors had to walk cautiously from larboard to starboard lest the boat sink? And then when the squall came down through the mountain gorge to the water, and Gennesaret with long white locks of foam rose up to battle it, and the vessel dropped into the trough, and shipped a sea, and the loosened sails cracked in the tornado, how Christ rose from the back part of the vessel, and came on across the staggering ship until he came to the prow; and, wiping the spray from his forehead, hushed the crying tempest on the knee of his omnipotence? Oh, was it a man who wrestled down the storm? Was it a man who with both feet trampled Gennesaret into a smooth floor?

But look at his mortuary achievements. Let all the psychologists and anatomists of the world go to Westminster Abbey, and try to wake Queen Elizabeth, or Henry VIII. All the ingenuity of man never yet brought the dead to life. But look at that dead girl in Capernaum. What a pity that she should die so early, and when the world is so fair! She is only twelve years old. Feel of the hands. Feel of the brow. Dead. Dead. The house is full of uproar and wailing. What does Christ do? He comes and takes that little girl by the hand, and no sooner has he touched her hand than her eyes open, and her heart starts, and the white lily of death flushes into the red rose of life, and she rushes into the arms of her rejoicing relatives. Who was it that raised her up? Was it a man, or was it a God?

What is that crying in Bethany? Mary crying, Martha crying, Jesus crying, and the neighbors crying. What is the matter? Lazarus is dead. The sisters think they will never again see him, never have him sit at the table again. Poor things! Since their father died they have depended upon Lazarus for almost every thing. Jesus comes down to the excavation in the rock, in one of the side niches of which Lazarus sleeps in death. Jesus generally spoke in gentle articulations, but now he lets out his voice to full strength, until it rings through all the labyrinths and avenues of the rock, "Lazarus, come forth!" And Lazarus slides down from the side niche into the main avenue of the rock, and stands a living man before the abashed and confounded spectators. Who was it that stood at the mouth of that cave, and uttered that potent word? Was it a man? Tell that to the lunatics in Bloomingdale Asylum. It was Christ, the everywhere-present, the everlasting, the omniscient, the omnipotent God!

But there is one test which will show you whether Christ is God or not. The recital of that verse ought to blanch the cheeks of some with alarm, and kindle the faces of others with eternal sunrise, "We must all appear before the judgment-seat of Christ." The world will be stunned by a blow that will make it stagger mid-heaven; the stars will scatter like dried leaves in an equinox; the grave-yards will unroll the bodies, and the clouds will unroll the spirits, and soul and flesh will come together in incorruptible conjunction. Hark to the loud wash of the retreating sea, and the baying of the advancing thunders, and the sweeping of winged cohorts! Smoke, and darkness, and fire, and earthquake, and shouting, shouting, shouting, wailing, wailing, wailing. On the one side, in piled-up galleries of light, are the one hundred and forty and four thousand—yea, the quintillions of the saved; and as they take their seats I feel as if I must drop under the insufferable radiance. On the other side are piled up, in galleries of thunder-cloud, the frowning, glaring, dying populations of the wrath to come. Before me, and between the two galleries, is a throne. It is very high. It stands on two burnished pillars—justice and mercy. It is stupendous with awards and condemnations. Look; but half hide your eyes, lest they be put out in the excess of vision. There is a throne, but no one is seated on it. Who shall occupy it? Will you go up and take it? "No," you say; "I am only dust and ashes." Show me some man that is fit to take it, in all the ages. Lord Mansfield? No. Solomon? No. Isaiah? No. Paul? No. Their foot would consume at the first touch of the step of that throne. Even Gabriel dare not go up on it. Michael, the archangel, would rather bow down, pulling his right wing over his left, and both over his face, and cry, "Holy!" But here is One ascending that throne. His back is toward us. He goes step above step, height above height, until he comes to the apex. Then, turning around, so that all nations can see him, we behold it is Christ; and all earth and heaven and hell fall on the knee, and cry out, "It is a God! It is a God!"

There is great comfort in my subject. It is God who came down from Jesus Christ to save us. Do you think only a man could have made an atonement for millions of the race? Does your common sense teach you that? I tell you if Christ is not God, the redemption of our race is a dead failure. We want a divine arm to lift our burden. We want a divine endurance to carry our pang. We want a divine expiation to take away our sin; and "Christ came, who is over all, God blessed forever. Amen."

God also comes down in Christ to comfort you. Sometimes our troubles are so great, human sympathy does not seem to be sufficient for them. O ye who cried all last night because of loneliness and bereavement, I want to tell you that it is your Maker and your God that comes this day to comfort you. When there are children in the house, and the mother dies, then you know that the father has to be more gentle than ever, and he has to act two parts in that household. And it seems as if the Lord Jesus Christ looked down and saw your helplessness, and he proposed to be both father and mother to your sick soul. He comes in the strength of the one, and in the tenderness of the other, and he says, "As a father pitieth his children, so I pity you." "As one whom his mother comforteth, so will I comfort you." Do you not feel the hush of that divine lullaby? Put down your tired head on the heaving bosom of that Divine compassion, and let him put his arms around you, and say, "O widowed soul! I will be thy husband and thy God. O orphaned ones! I will be your protector. Don't cry. Don't cry." And then he will put his hand on your eyelids, and sweep that hand down on the cheek, wiping away all the tears of loneliness and bereavement. Oh, what a loving, tender, sympathetic God has come for us! I do not ask you, this morning, to lay hold of God; you may be too weak for that. I do not ask you even to pray; you may be too bewildered for that. I only ask you just to let go, and fall back into the arms of Everlasting Strength.

You and I will soon hear the click of the latch of the sepulchre. We want an Almighty Christ to go with us. I wonder if the friend of Lazarus will be about. Our friends will take us with strong arms, and lay us down in the dust; but they can not bring us back again. I would be scared with infinite fright if I thought I should have to stay there forever. But no. Christ will come with a glorious iconoclasm, and split and grind up the granite, and let us come out. O the resurrection! What kind of a resurrection will it be?

A young woman was recently dying, without any hope, and she said to her mother, in the closing hour, "Mother, I am going away from you, and I am so afraid." When you leave this world, when you bid farewell to those with whom you have been associated, and in the last great day will you be afraid? If we have on that day Christ, the Omnipotent Saviour, on our side, all shall be well. If the resurrection comes upon a spring day, and all the flowers are blooming around our graves, how pleasant it would be to take up the brightest one of all those flowers, and put it in the scarred hand of Him who died for us! to gather up the most redolent of them all, and twist them into a garland for the brow that was stuck with the thorns! On that day, when Jesus is surrounded by all the dominions of the saved, we will see what an awful libel it was when men said that Christ was only a man; and then you will declare, with unparalleled emphasis, "Christ came, who is over all, God blessed forever. Amen." Oh, would you not like to join in that "Amen," ye who believe this Christ is the eternal God? You shall have my permission. Let your "Amen" be the doxology of this whole assemblage! "Christ came, who is over all, God blessed forever! Amen."

WRECKED FOR TWO WORLDS.

"Lest that by any means, when I have preached to others, I myself should be a castaway."—1 *Corinthians* ix., 27.

MINISTERS of religion may finally be lost. The apostle, in the text, indicates that possibility. Gown and surplice and cardinal's red hat are no security. Cardinal Wolsey, after having been petted by kings, and having entertained foreign embassadors at Hampton Court, died in darkness. One of the most eminent ministers of religion that this country has ever known, plunged into sin and died, his heart, in *post-mortem* examination, found to have been, not figuratively, but literally, broken. O ministers of Christ! because we have diplomas of graduation, and hands of ordination on the head, and address consecrated assemblages, that is no reason why we shall necessarily reach the realm celestial. The clergyman must go through the same gate of pardon as the layman. The preacher may get his audience into heaven, and he himself miss it. There have been cases of shipwreck where all on board escaped excepting the captain. Alas! if, having "preached to others, I myself should be a castaway." God forbid it.

I have examined some of the commentaries to see what they thought about this word "castaway," and I find that they differ in regard to the figure used, while they agree in regard to the meaning. So I shall make my own selection, and take it in a nautical and sea-faring sense, and show you that men may become spiritual castaways, and how finally they drift into that calamity.

We are a sea-board town. You have all stood on the beach. Many of you have crossed the ocean. Some of you have managed vessels in great stress of weather. There is a sea-captain; and there is another; and yonder is another; and there are a goodly number of you who, though once you did not know the difference between a brig and a bark, and between a diamond knot and a sprit-sheet-sail knot, and although you could not point out the weather-cross jack-brace, and though you could not man the fore clue-garnets, now you are as familiar with a ship as you are with your right hand, and, if it were necessary, you could take a vessel clear across to the mouth of the Mersey without the loss of a single sail. Well, there is a dark night in your memory of the sea. The vessel became unmanageable. You saw it was scudding toward the shore. You heard the cry, "Breakers ahead! Land on the lee bow!" The vessel struck the rock, and you felt the deck breaking up under your feet, and you were a castaway, as when the *Hercules* drove on the coast of Caffraria, as when the Portuguese brig went staving, splitting, grinding, crashing on the Goodwins. But whether you have followed the sea or not, you all understand the figure when I tell you that there are men who by their sins and temptations are thrown helpless! Driven before the gale! Wrecked for two worlds! Cast away! cast away!

By talking with some sailors, I have found out that there are three or four causes for such a calamity to a vessel. I have been told that it sometimes comes *from creating false lights on the beach.* This was often so in olden times. It is not many years ago, indeed, that vagabonds used to wander up and down the beach, getting vessels ashore in the night, throwing up false lights in their presence and deceiving them, that they might despoil and ransack them. All kinds of infernal arts were used to accomplish this. And one night, on the Cornish coast, when the sea was coming in fearfully, some villains took a lantern and tied it to a horse, and led the horse up and down the beach, the lantern swaying to the motion of the horse, and a sea-captain in the offing saw it, and made up his mind that he was not anywhere near the shore, for he said, "There's a vessel; that must be a vessel, for it has a movable light," and he had no apprehension until he heard the rocks grating on the ship's bottom, and it went to pieces, and the villains on shore gathered up the packages and the treasures that were washed to the land. And I have to tell you that there are a multitude of souls ruined by false lights on the beach. In the dark night of man's danger, Universalism goes up and down the shore, shaking its lantern, and men look off and take that flickering and expiring wick as the signal of safety, and the cry is, "Heave the main-topsail to the mast! All is well!" when sudden destruction cometh upon them, and they shall not escape. So there are all kinds of lanterns swung on the beach—philosophical lanterns, educational lanterns, humanitarian lanterns. Men look at them, and are deceived, when there is nothing but God's eternal light-house of the Gospel that can keep them from becoming castaways. Once, on Wolf Crag Light-house, they tried to build a copper figure of a wolf with its mouth open, so that, the storms beating into it, the wolf would howl forth the danger to mariners that might be coming anywhere near the coast. Of course it was a failure. And so all new inventions for the saving of man's soul are unavailing.

What the human race wants is a light bursting forth from the cross standing on the great headlands—the light of pardon, the light of comfort, the light of heaven. You might better go to-night, and destroy all the great light-houses on the dangerous coasts—the Barnegat Light-house, the Fastnet Rock Light-house, the Skerryvore Light-house, the Longship's Light-house, the Hollyhead Light-house—than to put out God's great ocean lamp—the Gospel. Woe to those who swing false lanterns on the beach till men crash in and perish! Cast away! cast away!

By talking with sailors, I have heard also that sometimes ships come to this calamity by the *sudden swoop of a tempest*. For instance, a vessel is sailing along in the East Indies, and there is not a single cloud on the sky; but suddenly the breeze freshens, and there are swift feet on the ratlines, and the cry is, "'Way! haul away there!" but, before they can square the booms and tarpaulin the hatchways, the vessel is groaning and creaking in the grip of a tornado, and falls over into the trough of the sea, and, broadside-on, rolls on to the beach and keels over, leaving the crew to struggle in the merciless surf. Cast away! cast away! And so I have to tell you that there are thousands of men destroyed through the sudden swoop of temptations. Some great inducement to worldliness, or to sensuality, or to high temper, or to some form of dissipation, comes upon them. If they had time to examine their Bible, if they had time to consult with their friends, if they had time to deliberate, they could stand it; but the temptation came so suddenly—a euroclydon on the Mediterranean, a whirlwind of the Caribbean. One awful surge of temptation, and they perish. And so we often hear the old story, "I hadn't seen my friend in a great many years.

We were very glad to meet. He said I must drink, and he took me by the arm and pressed me along, and filled the cup until the bubbles ran over the edge, and in an evil moment all my good resolutions were swept away, and, to the outraging of God and my own soul, I fell." Or the story is, "I had hard work to support my family. I knew that by one false entry, by one deception, by one embezzlement, I might spring out free from all my trouble; but the temptation came upon me so fiercely I could not think. I did wrong, and having done wrong once, I could not stop." Oh, it is the first step that costs; the second is easier, and the third, and on to the last. Once having broken loose from the anchor, it is not so easy to tie the parted strands. How often it is that men perish for the reason that the temptation comes from some unexpected quarter! as vessels lie in Margate Roads, safe from southwest winds; but the wind changing to the north-east, they are driven helpless, and go down. Oh that God would have mercy upon those upon whom there comes the sudden swoop of temptation, that they perish not, becoming, for this world and the world to come, cast away! cast away!

By talking with sailors, I have found out also that some vessels come to this calamity *through sheer recklessness.* There are three million men who follow the sea for a living. It is a simple fact that the average of human life on the sea is less than twelve years. This comes from the fact that men by familiarity with danger sometimes become reckless—the captain, the helmsman, the stoker, the man on the lookout, become reckless, and in nine out of ten shipwrecks it is found out that some one was awfully to blame. So I have to tell you that men lose their souls through sheer recklessness. There are thousands of my friends in this house to-night who do not care where they are in spiritual things. They do not know whether they are sailing toward heaven or toward hell, and the sea is black with piratical hulks that would grapple them with hooks of steel, and blindfold them, and make them "walk the plank." They do not know what the next moment may bring forth. Drifting in their theology. Drifting in their habits. Drifting in regard to all the future. No God, no Christ, no settled anticipations of eternal felicity; but all the time coming nearer and nearer to a dangerous coast. Some of them are on fire with evil habit, and they shall burn on the sea, the charred hulk tossed up on the barren beach of the lost world. Many of them with great troubles, financial troubles, domestic troubles, social troubles; but they never pray for comfort. With an aggravation of sin that stirs up the ire of God, they pray for no pardon. They do not steer for the light-ship that dances in gladness at the mouth of heaven's harbor; reckless as to where they come out, drifting farther from God, farther from early religious influences, farther from their present happiness, farther from heaven. And, what is the worst thing about it is, that they are taking their families along with them; and if one perish, perhaps they will all perish; and the way one goes, the probability is they will all go. Yet no anxiety. As unconscious of danger as the passengers on board the *Arctic* one moment before the *Vesta* crashed into her. Wrapped up in the business of the store, not remembering that soon they must quit all their earthly possessions. Absorbed in their social position, not knowing that very soon they will have attended the last levee, and whirled in the last schottisch. They do not deliberately choose to be ruined; neither did the French frigate *Medusa* aim for the Arguin Banks, but there it went to pieces. O ye reckless souls! I wish that to-night I could wake you up with some great perturbation. The perils are so augmented, the chances of escape are so few; you will die just as certainly as you sit there, unless you bestir yourself. I fear, my brother, you are becoming a castaway. You are making no effort, you are putting forth no exertion for escape. You throw out no oar. You take no soundings. You watch no compass. You are not calculating your bearings while the wind is abaft, and yonder is a long line of foam bounding the horizon, and you will be pushed on toward it, and thousands have perished there, and you are driving in the same direction. Ready about! Down helm! Hard down! or in the next five minutes, or four minutes, or three minutes, or two minutes, or one minute, you may be a castaway.

O unforgiven soul! if you could see your peril before God to-night on account of your lifetime sin and transgression, there would be fifty men who would rush through this aisle crying for mercy, and there would be fifty who would rush through that aisle crying for mercy, and they would be as men are when they rush across the deck of a foundering ship, and there would be thousands of arms tossed up from the galleries; and as these Christian men rose up to help them, it would be as when a vessel drives on the rocks, and on the shore the command is, "Man the life-boat! Man the life-boat! Pull, my lads, pull! A steamer with two hundred on board making the last plunge!" Why does your cheek turn pale, and your heart pound until, listening, you hear it? It is because, my dear brother, you realize that, owing to your lifetime sin and rejection of God's mercy, you are in peril, and I really believe there are thousands of people in this house this moment, saying within themselves, "What shall I do?" Do? Do? Why, my brother, do what any ship does when it is in trouble. Lift a distress-signal. There is a flash, and a boom. You listen and you look. A vessel is in trouble. The distress-gun is sounded, or a rocket is sent up, or a blanket is lifted, or a bundle of rags—any thing to catch the eye of the passing craft. So if you want to be taken off the wreck of your sin, you must lift a distress-signal. Rise. Lift your hand. Cry out for mercy. The publican lifted the distress-signal when he cried, "God, be merciful to me a sinner!" Peter lifted the distress-signal when he said, "Lord, save me—I perish!" The blind man lifted the distress-signal when he said, "Lord, that my eyes may be opened!" The jailer lifted the distress-signal when he said, "What must I do to be saved?" And help will never come to your soul until you lift such a signal as that. You must make some demonstration, give some sign, make some heaven-piercing outcry for help, lifting the distress-signal for the church's prayer, lifting the distress-signal for Heaven's pardon. Pray! pray! The voice of the Lord to-night sounds in your ears, "In me is thy help." Too proud to raise such a signal, too proud to be saved.

There was an old sailor thumping about in a small boat in a tempest. The larger vessel had gone down. He felt he must die. The surf was breaking over the boat, and he said: "I took off my life-belt that it might soon be over, and I thought somewhat indistinctly about my friends on shore, and then I bid them good-bye like, and I was about sinking back and giving it up, when I saw a bright star. The clouds were breaking away, and there that blessed star shone down on me, and it seemed to take right hold of me; and, somehow—I can not tell how it was—but, somehow, while I was trying to watch that star, it seemed to help me and seemed to lift me." O drowning soul! see you not the glimmer between the rifts of the storm-cloud? Would to God that that light might lay hold of you tonight!

> "Death-struck, I ceased the tide to stem,
> When suddenly a star arose,
> It was the Star of Bethlehem!"

O ye castaways! God is doing every thing to save you.

Did you ever hear of Lionel Lukin? He was the inventor of the insubmergible life-boat. All honor is due his memory by sea-faring men, as well as by landsmen. How many lives he saved by his invention! In after-days that invention was improved, and one day there was a perfect life-boat, the *Northumberland*, ready at Ramsgate. The life-boat being ready, to test it the crew came out and leaped on the gunwale on one side to see if the boat would upset; it was impossible to upset it. Then, amidst the huzzas of excited thousands, that boat was launched, and it has gone and come, picking up a great many of the shipwrecked. But I have to tell you to-night of a grander launching, and from the dry-docks of heaven. Word came up that a world was beating on the rocks. In the presence of the potentates of heaven the life-boat of the world's redemption was launched. It shoved off the golden sands amidst angelic hosannas. The surges of darkness beat against its bow, but it sailed on, and it comes in sight tonight. It comes for you, it comes for me. Soul! soul! get into it. Make one leap for heaven. This is your last chance for life. Let that boat go past, and there remains nothing but fearful looking-for of judgment, and fiery indignation which shall devour the adversary. I am expecting that there will be whole families here to-night who will get into that life-boat.

In 1833 the *Isabella* came ashore off Hastings, England. The air was filled with sounds—the hoarse sea-trumpet, the crash of the axes, and the bellowing of the tornado. A boat from the shore came under the stern of the disabled vessel. There were women and children on board that vessel. Some of the sailors jumped into the small boat, and said, "Now, give us the children." A father who stood on the deck took his first-born and threw him to the boat. The sailors caught him safely, and the next, and the next, to the last. Still the sea rocking, the storm howling. "Now," said the sailors, "now, the mother;" and she leaped, and was saved. The boat went to shore; but before it got to the shore the landsmen were so impatient to help the suffering people that they waded clear down into the surf, with blankets, and garments, and promises of help and succor.

I have to hope to-night that a great many of the families here are going to be saved, and saved altogether. Give us that child for Christ, that other child, that other. Give us the mother, give us the father, the whole family. They must all come in. All heaven wades in to help you. I claim this whole audience for God. I pick not out one man here nor one man there: I claim this whole audience for God. There are some of you who, thirty years ago, were consecrated to Christ by your parents in baptism. Certainly I am not stepping over the right bound when I claim you for Jesus. Then there are many here who have been seeking God for a good while, and am I not right in claiming you for Jesus? Then, there are some here who have been farther away. I saw you come in to-night in clusters —two, three, and four men together—and you drink, and you swear, and you are bringing up your families without any God to take care of them when you are dead. And I claim you, my brother; I claim all of you. You will have to come to-night to the throne of mercy. God's Holy Spirit is striving now with you irresistibly. Although there may be a smile on your lip, there are agitation and anxiety in your heart. You will not come at my invitation; you will come at God's command.

[At this point in Mr. Talmage's remarks, one of the windows in the rear part of the church was slammed down by some thoughtless person. The noise alarmed many in the vast congregation, and they made a rush for the doors. This had the effect of alarming others, and in a moment six thousand people were upon their feet. Mr. Talmage cried to them to "sit down." The president of the Board of Trustees ascertained the cause of the noise, and immediately informed Mr. Talmage, who announced it, and succeeded in bringing the people to order again. That part of the congregation who had wisely kept their seats were singing the Doxology during the uproar. Nearly all of those who had left the building returned when they learned the cause of their fright, and Mr. Talmage continued as follows:]

What! are you so afraid when there is no danger at all? Will the slamming-to of a window startle six thousand souls? Would God that you were as cautious about eternal perils as you are about the perils of time! If that slight noise sends you to your feet, what will you do when the thunders of the last day roll through earth and sky, and the mountains come down in avalanche of rock? You cry out for the safety of your body; why not cry out for the safety of your soul? You will have to pray some time; why not begin now, while all the ripe and purple clusters of Divine promise bend over into your cup, rather than postpone your prayer until your chance is past, and the night drops, and the sea washes you out, and forever and forever and forever you become a castaway?

THE END.

TALMAGE'S SERMONS.

SERMONS BY T. DE WITT TALMAGE, DELIVERED IN THE BROOKLYN TABERNACLE.

FIRST SERIES.
12mo, *Cloth* - - - - - - - - - - - - - - - - - - $2 00

SECOND SERIES.
12mo, *Cloth* - - - - - - - - - - - - - - - - - - $2 00

THIRD SERIES.
"*Old Wells Dug Out.*" 12mo, *Cloth* - - - - - $2 00

FOURTH SERIES.
"*Sports that Kill.*" 12mo, *Cloth*, $1 25 ; *Paper*, $1 00

The Sermons of T. De Witt Talmage have received much attention from the press and the public. Below are given a few of the notices:

A San Francisco (California) paper, speaking of Mr. Talmage's sermons in that city, says: "We believe that no such Christian preaching has been heard since the days when George Whitefield and the two Wesleys preached the Gospel on the shores of America. Sublime in his powers of pathetic and lucid description, terrible in the earnestness with which he pleads the cause of the undying soul, overwhelming with the tender overtures of redeeming mercy, and sparkling with graceful images and illustrative anecdote, the great multitude becomes as one man beneath his touch, and a silence broken only by an occasional gasping for breath from the whole assembly, attends his utterances from the first sentence to the last."

They are the keenest, sharpest, and most vigorous specimens of pulpit oratory we have yet read.—*St. Johns* (N. B.) *Globe.*

We believe that for originality, power, and splendor, these sermons will bear comparison with the greatest pulpit productions of any age or country. But for the knowledge of human life, and the adaptation of divine truth to the whole being of man—intellectual, emotional, moral, practical — and for the power of applying that truth, we know not his equal.—*Christian Age*, London.

These sermons I regard as among the best specimens of the simple, earnest, and pungent presentation of the solemn and precious truths of the Gospel that I have ever read, and having a fertility of illustration that is marvelous. I feel earnestly desirous that they should be in a form to preach to ministers of the Gospel, and so help them to preach to others.—Rev. E. D. G. PRIME, D.D., *New York Observer*.

Mr. Talmage is clear out of the old grooves and ruts of pulpit effort. You can not measure him by the books or criticise him by the schools. He is a law unto himself. In short, he is a mystery, a phenomenon, a contradiction of all the rules and books, and a most potent power for good. He speaks to more living people in this country than any other man; and his sermons being published both in this country and in England, his influence is wider felt than that of any other Protestant minister in the world.—*Central Christian Advocate*.

The *New York Independent* says: "The new Tabernacle is massive. It will hold nearly twice as many people as Plymouth Church. Mr. Talmage is a pulpit phenomenon. His conceptions of men and things are so vivid that he can not be said to possess them — they possess him. He is dramatic, and can not describe without acting. He has a clear, incisive mind, a broad and genial humor, a high and exacting conscientiousness, kindly sympathy, a vivid imagination, vehement passion, and every blow tells."

We found ourselves in Dr. Talmage's immense audience-room containing seats for 5000 persons, with decorated ceiling, brilliant chandeliers, and spacious galleries. When the exercises began, not a foot of sitting or standing room was anywhere visible. The whole scene of the evening proved that it does not require an intermingling of heresy to fill churches. Here were crowds flocking to hear the most plain and pungent preaching on the old theme of Gospel salvation.—*Advance*, Chicago, Ill.

Mr. SPURGEON, of London, says: "Mr. Talmage's discourses lay hold of my inmost soul. The Lord is with this mighty man of valor. So may he ever be till the campaign closes with victory! I am indeed glad of his voice. It cheers me intensely. He loves the Gospel, and believes in *something*, which some preachers hardly do. There are those about who use the old labels, but the articles are not the same. May the Lord win armies of souls to Jesus by this man! I am astonished when God blesses *me*, but somehow I should not be so much surprised if he blessed this man."

Mr. Talmage's sermons have ten readers in Great Britain where any other American sermons have one reader.—D. L. MOODY.

There is about Talmage a vehemence, an urgency, an earnestness, which sometimes carries him away as in a kind of wild whirlwind. He has immense command of words, and great fluency of speech. But he is not diffuse—any thing but that. His sentences, some of them especially, fall with a force and a strength which is sometimes almost painful. There is a reckless *abandon* about many of his sermons, a hearty outspokenness, which is as refreshing as a dip into a mountain stream on a hot summer's day. He has now the largest congregation and perhaps the most powerful church in America.—*Northern Echo*, Hartlepool, England.

With an earnestness of appeal and a power of awakening that we have never heard surpassed, Dr. Talmage preaches the Old Gospel that kindled the enthusiasm of the rustic and unlettered apostles of Galilee, and at the same time elicited the zeal and influenced the heart of the cultured Pharisee of Tarsus.—*London Christian World*.

Mr. Talmage's sermons are thoroughly evangelical, and are receiving the widest attention. He is the most popular preacher of the day.—*The Methodist*.

There is a tremendous nervous energy in Mr. Talmage's sentences. They startle by their very boldness. He does not know how to soften a denunciation, or kid-glove a lie, cheat, or sham.—*Providence* (R. I.) *Press*.

Glowing with impassioned fervor, Mr. Talmage wages a deadly war against the vices of the day in their most enticing forms.—*New York Tribune*.

Dr. Talmage went to and fro with quiet step on that large platform, sinking his voice, now full of melody, almost to a whisper, yet ever audible, now rising up into an impassioned burst of unmistakable eloquence, exceeding any thing we have ever heard since the early days of Father Gavazzi. When he had ended, it seemed like the ceasing of exquisite music. For two or three minutes there was a profound silence, until the congregation seemed to arouse themselves from the thrall. Then the vast multitude dispersed.—*Liverpool* (Eng.) *Weekly Mercury.*

In many respects Mr. Talmage stands at the head of American pulpit orators, and none excel him in dramatic force.—*St. Louis Times.*

We have known persons to drop the novel half finished, and take up Talmage's sermons, never to exchange truth for trash again.—*Pittsburg Methodist Recorder.*

They are brimful of vitality, intense dramatic power of description, and an earnestness of conviction in what is said that impresses the reader deeply.—*New Orleans Picayune.*

A Baptist pastor in Michigan says: "Within a distance of ten miles there are five places (some of them school-houses) where every Sabbath people come together to hear Dr. Talmage's sermons read. They have been blessed in many conversions."

Talmage is in some respects superior to any living preacher. His book is as readable as a romance, and a world more profitable.—*Ladies' Repository*, Cincinnati.

Do we consider the great influence of a popular preacher of the present day? Neither Jeremy Taylor, Smith, or even Whitefield, had the opportunities given to Mr. Talmage through the press.—*Union Advocate.*

That Mr. Talmage is a popular preacher can not be denied, as he addresses the largest audience in Brooklyn, and perhaps the largest regular audience in America. He fulfills Garrick's idea of a preacher, and talks of religion as if it were really a matter of supreme importance. His sermons read like plays, and must entertain, if they do not convert, his hearers; but we have no reason to doubt the latter, and commend them to such as enjoy this class of literature.—*Commercial*, Cincinnati.

What building would be big enough to hold the congregation if such sermons were preached in London?—*Congregationalist*, London.

The sermons by this celebrated divine are among the most admirable compositions in the language.—*Springfield Advertiser*.

Mr. Talmage's descriptive powers are unique and of a high order; in fact, we do not know of any preacher like him.—*Pittsburg Times*.

In the author's happiest style, and outside of its religious merits, which are of a high order, it is more interesting than a romance. Nothing but the breaking down of the press can prevent this book having an immense sale.—*Reading Times*.

Mr. Talmage is a finished speaker, with a terse and nervous style.—*Irish Citizen*.

Dr. Talmage's sermons are more interesting, simply as literary works, than many novels.—*Keystone*, Philadelphia.

Through this book Mr. Talmage will preach to nearly all the world.—*Turf, Field, and Farm*.

Their power for good can scarcely be overestimated. Whether heard or read, they produce a powerful impression, and are of the kind best adapted to reach the masses in these days of absorbing worldliness and eager pursuit of gain.—*Christian Advocate*.

Mr. Talmage has proved that he can gather a regular Sabbath congregation of five thousand hearers, and that he can make himself effectively heard by that number of people. He is one of those preachers who really belong to mankind at large. Most people who try to describe Dr. Talmage begin by saying that he is like somebody, or unlike somebody else. Now the fact is that he is not like any other person at all: he is just "Talmage" all over, with as much marked individuality as ever was concentrated in any one man.—*Union Era*.

Dr. Talmage is a star of commanding lustre in the pulpit of the North. His living thoughts and burning words, on the wings of the lightning and by the agency of the press, are borne to millions who have never heard his voice nor seen his face.—*Daily Sun*, Atlanta, Ga.

Not a single page of his books can be designated as superfluous or tiresome.—*St. Louis Republican*.

We doubt not that Dr. Talmage has gained greater celebrity than any man of his age.—*Christian Advocate*, Raleigh, N. C.

Mr. Talmage preaches twice every Sunday to immense audiences. Every seat up to the rafters is filled. His manner is so impassioned, his style so original, and his figures so vivid and startling, that he holds his hearers spell-bound to the end, and he moves them to tears or smiles at will.—*Charleston News and Courier.*

We thought last evening, as we looked over Mr. Talmage's audience, now hushed so that we could hear the clock's solemn ticking keeping time to the speaker's utterances—people seemingly afraid to breathe, lest they might lose a word—we thought to ourselves, here is the perfection of oratory; here is dominion, absolute and undisputed. The attempt to do any thing but listen to those sentences—now short, sharp, and ringing, and now drawn out with a plaintiveness that will linger after his voice has died away—is so vain that it needs only to be mentioned and tried to show his power.—*Free Press,* Easton, Pa.

Almost exactly such criticisms as are brought against him were brought against Luther, and against Whitefield and Wesley. But as in them all, so in Mr. Talmage, there are elements of power that the critics of words and phrases can not comprehend. Mr. Talmage is a genuine pulpit orator; and his oratory is none the less effective because it does not conform to pulpit canons. He wins his battles, as did Napoleon, by his violation of all rules. These sermons give a hint of the moral power that lies behind Mr. Talmage's burning eloquence and gives it force.—*Christian Weekly.*

In Dr. Talmage's sermons there are portions of writing which, for thrilling interest, are not surpassed by the pages of fiction.—*The Age,* Philadelphia.

There is apparently no hidden spring in the human heart that Dr. Talmage does not know how to reach.—*Occident,* San Francisco, Cal.

Mr. Talmage has two continents for a congregation. In addition to the host that greet him every Sabbath, the *Methodist* prints one of his sermons every week; the *Interior,* of Chicago, gives his "Friday Evening Addresses;" the *Christian Age,* of London, gets the advanced sheets of his sermons (phonographically reported) for weekly publication; and other foreign papers are publishing his sermons and addresses. His discourses have appeared in book form in London, and are securing wide transatlantic attention.—*Brooklyn Eagle.*

If ministers would more generally break away from the staid niceties and etiquetical mannerism of religious service, and cry aloud, using every opportunity and every available means to arrest the attention of the people, all the while, like Talmage, preaching the primitive Gospel of Jesus—telling the "old, old story," it would be far better for the Church in all its branches.—*Pittsburg Recorder.*

The sermons published in this series speak for themselves. They are printed exactly in the words delivered, and were all extempore. What precision, memory, directness, genius, and originality they reveal need not be stated. They are more condensed than theorems, as rounded, pointed, and polished as essays, yet extemporaneous, and their preservation dependent upon reporters' pencils. Considering that Mr. Talmage is still a comparatively young man, he has won a celebrity as a preacher of which the church represented by him with such intense, earnest, and fervent eloquence may well be proud.—*Chicago Inter-Ocean.*

Mr. Talmage is one of the most pathetic and eloquent men of the age. His published works are models of Anglo-Saxon style.—*Methodist Recorder.*

He is a fearless antagonist to all forms of sin—a writer who cares more for cleaving a helmet than for showing the jewels on the handle of his weapon. Blows are what he gives; and yet, as the blade goes swiftly down, the jewels frequently flash on the eye. The raciness and abandonment to his work, conspicuous in all the writer says, will find eager readers everywhere.—*Interior.*

These sermons certainly unveil to us the secret of Mr. Talmage's extraordinary power as a preacher. * * * The great themes of experimental piety and holy living are sent home upon the hearts of men with remarkable directness, force, and fervor. Mr. Talmage has a strong imagination, which seldom flags in word-painting, and usually arrays the most common truths in all the freshness of new discoveries, and all the glow of living reality. To this he adds a quick insight into human nature, the foibles, vices, and iniquities of the day, and the Gospel as the only remedy for human corruption. All is swayed by an overmastering Christian earnestness.—*Presbyterian Quarterly.*

Mr. Talmage's knowledge of human nature, his sparkling humor, his pruning-hook as well as his scalping-knife, his deep and clear comprehension of what is spiritually beautiful, as well as his hatred of all that is radically wrong, together with his own pure Christian life and experience—all conspire to make his utterances and practical work a blessing to those who hear or read his discourses.—*Industrial Monthly.*

A writer from South Australia says: "I read every Sabbath the choice and soul-stirring sermons of Dr. Talmage to the people. Every one is delighted to hear them."

They are the product of strong thought, a red-hot heart, a tremendous earnestness, and a determined purpose to do something for Jesus Christ. So he says many things that other men omit to say, and passes by many things that they do say. The book is a live one, and we welcome it.—*Northern Christian Advocate.*

Besides performing all the functions of a minister and pastor, Mr. Talmage conducts his "Lay College," and writes from four to five columns a week for his *Christian at Work*. Within five years he has built two immense and costly churches—the second replacing the first, which was destroyed by fire. Mr. Talmage works steadily on at the same high pressure, without giving the slightest evidence of fatigue.—*Zion's Herald*, Boston.

This book needs no recommendation. It recommends itself on every page. It is a scalpel—a two-edged sword. It dissects popular dissipations with an unsparing hand. It points out the mortification spots—the incipient gangrene—which are sure to spread because it is their nature, and finally kill. Put the book in every family, on every book and newspaper stand, and distribute it on every railroad and steamboat line.—*Christian Standard and Home Journal*, Philadelphia.

The *Bible Christian Magazine* of London, England, says: "There may be in them minor faults, as some critics assert; but in wealth of illustration, in graphic description, and faithful, powerful appeal, they are unequaled. It has been said that one Niagara is enough for a continent, or even for a world; but we wish that every country, and every city and large town, had such a preacher as the author of these sermons."

No sermons of Dr. Talmage's—and all of his sermons have received an unusual degree of notice—have attracted more attention than those which he has preached during the past winter on the theatre and other unhealthy amusements of modern society. Their force and truthfulness are illustrated not more by the obvious presence of those qualities in them than by the extent and bitterness of the denunciations they have received. After all that has been said against them, they, with the sermons preached in connection with them on other baleful sports, stand, with allowance for occasional extravagances, invincible assaults against the most injurious features of modern social life. The whole series are now published by the Harpers in a neat volume, under the title, *Sports that Kill*. The author takes the pains, which is not at all necessary with those who know him, to state that he has none of the disposition of the cynic. "Life is to me a rapture. I know of no one who laughs louder or more than I do. But for the sports and recreations of life, I should have been dead long ago. God has done everything to please and amuse us." He further explains his views on healthy, profitable sports in the sermon on "Christian Gymnastics," published in this volume, which we commend to all who are disposed to approach the extreme of austerity.—*The Methodist*, New York.

The *Congregationalist*, of London, England, says: "We wonder what building would be big enough to hold the congregation, if such sermons were preached in London."

Dr. Vincent's Sunday-school paper says: "Rhetorical, but practical; persecuted, but persistent; awkward, but eloquent. Talmage is the most widely read of all the pulpit orators in America. He is orthodox, extreme, intense, fearless. His is no sickly sentimentalism. He believes in a God of justice and wrath. He believes in the atonement. He believes in hell. He preaches hell-fire. He preaches full and free salvation. He preaches against all manner of social sins. He is a foe to theatres, to rum, and to every other form of evil. This book is an exploding bomb-shell—full of flash, and shot, and power."

www.ingramcontent.com/pod-product-compliance
Lightning Source LLC
Chambersburg PA
CBHW051735300426
44115CB00007B/579